AF572397

Peter Fjågesund

The Apocalyptic World of D. H. Lawrence

Peter Fjågesund

The Apocalyptic World of D. H. Lawrence

With a Foreword by
Frank Kermode

Norwegian
University Press

Norwegian University Press (Universitetsforlaget AS), 0608 Oslo 6
Distributed world-wide excluding Scandinavia by
Oxford University Press, Walton Street, Oxford OX2 6DP

London New York Toronto
Delhi Bombay Calcutta Madras Karachi
Kuala Lumpur Singapore Hong Kong Tokyo
Nairobi Dar es Salaam Cape Town
Melbourne Auckland

and associated companies in
Beirut Berlin Ibadan Mexico City Nicosia

Cover design by Ellen Larsen

Published with a grant from the Norwegian Research Council for Science and the Humanities

British Library Cataloguing in Publication Data

Fjågesund, Peter, 1959–
The apocalyptic world of D. H. Lawrence
I. Title
823.912

ISBN 82-00-21386-2

Typeset in the UK by Paston Press, Loddon, Norfolk
Printed in Norway by Tangen Grafiske senter, Drammen 1991

Contents

Foreword by Frank Kermode vii
Acknowledgements xi

Introduction 1

1. Lawrence's View of History 4
   General Remarks on Lawrence and Apocalypticism . . . 4
   Joachism 9
   The Organic-Cyclical View 13
   The Heroic-Totalitarian View 20
   History as a Movement of Blind Forces 23
   The Renunciation of History 24

2. Our Cosmos is Burst: The End of Civilization 27
   The First World War 27
   Lawrence's Letters from the War Years 28
   Women in Love 31
   Twilight in Italy 42
   Cultural Pessimism and Lawrence's Reading 45

3. A New Continent of the Soul: The Escapist Utopia 58
   Rananim 61
   History and Pre-History 67
   The Subconscious, Myth and Symbol 72
   The Sexual Act 79

4. The Background of Lawrence's Political Ideas 88
   European Society Around the First World War 89
   Political Vitalism 92
   Germany 94
   Italy 98
   Lawrence's Reading of Utopian Literature 102

5. The Mystery of Lordship: The Leadership Utopia . . 112
   The Leadership Ideas Before Aaron's Rod 115
   Aaron's Rod 121
   Kangaroo 123
   The Plumed Serpent 129

6. A Tragic Age and a Hopeful Heart:
The Double Vision of the Final Years 145
Lady Chatterley's Lover 146
Lawrence and Politics After *The Plumed Serpent* 158
Apocalypse 170

Notes 177
Bibliography 187
Index 195

Foreword

FRANK KERMODE

An interest in apocalypse seems to be practically universal, and is apt to become very strong at the ends of centuries as we shall no doubt see in the next few years, for the imminent end of a millennium will probably reinforce it.

Some people are more conscious of the myth, more superstitious one might say, than others. D. H. Lawrence was one such; throughout his work there is evidence that apocalypticism was in the grain of his mind. He concerned himself with almost all its aspects – millennialism, utopianism, communism (he wanted to set up a commune), sectarian leadership, whether political or spiritual (he saw himself as a leader of that stamp). He read many books about it, and was fertile in developing modern and personal versions of very old and widely entertained notions.

Apocalyptic theories have for many centuries imposed themselves on our attitudes to history, to social organization, to sexual behaviour. And although they could probably flourish in other contexts, in our culture they ultimately all derive in large measure from biblical apocalypse, and notably from the Revelation of St John.

It is possible that the history of the West would have taken a different course if that book, the end of the Bible, had been excluded from the canon, as it might well have been; even Luther, at one time, thought it should be treated as apocryphal. But by his time it had already been a powerful influence on thought. The Abbot Joachim of Fiore had extrapolated from it a tripartite scheme of world history so persuasive that he has been credibly described as having had more influence on subsequent political thought than Karl Marx. Not only was some version of his scheme the inspiration of those medieval sectaries so vividly studied by Norman Cohn in his *Pursuit of the Millennium*; it also animated the religious fervour of the English sects in the Commonwealth period, and survived to give inspiration to radical movements in the succeeding centuries. In the nineteenth century it recurred in sophisticated and secularized forms that were taken seriously by such eminences as

Saint-Simon, Comte and Renan, George Eliot, Yeats and Ibsen. It is still part of our thinking, whenever we speak of the ends of epochs, and of ages of transition.

In working-class, dissenting communities, such as that into which Lawrence was born, the message of apocalypse came not simply from the printed text but from chapel sermons and hymns. However he came to feel about them later, Lawrence never forgot them, and they were again vividly in his mind as he wrote his last book *Apocalypse*. The set of his mind was established by Revelation, though that was only the foundation. He knew about Joachim as he knew about Madame Blavatsky and about much else that enabled him to develop, in expository prose as well as in fiction, his own peculiar apocalypse. The many ways in which he did so are a subject of Peter Fjågesund's enquiries.

Previous critics have interested themselves in the writer's apocalyptic and utopian tendencies, and have studied that strange body of theoretical or, as Lawrence himself called it, 'pollyanalytic' prose (for example the *Study of Thomas Hardy* and 'The Crown'). They have combed Lawrence's available letters for comments on the subject, and examined the novels for apocalyptic structures or traces. Peter Fjågesund, however, may be said to have worked more systematically than his predecessors; and it is worth noting that while doing so he managed to keep his head. He writes with admirable sobriety on a subject quite likely to infect commentators with its enthusiasms, its wilder speculations. Fjågesund is not afraid to speculate, but he does so quite calmly.

We are always ready to say that we live in an age of transition; it is an idea of Joachim's that has dwindled into a commonplace. He thought there was a strictly defined period between the great epochs, and that he was living in the transition between the second and the third (and last). Each epoch was assigned to one of the Persons of the Trinity, and that of the Second Person was about to give way to the epoch of the Holy Spirit, a utopian epoch imagined according to Joachim's monastic ideal. Lawrence, like others in his time, gave the commonplace notion real force. Perhaps the true and violent end of the last century, or of the last age before our own, was the Great War. Lawrence experienced it as both horrible and transitional, a time of misery, the end of an epochal decadence that might, or must, give way to a new age, a new world – possibly not even a human world but a world renovated, a utopia even if inhabited only by plants and animals, purged of the ugliness with which human folly and machinery had surrounded our life.

In a spirit not wholly remote from that of the modern sects which isolate themselves to wait for the end – elect spirits who expect to survive it, expecting 'rapture', often by flying saucer – Lawrence formed a scheme for an ideal community, which he named Rananim, where congenial spirits would find an unspoilt place to live out these Last Days. At one moment he thought of Florida as a setting, possibly aware of the nineteenth-century American communes, with their strong leaders and enlightened, though not entirely libertine, views of sexual conduct. Such communities, like those of Cohn's medieval pilgrims, must have a strong leader, a charismatic man (certainly a *man*). Men of this type recur in the fiction, notably in *Aaron's Rod* and *Kangaroo*. Lawrence assumed that in life he would have the principal part, not because he sought the seigneurial sexual privileges enjoyed by some of Cohn's leaders, but rather to institute a new, more vital sexual order, with fruitful tensions between male and female, and a cult of *Männerbund* between males.

Readers of *Women in Love* will not need reminding of the prominence of these themes in that book. They imply an important but still subordinate role for women; some critics have supposed that he changed this view, but Fjågesund, considering the issues with his usual deliberation, decides that for Lawrence the male remained the superior sex.

Lawrence's apocalyptic ideas, though they always had the same roots, were copiously expressed and varied a good deal over time. Fjågesund does a good job of tracing their variations. He sees the war years as, for Lawrence, virtually pure apocalypse, and the postwar period as one in which the writer sought social, political and educational solutions to the world crisis that were often of a ruthlessly apocalyptic character and were normally based on some version of the leader principle.

He takes 1925, the year of *The Plumed Serpent*, as ending that phase. In the three versions of *Lady Chatterley's Lover*, and in *Apocalypse*, he finds evidence of a deepening despair, a sense of doom qualified by the old desperate hope that decadence, that brings an end, might give way to renovation, that the new age would provide its utopia.

He is right to warn us against reading out simple apocalyptic paradigms from the fiction. Lawrence was certainly capable of dropping apocalyptic hints – the falling star in *St Mawr* is merely an instance, an obvious borrowing from St John – and there are undoubtedly apocalyptic themes in the central masterpieces, *The*

Rainbow and *Women in Love* (certainly his 'war book'). But these books, and to a lesser extent the others, are too freely written, too concerned with their own growth and vitality, to be fully schematic. For anything remotely answering to that description one must look to the 'pollyanalytics'. Fjågesund is always respectful of that distinction.

Finally, it is good to have a view of Lawrence, of a cardinal issue in the interpretation of his work, from a young Norwegian scholar who can remind us that he has a different perspective; it enables him, for example, to suggest a connection between *Lady Chatterley's Lover* and Knut Hamsun's *Pan*. He also breaks new ground in his discussion of certain Italian and German intellectual influences. And he rightly stresses a point of which we may be aware, but are apt to neglect – that the sense of election, of possessing knowledge that would be terrifying to the masses, must have isolated this man, who indeed often complained of his isolation, in his struggle to understand, by means inherited from the Christian tradition, the terrible, obvious fact of the death of God.

Acknowledgements

I wish to express my gratitude to the British Council and to Lincoln College, Oxford, whose generous support made it possible for me to spend two years at the University of Oxford; to the Norwegian Research Council for Science and the Humanities for a publication grant; to Professor Keith Brown of the British Institute, the University of Oslo, for valuable discussions and criticism during the initial stages of the work; to Dr Stephen Gill of Lincoln College for the best of supervision and encouragement; to Professor Frank Kermode for his willingness to write a Foreword; and to Jonathan Jones for good friendship and a critical reading of the manuscript. Finally, I would like to thank my family and all our friends in Alan Bullock Close, Oxford, to whom this book is dedicated.

Introduction

Over the years several critics have pointed out the obvious connection between D. H. Lawrence and Christian apocalypticism. Frank Kermode has argued that the entire framework of Lawrence's thought relies on an apocalyptic interpretation of reality. A similar point has been made by L. D. Clark in his article 'The Apocalypse of Lorenzo', and Sarah Urang in her book *Kindled in the Flame*.

Essentially, apocalypticism is a view of universal history. In the *Encyclopaedia Britannica*, for example, it is defined as a term used to designate 'eschatological (end-time) views and movements that focus on cryptic revelations about a sudden, dramatic, and cataclysmic intervention of God in history; the judgment of all men, the salvation of the faithful elect, and the eventual rule of the elect with God in a renewed heaven and earth'.[1] Thus, in theological terms, apocalypticism does not only refer to the end of the world, but also to the millennium. It is this dialectic between forces of destruction and forces of renewal which forms the basic pattern of Lawrence's vision. However, this universal aspect of apocalypticism is closely parallelled, both in traditional Christian thinking and in Lawrence, by a personal and individual one, through ideas of sin and redemption, death and resurrection. In this way apocalypticism offers an entire framework for an interpretation of individual life as well as universal history.

However, there remains one marked and decisive difference between Lawrence and traditional apocalypticism. The Judaeo-Christian view of history depends upon an omniscient and omnipotent God who is above history and who at certain points in time intervenes directly in the temporal journey of mankind. Without God, traditional apocalypticism is meaningless. Yet, this God, who is at once personal and transcendent, is absent in Lawrence, and this absence points directly to a crucial problem in his works: the attempt to retain a vision of destruction and renovation in a godless universe. As a consequence, Lawrence is forced to transfer the individual as well as the cosmic process of salvation from God to man. He invests man with the divine attributes of the traditional God. Against this iconoclastic background, he ends up as both a prophet of doom and a utopian myth-maker and hero-worshipper.

The chief concern of this book will be to show the persistent presence in the cultural and political climate during the period of ideas which contributed to an apocalyptic sentiment; to examine Lawrence's relationship to the political and intellectual movements he encountered; and to show the logical continuity of his writings from the beginning of the First World War to the end of his career. The presentation focuses on the sense of doom which permeates his works from the period of the War and on his restless and worldwide quest during the 1920s. Partly, this was an individual, anti-social quest for a life of isolation away from the world, and partly a quest for a new vision of social and political organization. Particular attention will be paid to the political scene on the Continent and its significance for the development of the leadership ideas.

Lawrence made no claim to be a systematic thinker. As he says in the foreword to *Fantasia of the Unconscious*: 'This pseudo-philosophy of mine – "pollyanalytics", as one of my respected critics might say – is deduced from the novels and poems, not the reverse' (p. 15). Consequently, some would argue that Lawrence in the following is made subject to unfair treatment; that his fiction and his 'pollyanalytics' should be regarded as separate entities. It is the view of the present author, however, that Lawrence's critics have for too long ignored the intimate relationship – which Lawrence himself acknowledges – between the two. This does not mean forcing him into an intellectual framework which is essentially foreign to him or trying to establish once and for all what the writer's 'message' is. It simply means to follow his tracks in order to find the way in which he moves from one area of interest to another. Yet, at the bottom of Lawrence's kaleidoscopic artistic and intellectual odyssey, the apocalyptic interpretation of reality constitutes a sense of coherence and unity which has so far been largely neglected.

It should be mentioned, however, that there is one major aspect of Lawrence's apocalypticism which is not dealt with at all and which would clearly merit a separate study: his family background and his Congregational experience in Eastwood. Thus, in the present study Lawrence's life before the War and its obvious significance for his later development will simply be taken for granted and regarded as a fertile soil for the apocalyptic sentiments he encountered as an adult. The main focus, then, will be placed on the wider background of early twentieth century apocalypticism. However, an exhaustive description of the subject is not intended. As a general rule, only background material of direct relevance to Lawrence's works has been included.

[As to the texts of Lawrence's own works, the Cambridge edition has been used to the extent that this has been published. For the works not yet published in this series, recent Penguin editions have seemed to offer the most reliable alternative. There are, however, some texts which have been published neither in the Cambridge edition nor in Penguin. In these cases the first edition has been used – as with *The Escaped Cock* (*The Man Who Died*). Furthermore, a number of articles are still available only in *Phoenix* and *Phoenix II*, and letters from later than March 1927 only in the *Collected Letters*, edited by Harry T. Moore.

Due to the large number of references to Lawrence's works, these have all been included – when necessary with an abbreviation – in the running text. All abbreviations are given in the bibliography.]

1

Lawrence's View of History

General Remarks on Lawrence and Apocalypticism

The following is not an attempt to prove that D. H. Lawrence ever adopted a consistent philosophy of history. Unquestionably, he was so keenly aware of the sudden and inexplicable changes both in the individual and society as a whole that he would have felt such an ordering and systematization of history at large both as artificial and as an imaginative straitjacket. During important periods of his life, however, Lawrence was an ardent student of history, and frequently in his works he offers views and ideas concerning the forces of historical movement. This interest in the past must, of course, be seen in relationship with his view of life in general. Being an artist not primarily interested in the details of man's material and social welfare, but rather in his connections and relationships with his cosmic surroundings, Lawrence necessarily regarded history as a dramatic encounter of human aspirations and universal, non-human forces.

Lawrence was a spiritual revolutionary, calling for fundamental and far-reaching changes in a world which, he claimed, would otherwise be destined for final doom and destruction. His missionary zeal for change necessarily had to include a vision of some greater framework within which such a transformation of life could take place. Also, such a framework or body of ideas would serve to explain the urgency and the scale of the proposed saving operation. Thus, when reading Lawrence, one would expect to find a view of universal history which would match his view of man's individual destiny, that is, a view of history which could account for sudden and radical movements as well as explain that the world is now in the midst of such a decisive and critical upheaval.

Again, this does not suggest that Lawrence was searching for, or that he ever adopted, a unified system of thought concerning the movement of history. Still, it is the contention of this book that the broad outline of history inherent in Christian apocalyptic thought offers the most convincing model by which a modern reader can come to an understanding of Lawrence's mental horizon and of his life-long quest for a solution to the existential problems he encountered. Naturally, it is not meant to reduce to a simple formula Lawrence's total contribution as an artist, but rather to indicate the background against which the complexities of his message should be evaluated. To put it in a more Lawrentian manner, apocalypticism is the soil in which the flowers of his art are most firmly rooted, or in the words of Frank Kermode, 'the chief mould of [his] imaginative activity'.[1]

Apocalypticism, then, should not be regarded as a paradigm or pattern which Lawrence deliberately and consciously imposed on his writings. Indeed, it may be argued that every culture has its own deeply inculcated view concerning history and its essential significance, even when this view is not explicitly formulated or expressed. For instance, the Christian culture of Western Europe may be said to have adopted the Jewish or Biblical linear view, whose most important characteristic is the apocalyptic element. In Lawrence, however, this element is both radicalized and applied directly to the present, a present which is seen as enmeshed in an acute historical crisis; it is not, as is frequently the case, regarded as a vague idea of events confined to a distant past or a distant future.

By thus placing himself and his generation at the very centre of apocalyptic upheaval and change, Lawrence inevitably assumed the role of a prophet of doom, declaring to a largely unheeding world that the present form of life was bound to collapse. In this respect he joined a long and powerful tradition going back all the way to the great prophets of the Old Testament. Norman Cohn, in his book *The Pursuit of the Millennium*, describes the cultural atmosphere in which 'revolutionary chiliasm' is likely to appear:

> Whether in the Middle Ages or in the twentieth century, revolutionary chiliasm has flourished only where the normal, familiar pattern of life has already undergone a disruption so severe as to seem irremediable. When a way of living which has long been taken for granted is called in question, invalidated or simply rendered impracticable, a situation of peculiar strain is created.[2]

This would certainly seem to describe the general mood around the First World War. Still, it has to be added that both in Lawrence and in traditional apocalypticism this strain is rivalled and to an extent neutralized by a faith which claims that corruption and decay are only the last stages before a renewal of life. As Lawrence himself wrote: 'If we have our fill of destruction, then we shall turn again to creation' ('The Crown', *RDP*, 294). Thus, the prophet of doom also carries a message of hope and expectancy. According to Hans Blumenberg in his book *The Legitimacy of the Modern Age*, 'acute "immediate expectation" tears the individual free even from the historical interests of his people and presses upon him his own salvation as his most immediate and pressing concern'.[3] No doubt this is also the case with Lawrence. As will be shown in the next chapter Lawrence, especially during the war, considered his own country and people cast adrift in the 'river of corruption' (*WL*, 172), and as a consequence he left Britain immediately after the war to seek his personal salvation beyond the barriers of his own society and culture.

Still, the important point is that Lawrence, despite being a prophet of doom, stubbornly retained the conviction that a revitalization was somehow bound to come, and that these two elements, destruction and creation, were inextricably linked. There is, then, a suggestion of a faith in an underlying pattern, or logic, to the complex movements of history.

This leads on to the question of who or what is the driving force behind historical change. Traditional apocalypticism of course relies on the existence of God and his power to uphold, transform and bring to an end the temporal odyssey of man. God is over and above history; he creates it and can interfere with its movement, which is beyond human comprehension. From this point of view, man is left in total ignorance as to the course of universal history. However, a certain pattern is introduced, by the 'apocalyptic types', as Frank Kermode calls them, of 'empire, decadence and renovation, progress and catastrophe',[4] which are generally seen as more or less set periods of time occurring in a predetermined sequence. These, it seems, are man's only clue to an interpretation of the direction and end towards which history is ultimately moving. As suggested before, this sequence of apocalyptic types is the basic paradigm of most historical thinking in the Western world.

In Lawrence the apocalyptic framework can be discerned on different levels and in different versions. In several of his works there is a close relationship and a clear similarity between the individual and the cosmic levels. Both the characters and the world in which they live are caught in an apocalyptic maelstrom. Individual death, for instance, is clearly linked with social corruption.

However, this 'downward rhythm' is not entirely irreversible; there are clues to a possible turning of the tide. But for Lawrence these clues are human in origin, not divine, as in traditional apocalypticism. The resurrection of man from his doom, exemplified by the 'Risen Lord' ('Resurrection', *RDP*, 233) and the 'new-created' lover ('The Crown', *RDP*, 266), goes hand in hand with utopian ideas of a social millennium. Indeed, in Lawrence's celebration of hero worship, one finds in the ability of the perfect leader to change the course of history, a melting together of individual and universal forces. The further implications of these views will be dealt with more extensively later. Let it suffice at this point to say that apocalypticism constitutes in Lawrence the pivotal point, the coordinating principle in the relationship between man and the world, the individual and the universe. Only through death and rebirth can man and society once more come to be 'breast to breast . . . with the cosmos' (*Ap*, 130).

Any view of history is an attempt to stabilize the ephemerality of existence, to put the present into a meaningful relationship with the past and the future. Stephen Spender, discussing this obvious need in man to see himself as part of a greater whole, says that 'it is almost impossible for an artist to-day – a believing artist, one who is not simply an individualist-anarchist – to live entirely in the present, because the present is chaotic. If we want beliefs, or even a view of history, we must either turn back to the past, or we must exercise our imaginations to some degree, so that we live in the future'.[5] Lawrence, living in such a period of chaos and confusion, shows in his works a familiarity with several views of history; indeed, few writers seem to 'move about in time' with greater ease than Lawrence. A certain understanding of these views is needed, and for two reasons: (1) seeing Lawrence as a representative figure of the period, it gives an impression of which ideas regarding history and historical change were current, and (2) it will show how traditional apocalypticism serves as a common denominator for the seeming heterogeneity of historical views appearing in Lawrence's works.

However, before embarking on the discussion of the various views of history known to and expressed by Lawrence, it should be mentioned that the following presentation is largely based on the widely accepted theories of Karl Löwith. In his book *Meaning in History*, Löwith argues that most of the important post-Renaissance philosophies of history are actually secular variants of the Christian or Biblical view of history, thus containing patterns of historical movement related to or similar to traditional apocalyptic and millennial thinking. Admittedly, Löwith's ideas have been under attack, particularly from Hans Blumenberg in his book *The Legitimacy of the Modern Age*, but that is a separate issue, and my exposition will support Löwith's overall thesis. This does not mean that I will attempt to force any theory of history into an essentially Biblical or religious model. As will be shown there are, for instance, other conceptions of history whose origin should be sought in myth rather than in orthodox religion. Nevertheless, these views of history are very easily assimilated into the rather loose and open categories offered by the 'apocalyptic types', and in my opinion this is exactly what happens in Lawrence.

Furthermore, when describing Lawrence's approach to history, it should be kept in mind that the standards of historical scholarship at the time were slightly different from what they are today. Whereas modern historiography, which is strongly influenced by Marxist thinking, may be said to take an almost exclusive interest in the faithful recording of fact and detail, the historians at the turn of the century still allowed themselves to take a broader and more interpretative view of history. This was especially the case with the school of comparative studies, which reached a peak at this period, and there is no doubt that Lawrence was strongly influenced by several such works in cultural and religious history, particularly those by Frazer and Tylor. In *Apocalypse* he says: 'It was not till many years had gone by, and I had read something of comparative religion and the history of religion, that I realised what a strange book it was that had inspired the colliers on the black Tuesday nights in Pentecost or Beauvale Chapel . . .' (64). Evidently, Lawrence's opinions and speculations concerning man's place and role in the great cosmic processes were encouraged by his reading of professional scholars. And this is even more the case, of course, with the quite considerable number of unscholarly works which attracted Lawrence's attention, some of which will be dealt with in the next chapter.

In an attempt to create a reasonably clear picture of Lawrence's conceptions of history, I have divided them into five types, the first three of which are the 'Joachite', the 'organic-cyclical' and the 'heroic-totalitarian' views. Then follows a fourth conceiving history to be a movement of blind forces, and a fifth on the renunciation of history. What is meant by the various categories will be explained in due course. It should be stressed, however, that this division is made for the sole purpose of clarity of exposition, and does not suggest that Lawrence's thinking was similarly divided into clear-cut bodies of thought. Indeed, it is my contention that all these views come together under the umbrella of an apocalyptic-millennial framework.

Before turning to a discussion of the Joachite view of history, a general characteristic of Lawrence's writing, and of his view of history, should be mentioned. As briefly suggested above, Lawrence's message is fundamentally 'this-worldly'.[6] He may be said to represent a view which, in Löwith's terms, would place him in the secular, as opposed to the Christian camp. But such a conclusion is not entirely convincing. What seems to happen is that the traditional conceptions, which regard both the apocalypse and the following millennium as the products of divine interference in history, are in Lawrence transferred from their other-worldly dimension to an earthly vision of a similar quality. The coming drama – as envisaged by Lawrence – is brought about by man himself, but with the semblance of a divine figure lurking in the wings. Again, according to Löwith, it is historically correct to interpret decadent and utopian thought as a secular continuation of religious apocalyptic and millennial ideas. Thus, Lawrence somehow succeeds in retaining a belief in God (or the gods, the Unknown), while at the same time pulling the object of this belief down from its obscure celestial pedestal to the tangible reality of the here and now. Unfortunately, this position is logically unsatisfactory and therefore difficult to defend. Incapable of taking a clear stand – as for instance abandoning the notion of God altogether – Lawrence finds himself on the uncertain threshold between two conflicting world-views: on the one hand, a view which includes as an essential element an extra- and superhuman power; and on the other, the purely *homo mensura* view represented in philosophy by *Lebensphilosophie* and later Existentialism. This fundamental conflict is constantly resurfacing in Lawrence's writings, and it is crystallized in his attempts to come to grips with the problems of historical movement.

Joachism

Joachism is probably the most easily discernible influence on Lawrence's ideas of history, primarily because the Joachite terminology is so clearly distinguishable from that of other philosophies of history. Joachim of Fiore was an 'Italian mystic, theologian, biblical commentator, philosopher of history, and founder of the monastic order of San Giovanni in Fiore'.[7] At his death in 1201, Joachim was widely regarded as an influential but controversial figure, and throughout the medieval period, and even later, the Catholic Church made curiously half-hearted and indecisive attempts to curb the influence of his ideas. However, the book *The Everlasting Gospel*, which was probably written by one of his followers after Joachim's death, for centuries gave nourishment to a peculiar but officially discredited undercurrent in the Church. Karl Löwith describes the Joachite doctrine as follows:

> The general scheme of Joachim's discriminating interpretation is based on the trinitarian doctrine. Three different dispensations come to pass in three different epochs in which the three persons of the Trinity are successively manifested. The first is the dispensation of the Father, the second that of the Son, the third that of the Holy Spirit. The latter is beginning just now (i.e., toward the end of the twelfth century) . . . [It] will come to pass with the reappearance of Elijah at the end of the world. The three stages are overlapping, since the second begins to appear within the first and the third within the second.[8]

It should also be added, apropos of Lawrence and his *Apocalypse*, that Joachim received the scheme as a divine inspiration while reading the Revelation of St. John.

The vision of a new and perfect reign of the Holy Spirit implicitly threatened to render unnecessary the entire function of the Church. Moreover, according to Frank and Fritzie Manuel in *Utopian Thought in the Western World*, the 'great expectation for which Joachim [prepared] the faithful [was] not an apocalyptic end of the world and a transcendent resolution in heaven, but a more immediate event, the appearance within a generation of the Holy Ghost on earth'.[9] Such a 'this-worldly' account of an otherwise distant and esoteric millennium naturally appealed to Lawrence's imagination, and was probably an important reason for his obvious sympathy with the Joachite doctrine. Furthermore, the questions arising from Joachim's position are equally present in Lawrence. Manuel and Manuel claim that 'with doctrines of renewal and progression there is always a problem as to whether renovation can take place within the establishment or whether the order has to be completely refashioned'.[10] Though for Lawrence there is a clear demand for a total renovation, the question still remained throughout his life as to how such a universal change could possibly come about.

It is not known exactly when Lawrence became acquainted with Joachim and his view of history. In the parts of *Twilight in Italy* which were added before publication in book form in 1915, there is a use of imagery which may point to a knowledge of Joachim.[11] Claiming that the Infinite consists of the Father and the Son, Lawrence writes: 'They are always opposite, but there exists a relation between them. This is the Holy Ghost of the Christian Trinity' (*TI*, 46). By 1916, however, Lawrence is definitely well informed about Joachite ideas. In February that year he read *From St. Francis to Dante*, a translation by G. G. Coulton of the chronicle of the Franciscan Salimbene.[12] Apart from a great number of scattered references to Joachim, this book also contains an entire chapter on the life and ideas of the abbot from Fiore. In March, Lawrence wrote to Ottoline Morrell: 'I *love* Salimbene: I liked the book *very much* indeed. It gives one such a robust belief in life' (*Le II*, 572). Joachim is briefly mentioned in *Movements in European History*, written in 1918 and 1919, and this is the only direct reference to Joachim in all of Lawrence's works.[13] Yet there are instances of Joachite influence in other works. In *Studies in Classic American Literature* Joachite imagery is used as an explanatory key to the literature in question. Discussing Hawthorne, for instance, Lawrence says: 'The Father had his day, and fell. The Son has had his day, and fell. It is the day of the Holy Ghost. . . . These people in *Blithedale Romance* have sinned against the Holy Ghost, and corruption has set in' (117). In the chapter on Edgar Allan Poe he writes: '. . . it is the Holy Ghost we must live by. The next era is the era of the Holy Ghost. . . . The Ushers, brother and sister, betrayed the Holy Ghost in themselves' (85).[14] And in the final discussion in *Aaron's Rod* between Aaron and Lilly, the latter says: '"Somewhere within the wholeness of the tree lies the very self, the quick: its own innate Holy Ghost. And this Holy Ghost puts forth new buds, and pushes past old limits, and shakes off a whole body of dying leaves"' (296).

In *The Plumed Serpent*, the influence of Joachite thought is more consistently reflected. As Marjorie Reeves and Warwick Gould point out, the name of Kate's second husband, who had died during the Irish rebellion, is Joachim.[15] But they have failed to grasp the further implications. If we keep in mind the triadic pattern of Joachism, a number of other and seemingly random details are brought to light via this link offered by Joachim's name. To repeat, the first stage of Joachim's scheme is that of the Father, a stage which is connected both in Lawrence and in Joachite thinking with the period of the Old Testament, or the Law. As might be expected, therefore, Kate's *first* husband was a lawyer (70). Also he was the father of her son and daughter. As Kate tells Cipriano: '"I liked him. But I never felt anything very deep for him. I married him when I was young, and he was a good deal older than I"' (ibid.). The second stage of the Joachite pattern, that of the Son or Christ, is connected with Love, self-sacrificing Love, and Joachim, Kate's second husband, loved his country and people so deeply that he, like Christ, was willing to give his life for their freedom. He let 'himself be bled to death for people who would profit nothing by his sacrifice. . . . He was one of the white, self-sacrificing gods' (ibid., 388). Also, like Christ, he had no children. Having left these two stages behind, Kate is ready for what Lawrence described a decade earlier, in the 'Study of Thomas Hardy':

> Now the aim of man remains to recognise and seek out the Holy Spirit, the Reconciler, the Originator, He who drives the twin principles of Law and Love across the ages. Now it remains for us to know the Law and to know the Love, and further to seek out the Reconciliation. It is time for us to build our temples to the Holy Spirit, and to raise our altars to the Holy Ghost, the Supreme, Who is beyond us but is with us ('Study of Thomas Hardy', *SThH*, 126).

In *The Plumed Serpent* this stage in Kate's life is initiated when she makes her final entry into the cult of Quetzalcoatl by marrying Cipriano, the embodiment of the resurrected god.

Thus there is in *The Plumed Serpent* an underlying Joachite pattern to the life of the main character. But it is not just confined to individual lives. It is also present, although more loosely, in the whole structure of the novel. Cipriano, by claiming to be the resurrected Quetzalcoatl and by forcing the new religion on the Mexican people, actually leaves behind the religious stage represented by Christianity and announces the coming of a new and universal era of the Holy Ghost. Thus Lawrence uses the entire religion of Christianity, instead of one of the persons in the Trinity, as one stage in a new and idiosyncratic Lawrentian version of the Joachite doctrine.

Leaving *The Plumed Serpent*, another aspect of Joachism should be mentioned which was certainly appreciated by Lawrence. Joachim regarded 'the persons of the Trinity not only as theological, but also as historical realities', an idea 'flagrantly diminishing the position of Christ . . .'.[16] This introduction of relativity into divine history, which of course was also an essential feature of the historicism of the Romantic period, is reflected in views launched by Lawrence in, for instance, his essay 'On Being Religious', published in 1924: 'As a matter of fact, never did God or Jesus say that there was one straight way of salvation, forever and ever. On the contrary, Jesus plainly indicated the changing of the way' (*RDP*, 191). And in 'Resurrection' from 1915: 'Put away the Cross, it is obsolete. Stare no more after the stigmata. They are more than healed up. The Lord is risen, and ascended unto the Father. There is a new Body, and a new Law' (*RDP*, 233).

The fact that Lawrence made such varied use of Joachite ideas does not prove that he personally believed in such a rigorous pattern of historical change. But it certainly does show that he found it natural to think along similar lines and that these ideas therefore were perfectly suited to emphasize the fundamental content of his writing.

The Organic-Cyclical View

The second view of history relevant to Lawrence I have called the organic-cyclical view. Admittedly, most studies in the philosophy of history make a sharp distinction between so-called linear and cyclical conceptions of history. It may be surprising, therefore, having just placed Lawrence in the mainstream of the traditional linear view, to find that he was equally interested in the cyclical interpretation of historical movement. Again it must be emphasized that Lawrence neither expresses nor claims to express a systematic exposition of history. But at the same time, it should be added that the difference between the two models is not as great as one would expect. Indeed, according to Arnold Toynbee, they have several features in common:

> Shall we opt . . . for the Jewish-Zoroastrian view of history as against the Graeco-Indian? So drastic a choice may not, after all, be forced upon us, for it may be that the two views are not fundamentally irreconcilable. . . . While civilizations rise and fall and, in falling, give rise to others, some purposeful enterprise, higher than theirs, may all the time be making headway, and, in a divine plan, the learning that comes through the suffering caused by the failures of civilizations may be the sovereign means of progress.[17]

When seen from a slightly different point of view, there is in both conceptions a marked element of a struggle between forces eternally opposed to each other, a dialectical movement whose inherent polarity forces history into ever new and radically different stages. Surely, the cyclical conception, as opposed to its linear counterpart, contains the element of repetition. However, this hardly has any significant influence on the mental horizon of the individual, as long as each historical cycle is thought to last for as long as 2,000, 6,000, or even 18,000 years. Consequently, Lawrence's interest in the cyclical view is not necessarily opposed to what has been called his apocalyptic framework.

Actually, it is tempting, as a continuation of Löwith's argument, to consider the turn of the century interest in cyclical theories of history as a secular, intellectual reinterpretation or variant of a traditionally apocalyptic sentiment. Though the two theories are markedly different by the fact that the cyclical view substitutes the personal god with an impersonal fate, this was a time when the nonconformist preachers of fire and brimstone were standing side by side with the intellectual elite in a common prophecy of the final conflagration. The point is that their diagnoses for the future were almost identical despite a seemingly very different background. Also, with respect to Lawrence's works, it is quite futile to look for a consistent distinction between the two views, as he was obviously indebted to both.

Lawrence's interest in the cyclical theory seems to have a twofold origin: on the one hand, the Romantic heritage; and on the other, a fascination with mythology and distant cultures.

There is an uninterrupted tradition all through the nineteenth century, stemming from the Romantic movement, of looking at the world and the cosmos as a living unity, whose life is subject to organic laws rather than to the laws of a personal god. In the philosophy of history, these ideas were a basic ingredient in the works of Herder, Schelling, and finally Hegel, and along with the rest of the Romantic movement they form the ideological basis of the nature tradition in literature, of which Lawrence is a late representative. The cyclical element is particularly evident in the use of analogy. Historical and individual processes are systematically expressed in imagery relating to the life of plants, the seasons of the year, the movements of the planets and so forth. Similarly, contrasts are rendered as an opposition between birth and death, growth and decay, light and darkness. For the Romantics the organic ideas were an attempt to restore a sense of connection between man and the world around him, and at its most optimistic Romantic literature celebrates this very restoration of natural harmony in a world where traditional religion is in decline. Yet simultaneously, the nervous, elusive and somewhat strained aspects of Romanticism testify to an inherent doubt and anxiety as to the possibility of achieving such a lofty goal. In Lawrence the note of optimism is largely subdued and vague anxiety has turned into frank despair. In 'The Crown' he still uses the Romantic language of analogy to natural phenomena, but the message offers no possibility of harmony:

> [We], the peoples of the world, we are enclosed within the womb of our era, we are there begotten and conceived, but not brought forth. . . . We roam within the vast walls of the womb, unnourished now, because the time of our deliverance is ripe, even overpast, and the body of our era is lean and withered because of us, withered and inflexible (*RDP*, 255).

Here the writer's despair is based on the realization that the organic dialectic has been brought to a suicidal standstill. The ordering principle of the universe, the cosmic law governing the life of man and nature, is threatening to collapse. Thus Lawrence sets the scene for an apocalyptic blow to an entire conception of man and his physical surroundings, but he is nevertheless so much a part of its heritage that he retains the language and the ideological frame of reference inseparably connected with it. Although he has no greater wish than to see the wheel of creation moving towards a new spring, a gloomy reality shows the futility of clinging to any faith in progress.

The other and perhaps more important clue to Lawrence's attraction to cyclical theories was the general revival during the late nineteenth and early twentieth centuries of an interest in ancient mythology, together with a new and widespread curiosity for distant cultures and esoteric doctrines. The deliberate turning away from the great heritage of Western civilization was, of course, part of a desperate search for meaningful alternatives to a culture which, according to common consent, had entered its final phase and was about to collapse. This new field of interest also offered alternative views of history, and it is not surprising that the cyclical view attracted particular attention. First, it was a welcome challenge to the traditional scheme of linear movement; second, it offered a remarkably credible account of what processes were actually at work at the present time, and *that*, after all, is the main function of any philosophy of history. At the same time, however, it did not demand an entirely new approach to history. As suggested already, it could, with relative ease, be assimilated into the frame of reference with which everyone in the West was familiar. It would seem that this is exactly what happened with Lawrence.

First, however, a closer look is needed at Lawrence and the revival of ancient mythology. When in 1915 he read John Burnet's *Early Greek Philosophy*, he seemed, judging from his letters at the time, to have completely accepted the entire world view of the ancient Greeks. Before reading Burnet, however, he had also read a substantial amount of Greek drama, and together these encounters with the distant past had a significant effect on his later views. In the field of history, according to Daniel Schneider, a 'Greek idea that influenced Lawrence is that of the alternation of historical periods. Followers of Heraclitus called each period "the Great Year", a period held by some stoics to be that "between one world-conflagration and the next"'.[18] Similarly, Schneider describes the influence derived from Lawrence's reading of Greek drama, represented especially by Empedocles:

> The alternation of Love and Strife is . . . basic in Empedocles' picture of cosmic change; and the idea of such an oscillation in history was accepted by Herbert Spencer in his *First Principles*. Lawrence made the idea central in his *Movements in European History*, where he speaks of movements in the hearts of men . . . 'sweeping them apart for ever on the tides of opposition' . . . . Thus the Heraclitean and Empedoclean oppositions are built into history. And they are built into the organic rhythms of healthy individuals, who, as Lawrence argued in *Women in Love*, must both come together and remain separate.[19]

Besides familiarizing himself with cyclical theories from the ancients themselves, Lawrence was also influenced by similar ideas in more recent writers. As early as 1914 he was aware of Nietzsche's idea of the eternal recurrence,[20] which was no doubt itself inspired by Nietzsche's thorough knowledge of the ancient Greek culture. Lawrence's early acquaintance with this theory is significant, since according to Frederick Copleston, it 'expresses Nietzsche's resolute will to this-worldliness, to *Diesseitigkeit*. The universe is shut in, as it were, on itself. Its significance is purely immanent'.[21] As already mentioned, this is also a persistent theme in Lawrence.

Another source from which Lawrence may well have received similar ideas is the works of Madame Blavatsky. The cycle is a basic symbol in theosophical and other esoteric doctrines, and in *Isis Unveiled*, with which Lawrence seems to have been familiar, Blavatsky asserts with unwavering conviction the universal validity of the cyclical conception of history. Her exposition is quoted at some length because it seems that both her style and content are clearly echoed in Lawrence, notably in such polemical writings as *Fantasia of the Unconscious* and *Apocalypse*.

> To our mind, no stronger proof of the theory of cyclical progression need be required than the comparative enlightenment of former ages and that of the Patristic Church, as regards the form of the earth, and the movements of the planetary system. . . . The 'coats of skin', mentioned in the third chapter of *Genesis* as given to Adam and Eve, are explained by certain ancient philosophers to mean the fleshy bodies with which, in the progress of the cycles, the progenitors of the race became clothed. They maintained that the god-like physical form became grosser and grosser, until the bottom of what may be termed the last spiritual cycle was reached, and mankind entered upon the ascending arc of the first human cycle. Then began an uninterrupted series of cycles or *yugas*. . . . As soon as humanity entered upon a new one, the stone age, with which the preceding cycle had closed, began to gradually merge into the following and next higher age. With each successive age, or epoch, men grew more refined, until the acme of perfection possible in that particular cycle had been reached. Then the receding wave of time carried back with it the vestiges of human, social, and intellectual progress. Cycle succeeded cycle, by imperceptible transitions; highly-civilized flourishing nations, waxed in power, attained the climax of development, waned, and became extinct. . . . How analogous this theory is to the law of the planetary motion. . . .[22]

This definitely agrees with the organic principle of waxing and waning which is a recurrent theme in Lawrence. In *Apocalypse* he remarks:

> The good potency of the beginning of the Christian era is now the evil potency of the end. This is a piece of old wisdom, and it will

> always be true. Time still moves in cycles, not in a straight line. And we are at the end of the Christian cycle. And the Logos, the good dragon of the beginning of the cycle is now the evil dragon of today (125).

In the above discussion of Joachism, *The Plumed Serpent* was used as a case in point. It is characteristic of Lawrence's eclectic attitude to systematic bodies of thought, however, that the same novel also contains elements of the organic-cyclical conception of history. In *The Plumed Serpent*, according to Baruch Hochman,

> the life of civilizations – any civilization – depends on the cosmic life outside it and is ultimately controlled by that life. This idea is ordinarily expressed in the imagery of the ocean or tree of life – of the great oceanic womb of all things, or the tree of life whose roots reach down into the nest of dragons at the heart of the cosmos. . . . The fully developed tree-of-life imagery directly implies a cyclic conception of history'.[23]

Again, Lawrence must have drawn heavily on his reading of comparative studies in mythology and cultural history. Tylor, Frazer and Blavatsky all discuss in relative detail the symbolism connected with the tree in different cultures. Blavatsky, for instance, mentions the Yggdrasill, the tree of life in Norse mythology, which has three roots. 'Under the first root runs the fountain of life, Urdar; under the second is the famous well of Mimer' (containing Wit and Wisdom) and under the third is 'the monster Nidhögg, who constantly leads mankind into evil'.[24] As in the passage from *Apocalypse*, the constant dialectic between opposing forces is clearly suggested. Another episode from *The Plumed Serpent* also shows that ideas of cyclical movement were a constant presence in Lawrence's mind when writing the book. As Kate says of her Indian servant Juana: 'Ah, the dark races! . . . The dark races belong to a bygone cycle of humanity' (148). And finally, in Zelia Nuttall's *The Fundamental Principles of Old and New World Civilizations*, which Lawrence read the same year that he wrote *The Plumed Serpent*, there are references to cyclical ideas in the old Mexican religion:

> The Mexicans believed that four great eras had passed since the creation of the world and designated these as the earth, air, fire and water eras. They believed that, although humanity had always escaped utter annihilation, the world had been almost

> completely destroyed by three of the elements in succession at the end of these eras. At the time of the Conquest, the Mexicans supposed themselves to be living in a fourth age which was doomed to perish by fire.[25]

In *Mornings in Mexico* Nuttall's information reappears as Lawrence's own view of history: 'I prefer to believe in what the Aztecs called Suns: that is, Worlds successively created and destroyed' (12). And a couple of pages later:

> The Aztecs say there have been four Suns and ours is the fifth. The first Sun, a tiger, or a jaguar, a night-spotted monster of rage, rose out of nowhere and swallowed it, with all its huge, mercifully forgotten insects along with it. The second Sun blew up in a great wind. . . . The third Sun burst in water, and drowned all the animals. . . . Out of the floods rose our own Sun, and little naked man (14).

Before leaving the organic-cyclical view of history, it should be noted that Lawrence was far from the only writer of the period who employed these ideas. It should be sufficient to mention but two of his great contemporaries, Joyce and Yeats. As to Joyce's *Finnegans Wake*, John Gross remarks that the 'two most fundamental axioms of the [book] are that history endlessly repeats itself, and that the part always implies the whole. Civilizations rise and fall according to a preordained cyclic pattern, and as the wheel turns the same characters, events, and institutions come round again under different guises'.[26] Similarly, Yeats 'shares with the Hindu conception the unteleological feeling: there is no goal for humanity . . ., history moves in a circle and civilizations only emerge from the womb to sink into it again'.[27] This connects with Lawrence's fundamental 'this-worldliness'. If one could only break through the barriers of the present, one would find that the universe is open-ended. It has no *telos*, no grand finale attached to it. New opportunities are constantly appearing out of the Unknown. In Lawrence's own words: 'It is never finished. That is one thing where Jesus spoke a fatal half-truth, in his *Consummatum Est!* Death consumes nothing. It can but abruptly close the individual life. But Life itself, and even the forms men have given it, will persist and persist and persist' ('The Crown', *RDP*, 292).[28]

In addition, possibly the most important and most controversial philosophy of history launched during the first decades of our century was based on the cyclical pattern. Oswald Spengler's *Der Untergang des Abendlandes* (*The Decline of the West*) was, according to the author, 'eine Analyse des Unterganges der westeuropäischen, heute über den ganzen Erdball verbreiteten Kultur'.[29] In Spengler's vision of history, every culture goes through an organic process of growth and decline, and is 'destined to pass away when its appointed time [has] been completed', that is, after a period of about two thousand years.[30] Though Lawrence is not known to have read Spengler's work, which was first published in 1918, its sheer notoriety cannot have escaped his notice. He also mentions it in the first two versions of *Lady Chatterley's Lover* (*FLC*, 18 and *JTLJ*, 11).

The Heroic-Totalitarian View

Turning now from the organic-cyclical conception of history to what has been called the 'heroic-totalitarian' view, a few words of explanation are probably needed.[31] In the minds of most people the word 'heroic' somehow carries connotations of the nineteenth century, whereas 'totalitarian' is rather more connected with political movements of the twentieth century. From an historical perspective, however, they are closely related, and the works of Lawrence clearly reflect this relationship when dealing with ideas and ideologies of this kind. Furthermore, the following examination argues that there exists a fundamental relationship between Lawrence's apocalyptic framework and these ideas, which he expressed most clearly during the last ten years of his life. But in order to evaluate the importance of heroic-totalitarian ideas for Lawrence's view of history, a certain knowledge of their background and origin is required.

First of all, as to the hero worship of the nineteenth century, a point of departure is provided by the close resemblance and connection between heroic and religious ideas. In his book *The Victorian Frame of Mind*, Walter E. Houghton says:

> If by act and word the hero is a revelation of God, hero worship is a religion; or more exactly, the basis of all religion. . . . Behind this quasimystical point of view, so difficult for us to understand, lay various ideas which are now largely dead: the prophetic tradition of the Old Testament, the religious reading of history, . . . and the powerful strain of pantheism in transcendental thought.[32]

The essential divinity of the genius and the hero is typical of the Romantic sentiment. In the philosophy of history this idea reaches its climax in Hegel's strangely human-divine term of the *Weltgeist*, which is the human embodiment in great individuals – such as Napoleon – of the divine spirit of historical movement and change. These individuals are themselves the vehicles by which history changes its course.

A rebellious variant of the hero, striking an anticipatory note of the twentieth century, is found in the Romantic versions of the Faust myth, in which a defiant individual – Byron's Manfred is probably the most extreme example – 'knows no pardon and asks no forgiveness, either from God or man',[33] and refuses to conform with the standards of religion and society. Generally, however, during the Romantic and Victorian periods, the cult of the hero was regarded as a positive and genuinely healthy reaction against 'the conception of man as a human automaton, whose actions and thoughts were controlled by the total physical environment. . . . In such a state of apprehension the hero embodies everything one longs to hold on to: the self-reliance, the moral character freely choosing the nobler course of action, the dynamic power of the human will'.[34] It is in this tradition that a figure like Thomas Carlyle, eagerly read by Lawrence from an early age, must be seen. This entire heritage, with its uncritical celebration of the heroic individual, is both an essential part of the cultural atmosphere in which Lawrence grew up and one of the pillars on which he later built his criticism of modern industrialism and democracy.

During his formative years, however, Lawrence was also exposed to new and more radical ideas which in many respects continued the nineteenth-century heroic and anti-democratic tradition. And it is not surprising to find that Germany and the Continent again provided a considerable amount of the intellectual ammunition for this clandestine attack on the foundations of Western civilization. Whereas nineteenth-century hero worship was largely an accepted and integrated part of both religious and non-religous views of life and history, this was definitely not the case with the new and more aggressive ideas which were launched in the late nineteenth century, but whose full impact was felt only during the early decades of the twentieth. Naturally, it is not easy, in such a condensed survey, to do justice to the issues in question, but in terms of intellectual history it is undoubtedly correct to consider Nietzsche as the most influential figure. As one would expect, his views of historical change, brought about by heroic individuals, in several respects coincide with those of Lawrence. As with Lawrence, the feeling of impending doom is paramount, but this doom will clear the way not only for a new world but also for a new type of man: 'Behold, I teach you the Superman. The Superman is the meaning of the earth'.[35] Significantly, Nietzsche's vision contains no trace of a god or of divine interference. It is man who will himself bring about the apocalypse and it is man who must make the new dawn possible by creating a new code of values suitable to a godless universe. Nietzsche, in other words, is forced to seek individual greatness, which he sees as the source of historical change, *in* man rather than outside man, which is also the task Lawrence set himself. Also, Nietzsche and Lawrence agree in regarding the collapse of the old order as necessary in order for the hero to bring about positive change. Here we are clearly back in a quasi-religious line of thought: the hero or the Nietzschean superman becomes the saviour who can carry out his mission only when freed from all moral limitations and restrictions. He becomes in short a human substitute of God's omnipotence, promising the millennium as the reward for total allegiance. The Nietzschean hero may be seen as born from despair, a voice calling for some sort of salvation in an empty universe. Still, he proudly asserts *human*, as opposed to divine greatness. No wonder then that Nietzsche, as he himself put it, had 'only a look for those who dare to say the word Faust in the presence of Manfred'.[36] Undoubtedly, Byron's uncompromising hero was closer to his heart than Goethe's.

Marxism is another body of ideas based exclusively on human and materialistic principles but at the same time clearly marked by apocalyptic features. There is no need to go into any detail about the view of history found in Marxist thinking, but its basic elements, the apocalyptic drama of the revolution, the dictatorship of the proletariat – the chosen people – and the utopian vision of the subsequent 'supreme community of communist character'[37] are all very clearly secular accounts modelled on a religious original. In addition, it gives room for the great heroic act in that the proletariat in one decisive and courageous move annihilates the very source of evil, the bourgeois establishment. Though Lawrence does not seem to have shown any particular interest in Marxism, it has to be kept in mind that the overall impact of Marx was such that 'his ideas, like musk, had begun to suffuse the intellectual atmosphere'.[38] Together with the ideological offshoot called syndicalism, which will be described in some detail in chapter 4, Marxism can be regarded as one of the most important contributions to the views of historical movement during this period. No doubt also the practical application of Marxist ideas in the Russian revolution was part of the reason for Lawrence's post-war interest in political measures radical enough to influence the course of history at large.

History as a Movement of Blind Forces

Given the claim that an apocalyptic-millennial framework constitutes the core of Lawrence's view of history, it may seem inconsistent to then argue that his writings also reflect a feeling that history is a series of accidental or even meaningless events, that it is simply a movement of blind forces. The somewhat paradoxical point, however, is that the forces of chaos form an integral part of this basic scheme. The going asunder, the falling apart, the 'reduction of old tissue' ('The Crown', *RDP*, 295) are the manifestations of the apocalypse itself. The very nature of the apocalypse is the free play, the letting loose, like water from a broken dam, of the destructive forces. The only thing to counteract this seeming blindness and futility is a faith which persistently claims that the apocalypse is a temporary incident (though it heralds the end of time) and itself the sign of approaching renewal. This is Lawrence's stubborn position from the war onwards. The end of the world is, so to speak, the point from which he sets out on his quest for a new footing. This sense of enduring a real social and spiritual collapse will be the main topic of the next chapter, but some of the intellectual background referring specifically to the view of history, should be dealt with here in order to get an understanding of how the feeling of approaching doom could reach such proportions.

One important element in the break-up of the traditional view of history as an ordered and meaningful process is the impact of Darwin. According to John A. Lester Jr. in his book *Journey Through Despair 1880–1914*, 'Darwin left no room whatever for purpose in the world, human or divine, or for any free will to pursue such a purpose if there was one. He posited only, in the infinitely remote past, an initiating First Cause. Thereafter, the impersonal, predetermined, external forces of the material world shaped all that man has become and can be'.[39] Consequently, well before the turn of the century the scene was set for a view of history which had to abandon the notion of purpose and design. Later scientific discoveries simply served to emphasize the only remaining certainty – that everything is uncertain.

In the writings of perhaps the three major philosophers of the period, there is a similar stress on the lack of an ordering principle in the movement of history. Schopenhauer's irrationalism, Nietzsche's nihilism, and Bergson's intuition are all based on the painful realization that history is ultimately the product of forces within each individual being, forces of which we only have a very limited knowledge and which lack a common and unifying purpose. The same sense of being caught in an historical holocaust or at least accidental processes is evident, as suggested earlier, in Spengler's cyclical structure, which is 'based on the assumption that "real history is heavy with fate but free of laws"'.[40]

Further examples should not be needed. The point is that such a social and intellectual climate clearly leaves the doors wide open for reactions similar to those of Lawrence. In effect, the apocalyptic tendency had been underway for several decades before 1914, but it seems that the war finally brought to the attention of society as a whole irrefutable evidence of a general decline into chaos. The explosive outburst of despair, which was a result of this experience, is clearly reflected in Lawrence's writings from the war years. This is not to suggest that the war alone brought about this radical shift in his artistic and intellectual development, but it was most certainly of major importance. Moreover, it was a kind of physical, immediate manifestation of the traditional vision of the final days. However, Lawrence also tried to channel his grief and agony into a hope for the future, and it is part of his greatness that he never fully subscribed to the view of life and history as a chemical lottery. Still, especially in 'The Crown', he remained dangerously close to regarding the world as finally consigned to the bottomless pit.

The Renunciation of History

The final element relating to Lawrence's view of history has been called the 'renunciation of history'. This refers to the urge present in many of his works to withdraw from society and to create an alternative life which is wholly independent from the historical reality of the world at large. This, of course, includes Lawrence's entire utopian vision. Like millenniarism, utopianism has for centuries been seen from two radically different positions: positively, as a source of hope and salvation; and negatively, as a romantic and escapist attempt to seek refuge from an unbearable reality. Reading Lawrence one is constantly reminded of this conflict. In later chapters a closer examination will be made of Lawrence's struggle to retain an acceptable balance between a realistic attitude to the world as it is, and the dream and the vision of a better world to come. What seems to be important at this point is to sort out the difference in Lawrence between the so-called utopian and millennial ideas. It has already been claimed that secular utopianism is ultimately rooted in the tradition of religious millenniarism. Nevertheless, they are to be seen as rather distinct variants, the former being a purely earthly vision of an alternative reality in this world, and the latter a vision confined to a *post-mortem* existence in a world renewed by the interference of God in history. Most critics seem to place Lawrence in the secular, utopian tradition while including a touch of diluted religion in the background.

However, as mentioned earlier in this chapter, such a conclusion may prove too simple. First, the utopian tradition as it appears after the Renaissance is concerned primarily with the material and social well-being of the people, whereas the spiritual superstructure is generally of minor importance. The main point is not to seek monastic seclusion in order to live in accordance with a higher and purer reality, but rather to live well, in a society of justice, liberty and comfort. For Lawrence the case is rather different. Being primarily a spiritual revolutionary, he regards man first and foremost as a being hungry for *spiritual* freedom and salvation. The material fulfilment, the need for the bread and butter of existence, plays only an insignificant role in his works. Thus, in novels like *Kangaroo* and *The Plumed Serpent*, even a political revolution is considered only as a means towards achieving spiritual freedom. When in the latter novel Cipriano has brought about the revolution, his first priority is not to provide food and shelter for the poor, but to preach the gospel of the new religion.

Second, what could be called Lawrence's 'utopian vision' is inseparably connected with a violent process of rebirth and resurrection, which is again part of a fundamentally apocalyptic and religious view of life. His utopianism, therefore, carries important elements from both traditions, and should be seen, along Löwith's line of argument, as a secular, 'this-worldly' version of the religious, other-worldly millennium. The apocalyptic tradition, which includes visions of perfection as well as of destruction, is the ultimate point of reference for the display of extremes in Lawrence's writings; extremes, that is, which would otherwise appear as separate and even unrelated to one another. This emphasis on apocalypticism does not mean, of course, that Lawrence was untouched by the utopian tradition in Western thought. On the contrary, this influence is essential for a proper understanding of his works, but, like his view of history as a movement of blind forces, it is made to play a subsidiary role in a greater scheme. This seems the only way to grasp Lawrence's constant preoccupation with death and rebirth on the individual level, and, on the cosmic level, with doom and destruction alongside a vision of a resurrected humanity.

This chapter has offered a deliberately general outline of a number of ideas concerning historical change which Lawrence was either directly acquainted with or aware of as an intellectually minded person of the early twentieth century. Therefore, apart from the discussion of Joachism, which is a rather special case, I have quoted sparingly from Lawrence's own works. Also, when writing about Lawrence's view of history, one is necessarily thrown into the middle of his entire work, which makes a relatively broad view inevitable. It is to be hoped, however, that such a provisional outline gives an indication of how the most diverse ideas about historical movement are actually brought together in Lawrence's apocalyptic-millennial framework, thus creating – despite the writer's strongly inconsistent mind – something like a frame of reference. Granted this, it should be possible to take a closer look at the way in which the various elements of the apocalyptic scheme not only retain their universal dimension, but are also transferred into an underlying principle for Lawrence's view of individual as well as social and political life. This will be the main concern of the chapters that follow.

2

Our Cosmos is Burst: The End of Civilization

The First World War

Apocalyptic thinking is not primarily the result of a cool and rational analysis of reality. On the contrary, it is an emotional attitude, relying on subjective factors such as hope, fear and faith. Consequently, apocalypticism takes different courses at different times. One common point of reference, however, seems to be a sense of the very inevitability of the coming disaster. There always seems to be some cosmic law, some invisible hand with its own inherent logic, with which the human will cannot interfere. Escaping the apocalypse, therefore, requires an attempt to actually turn the tide of history. This then is the situation in which the prophet of doom finds himself.

In Lawrence there is just such a feeling of being part of a greater cosmic process, and during the whole period of the war this process is considered to be almost exclusively destructive. It was inevitable that Lawrence should draw a connection between a war-ridden Europe and the apocalyptic element in his conception of history, and he ultimately came to identify the war as the manifestation of the Armageddon itself. In this way the sense of apocalypse came to dominate Lawrence's view, not only of universal history, but also of the whole range of social and individual relationships struggling to survive under this all-encompassing doom.

For Lawrence the apocalypse is twofold, though essentially the two elements have a common root. First, he maintains that we live in the final stages of the Christian era. This coming asunder of the traditional faith and the values it has created is, of course, tragic and painful. But at the same time, death also carries the promise of a new birth. In 'The Crown' he says: 'The spirit of destruction is divine. . . . In corruption there is divinity. . . . In the soft and shiny voluptuousness of decay, in the marshy chill heat of reptiles, there is the sign of the Godhead' (*RDP*, 292 and 476). The second and complicating element is that the death process has come to a halt, the cycle does not turn, and suddenly the expectation of renewal seems to be based on an illusion. 'The process of birth had been arrested, . . . the past was taut around us all. Then began the chaos, the going asunder, the beginning of nothingness' (ibid., 260). The horror of the apocalypse is further increased by its failure to come to an end and give room to a new world. With such a sense of utter hopelessness, Lawrence wanted *Dies Irae* as the title of the novel which was eventually published as *Women in Love*, and of which he said: 'The book frightens me: it is so end-of-the-world' (*Le III*, 25).

Still, even amid chaos and confusion, Lawrence never abandoned his great vision: to get the wheel of creation moving again. But it is the failure to achieve this goal which is the driving force behind the apocalyptic frenzy of the war years. The first part of this chapter will discuss the presence of apocalyptic thought in Lawrence's works from the period of the war, particularly in the letters and *Women in Love*. 'The Crown' will be used as a more philosophical point of reference. Realizing, however, that the war itself cannot be seen as the sole factor in this development, in the second part I will examine aspects of the literary and intellectual tradition which led up to the war and which surely influenced the overall character of Lawrence's writing.

Lawrence's Letters from the War Years

During the First World War Lawrence wrote two important works which both deal with the death of the Christian civilization: *Women in Love* and 'The Crown', one fictional and one – in the rather loose meaning of the term – 'philosophical' work.[1] In addition, there is *Twilight in Italy*, which was prepared for book publication during the war, and the letters, which provide an invaluable source of information about his more immediate and impulsive reactions to the world around him. Since this 'instinctive' side of Lawrence is often decisive for his ideas in general, starting with a survey of the letters should offer a reasonably accurate clue to his general mood and concerns during the period in question.

Undoubtedly, Lawrence saw the beginning of the war as a disastrous event. Looking back on it a few months later, he wrote in a letter to Lady Cynthia Asquith from January 1915: 'The War finished me: it was the spear through the side of all sorrows and hopes. I had been walking in Westmoreland, rather happy, with water-lilies twisted round my hat. . . . Then we came down to Barrow in Furness, and saw that war was declared. And we all went mad' (*Le II*, 268).

A general characteristic of Lawrence's letters from the war years is his seemingly natural inclination to interpret both personal and political events in apocalyptic terms. In May 1915 he visited Bognor in Sussex, and in a letter to Lady Ottoline Morrell wrote about the 'powerful sea':

> It seemed to me anything might come out of that white, silent, opalescent sea; and the great icy shocks of foam were strange. I felt as if legions were marching in the mist. I cannot tell you why, but I am afraid. I am afraid of the ghost of the dead. They seem to come marching home in legions over the white, silent sea, breaking in on us with a roar and a white iciness' (342).

In September the same year, Lawrence had another experience which obviously made a deep impression on him, because he repeated it in several letters. Again to Lady Ottoline, he wrote:

> Last night when we were coming home the guns broke out, and there was a noise of bombs. Then we saw the Zeppelin above us, just ahead, amid a gleaming of clouds: high up, like a bright golden finger, quite small, among a fragile incandescence of clouds. And underneath it were splashes of fire as the shells fired from earth burst. Then there were flashes near the ground – and the shaking noise. It was like Milton – then there was war in heaven. But it was no angels. It was that small golden Zeppelin, like a long oval world, high up. . . . Then the small long-ovate luminary . . . disappeared again (389–90).

To which he appends this significant remark: 'So it seems our cosmos is burst, burst at last, the stars and moon blown away. . . . So it is the end – our world is gone, and we are like dust in the air' (390).

In other ways as well, Lawrence transforms his own fears into universal significance. During his stay in Cornwall, for instance, he repeatedly maintained that he could not come to London. 'I dare not come to London, for my life. It is like walking into some horrible gas, which tears one's lungs. Really – Delenda est Carthago' (650). And in April 1917 he predicted that 'there will fall a big fire on the city before long, as on Sodom and Gomorrah . . . ' (*Le III*, 118).

As one would expect, political events are viewed in much the same manner. In May 1916 Lawrence commented on the Easter rising in Ireland: 'I must say the Irish rebellion shocked me – another rent in the old ship's bottom' (*Le II*, 611–12). In December the same year, with signs of increasing despair, he told Lady Cynthia Asquith about the state of British politics: 'Here's a pretty state of affairs – Messrs Lloyd George and Lord Derby – funny – pretty! This is the last stage of all, that ends our sad eventful history. So be it. It is what the countryful of swine wanted' (*Le III*, 49). Commenting further on Lloyd George, Lawrence claimed that he will steer

> the ship of the State on to such a wonderful Goodwin Shoal of submerged opposition, that she will split in two like a walnut, and the waters will be over our heads. Good! – so be it. If there is no other way to get rid of their folly, drown it. But we are running rapidly into the jaws of hell, as a country. I am glad. I want now to see the jaws of hell crack our little island like a nut . . . (56).

Even more ferocious, however, is the final judgment Lawrence passed upon England in February 1917, during the most hopeless period of the war:

> I curse my country with my soul and body, it is a country accursed physically and spiritually. Let it be accursed forever, accursed and blasted. Let the seas swallow it, let the waters cover it, so that it is no more. And let it be known as accursed England, the country of the damned. I curse it, I curse England, I curse the English, man, woman, and child, in their nationality let them be accursed and hated and never forgiven (92).

But Lawrence was not solely concerned about the fate of his own country. In March 1917 he wrote to his friend Koteliansky about recent events in Russia. 'What is happening in Russia? Is the world coming to an end?' (102). In a later letter he assured Koteliansky that 'chaos is necessary for Russia. Russia will be all right – righter, in the end, than these old stiff senile nations of the West', adding: 'I don't think chaos is any good for England. England is too old' (284–85). This last remark, however, is curious in the light of what Lawrence wrote to Mark Gertler a few months earlier: ' . . . I feel that nothing but a quite bloody, merciless, almost anarchistic revolution will be any good for this country, a fearful chaos of smashing up' (215). Perhaps the best summation of his feelings came in a letter to Edward Marsh: ' . . . I feel as if the whole thing were coming to an end – the whole of England, of the Christian era: as if ours was the age only of Decline and Fall' (*Le II*, 433).

Thus there is a strong insistence of apocalyptic imagery throughout Lawrence's letters during the war. But as a prophet of doom he runs into obvious difficulties in deciding, for example, which criteria to use to pass the final verdict on Western civilization. Here the letters bear painful testimony as to how the flow of external events throws him into confusion and contradiction, forcing him from one position to the next. Over a short period of three months, Lawrence moves from believing 'an end is coming: the war, a plague, a fire, God knows what' (426) to feeling 'so sad, for my country, for this great wave of civilization, 2000 years, which is now collapsing' (431), before concluding: 'The world is gone, extinguished, like the lights of last night's Café Royal – gone for ever' (499). The timing of the end, whether it *will* take place, *is* taking place, or *has* already taken place, seems to vary from letter to letter. Only a few months later, the final crack of doom is again postponed for a future occasion: 'I do really think we shall see this old order collapsing – even in the outer world – smashing right down' (622).

Women in Love

On the one hand, *Women in Love* is an essay of cultural criticism about the tragic fate of modern Europe. Many of the dialogues in the book relate to this superstructure of ideas. From another point of view, it is a novel developing its fictional plot by means of an elaborate interplay of symbol and imagery. The success of the novel depends on the constant interaction between the two or to what extent Lawrence is able to fuse them into an artistic whole.

On the level of ideas, Lawrence frequently includes material to be found in his letters and other works of factual prose. In the above survey of his letters, Lawrence's fear of London was mentioned. In *Women in Love* this fear is glimpsed in a discussion between Gerald Crich and Birkin as they are travelling in the train to London. As Birkin says: '"I always feel doomed when the train is running into London. I feel such a despair, so hopeless, as if it were the end of the world"' (*WL*, 61). The continuation of their discussion touches upon the very essence of the 'Crown' essay: the failure of our civilization to die finally and give room for a new world. '"Really!" said Gerald. "And does the end of the world frighten you?" Birkin lifted his shoulders in a slow shrug. "I don't know," he said. "It does while it hangs imminent and doesn't fall . . ."' (ibid.). Similarly, in the same scene, Birkin, looking at the land from the train window, thinks to himself: 'if our race is destroyed like Sodom . . .' (59). This idea is also referred to above, precisely in connection with London.

A further parallel to Lawrence's visions of cosmic disaster, such as those found in his letters, can be seen in the grotesque game played by Gudrun and Loerke towards the end of *Women in Love*:

> As for the future, that they never mentioned except one laughed out some mocking dream of the destruction of the world by a ridiculous catastrophe of man's invention: a man invented such a perfect explosive that it blew the earth in two, and the two halves set off in different directions through space, to the dismay of the inhabitants: or else the people of the world divided into two halves, and each half decided *it* was perfect and right, the other half was wrong and must be destroyed; so another end of the world. Or else, Loerke's dream of fear, the world went cold, and snow fell everywhere, and only white creatures, Polar bears, white foxes, and men like awful white snow-birds, persisted in ice cruelty (453).[2]

The intellectual superstructure of *Women in Love*, however, is generally dominated by ideas similar to those presented in 'The Crown', which was written in 1915, after the publication of *The Rainbow* but before Lawrence began writing *Women in Love*. In *Women in Love* Birkin is invariably the mouthpiece for ideas found in 'The Crown'. In his first serious discussion with Ursula, he asks: '"Why? Why are people all balls of bitter dust? Because they won't fall off the tree when they're ripe. They hang on to their old positions when the position is overpast, till they become infested with little worms and dry-rot"' (126). In 'The Crown' Lawrence claimed that 'the fruit of darkness, unable to fall from the tree, has turned round towards the tree and is become mad, clinging faster upon the utter night whence it should have dropped away long ago' ('The Crown', *RDP*, 259).

In a later and crucial discussion with Ursula, during the water-party held by the Crich family, Birkin talks insistently about the necessity of recognising the river of darkness, the downward rhythm, those forces which will eventually bring about the collapse of civilization. It is important, he says, because it is '"our real reality"' (*WL*, 172). It is also our *only* reality, since even '"our white phosphorescent flowers of sensuous perfection"' (ibid.) belong ultimately to the death process, and failing to admit the presence of it is both escapist and illusory. This echoes what Lawrence said in 'The Crown': 'Whatever single act is performed by any man now, in this condition, it is an act of reduction, disintegration. . . . The activity of death is the only activity' ('The Crown', *RDP*, 281).

It has already been suggested that apocalyptic thinking contains an element of inevitability, a one-way movement which cannot be reversed. This is also Birkin's point when he explains the mystery of dissolution to a sceptical Ursula. 'Dissolution rolls on, just as production does,' he said. 'It is a progressive process – and it ends in universal nothing – the end of the world, if you like' (*WL*, 173). Then, as an afterthought, he adds: 'But why isn't the end of the world as good as the beginning?' 'I suppose it isn't,' said Ursula, rather angry. 'Oh yes, ultimately,' he said. 'It means a new cycle of creation after – but not for us' (ibid.). Essentially, the death process is necessary and good, because it is a prerequisite for a new cycle of creation. This is quite in agreement with Christian apocalypticism: the millennium is possible only after the apocalypse. It also explains Ursula's reaction at the end of the discussion. '"You are a devil, you know, really," she said. "You want to destroy our hope. You *want* us to be deathly"' (ibid.). Ursula thus accuses Birkin of being in love, not with this world, but the next, an accusation Lawrence himself raised nearly fifteen years later against certain groups of Nonconformist Christians, in his last prose work, *Apocalypse*. The accusation is interesting because it points to a painfully close relationship between Birkin and low church prophets of doom, the very people Lawrence so strongly attacked. As was suggested in the previous chapter, his fiercely defended 'this-worldliness' constantly shows itself to rely on a vision of the beyond.

Ursula's statement is given further weight by comparing it to what Lawrence says of the war in 'The Crown':

> So we have gone to war. . . . There remains only the last experience, the same to all men, and to all women, the experience of the final reduction under the touch of death. . . . The great thing is that this desire for the consummation in reduction, utter

> reduction, death, may at length be satisfied, before we have lost control, and our living impulse is slipping over the edge, into the void ('The Crown', *RDP*, 475–76).

The process of reduction is seen as necessary for the 'living impulse' to recover, an interpretation very close to certain versions of Christian pietism, which regard the death from this fallen world as a blessing and preparation for the splendour beyond.

The fact that Lawrence actually *wants* this disintegration to complete its course is a significant contradiction, since he is generally said to glorify the life and the opportunities of this world. The reason for this contradiction lies at the heart of his apocalypticism: when Lawrence glorifies the beauty of human life here on earth, he does not glorify it for the way it is actually being lived around him. Rather he praises his *own* vision of what it could be like if it had not been the life of a fallen world. The only logical conclusion to such a contradiction is to try and resolve it through a vision of radical change, a cleansing, a painful process of purification: an apocalypse. This is what Lawrence is desperately hoping for. Without such hope, life remains in a comatose state, nothing but a meaningless waiting for Godot.

Another important aspect of *Women in Love* is the seemingly insignificant role the war plays in the novel. The reason for this is simple: Lawrence's apocalyptic interpretation of the war offered the perfect excuse for not becoming directly involved with it. To him the war was the apocalypse, literally the end of the world. The war is expanded beyond a political struggle between nations into an event of universal proportions. The individual cannot interfere, he can merely witness the cruel logic of history, and this explains Lawrence's numerous withdrawals from public action during the war. Once again the old contradiction emerges: Lawrence's secular, godless universe places man as the master of his own fate. But at the same time historical forces exist of a magnitude beyond human control. No doubt, this conflict explains Lawrence's almost pathological fury against humanity and the world in general during the war. If there is no god who is responsible for the apocalypse, then there is only humanity itself to blame for its own collective suicide.

Turning now to the deeper strata of *Women in Love*, to symbol and mythological imagery, clear-cut thoughts and ideas are exchanged for scenes whose ultimate meaning and significance are more difficult to grasp. To some extent, however, the critical aspect of the book, with its relatively straightforward discussions, can be regarded as a kind of Greek chorus, commenting upon and illuminating the more obscure – and at times almost non-verbal – events.

It seems natural, when dealing with *Women in Love* in terms of the death of Western civilization, to concentrate on the Crich family and the relationship between Gerald Crich and Gudrun Brangwen. After all, the Criches are portrayed as the carriers of the disease of the modern world, and it is clear early on that they are marked by death. In childhood, Gerald accidentally kills his brother, thus acquiring the curse of Cain; Gerald's sister Diana drowns in the lake at the water-party; his father dies a slow and painful death as an old man; his mother is a living ghost; and Gerald himself freezes to death in the Alps at the end of the novel. Moreover, Gerald is described as a living representative of a dying way of life, and his final fate, Lawrence warns, is going to be the fate of the world at large. 'The world of *Women in Love* is . . . a fallen world, almost a demonic world, where evil is a necessary concomitant of experience, and where salvation is possible only for those who are willing to renounce that world completely'.[3] This salvation is what Birkin, and to a certain extent Ursula, are trying to achieve. Thus Lawrence offers a black and white picture in terms of the two couples: Gerald and Gudrun embodying the embrace and acceptance – however hesitant – of this world, and Birkin and Ursula its renunciation.

The symbolism and imagery surrounding Gerald and his family complements what is elsewhere expressed in more direct language. Lawrence employs a great variety of images, such as underworld, flood, 'ice-destruction', steel, cold, snow, etc., to reinforce the sense of the characters being helplessly caught in the death process. Some examples of this apocalyptic imagery will be analysed in the following.

But before turning to a discussion of the Criches, it seems appropriate to consider another central character in the novel, Hermione, and the subtle relationship which exists between her and the forces of darkness. To begin with, her very name is a puzzle. Not even the new Cambridge edition of *Women in Love* attempts an explanation of such a strange choice. There is, of course, Queen Hermione in Shakespeare's *A Winter's Tale*, a play which is saturated with imagery connected with death and rebirth. But there is also an interesting connection directly to Greek mythology. Most commonly, Hermione is known as the daughter of Helen and Menelaus of Troy. More interestingly, however, the shrine of the marine Aphrodite was placed in a town called Hermione, and this direct link with the major Greek goddess opens up a number of possible interpretations of various scenes in *Women in Love*. If Lawrence was aware of what connotations the name had (and most probably he was) – in *Kangaroo* he reveals an awareness of the maritime Aphrodite, and in the 'Prologue to *Women in Love*' he says about Hermione that she is a maker of gods – then it is natural to regard Hermione both as representing the values of Aphrodite and as offering a place in which these values are worshipped (*Ka*, 189 and *WL*, 494). This seems to be exactly the case in the novel.

First, although Aphrodite is a goddess of love and fertility, she is also the goddess of degraded love. But Lawrence goes a step further. In Birkin's words, she is the '"flowering mystery of the death-process. . . . Aphrodite is born in the first spasm of universal dissolution – then the snakes and swans and lotus – marsh-flowers – and Gudrun and Gerald – born in the process of destructive creation"' (*WL*, 172). In 'The Crown', Aphrodite is seen as 'The great goddess of destruction in the sex' (*RDP*, 292 and 476). While in *Twilight in Italy*: 'Aphrodite . . . is goddess of destruction, her white, cold fire consumes and does not create' (*TI*, 35). Comparing these statements with the description of Hermione, one finds interesting similarities. Early in the novel Birkin rejects Hermione's so-called *love*: '"Even your animalism, you want it in your head. . . . It is all purely secondary – and more decadent than the most hide-bound intellectualism. What is it but the worst and last form of intellectualism, this love of yours for passion and the animal instincts?"' (*WL*, 41). Later in the book it is said of her that she 'suffered the ghastliness of dissolution, broken and gone in a horrible corruption' (89). Clearly, Hermione's love is here seen as destructive, a fact which is most strongly expressed by her attempt to kill Birkin with the ball of lapis lazuli.

Second, as in Greek mythology, Hermione offers a place of worship, and in the novel Breadalby is the place where the future lovers Ursula/Birkin and Gudrun/Gerald are brought together. Hermione, the character, and Breadalby, the place, constitute therefore, especially in the early part of the book, the mental and physical atmosphere in which the lovers become acquainted. Further interesting parallels can be drawn to events surrounding Lawrence. To some extent Hermione in the novel was based on Lady Ottoline Morrell, and Breadalby on her manor at Garsington outside Oxford. Here Lawrence was a frequent guest, and as late as March 1915 he wrote in a letter to Lady Ottoline: 'Primarily, you belong to a special type, a special race of women: like Cassandra in

Greece, and some of the great women saints. They were the great *media* of truth . . .' (*Le II*, 297). However, their relationship rapidly deteriorated, and it was brought to an abrupt end when Lady Ottoline read a draft of *Women in Love*. During the actual writing of the novel Lawrence must have revised his view of Lady Ottoline. At a certain point, Lawrence had even suggested Garsington as a place for his Rananim, but obviously by the time of *Women in Love* these plans had been abandoned. This, again, points to a rather drastic change in Lawrence's view of his patron during the first years of the war, Lady Ottoline turning, so to speak, from a goddess of creation to a goddess of destruction.

As to the Criches, a striking parallel is to be found between Gerald Crich and the Greek god Hades, the king of the Underworld.[4] First of all there are constant comparisons between Gerald's professional position as a mine owner and his personal characteristics connected with the underworld and a 'dreadful subterranean activity' (353). Both Hades and Gerald, in other words, are masters of the underworld. Second, it is hardly a coincidence that whereas Hades had a brief affair with a nymph called Minthe, Gerald had a similar affair with a girl of a similar name, Minette.[5] Third, there is a curious similarity between the story of Hades' abduction of his future wife Kore (Persephone) and the chapter 'Sketch-book' in *Women in Love*, which describes one of the first serious encounters between Gudrun and Gerald. In the Greek story 'Kore was gathering flowers in the fields of Nysa with her companions when she suddenly noticed a narcissus of striking beauty'.[6] Gudrun, similarly, is out by the lake together with Ursula, not gathering, but drawing flowers, and she sat 'staring unconsciously, absorbedly at the rigid, naked, succulent stems' of the water-plants (119). Then, in the myth, as Kore bent down to pick the flower, 'the earth gaped open and Hades appeared. He seized her and dragged her with him down into the depths of the earth'.[7] In the novel Gerald and Hermione appear in a boat, and wanting to look at Gudrun's sketch-book 'Gerald stretched from the boat to take it. . . . And as if in a spell, Gudrun was aware of his body, stretching and surging like the marsh-fire, stretching towards her, his hand coming straight forward like a stem. Her voluptuous, acute apprehension of him made the blood faint in her veins . . .' (120).[8] The episode is clearly decisive for the relationship between them, just as decisive as Kore's abduction to the underworld. 'The bond was established between them. . . . [They] were of the same kind, he and she, a sort of diabolic freemasonry subsisted between them'

(122). In this episode one should also remember the presence of Hermione. One of the most well-known attributes of Aphrodite is her ability to fill 'women's hearts with the frenzy of passion',[9] which is what happens to Gudrun.

Thus, in *Women in Love* Lawrence seems to use elements from Greek mythology to emphasize the relationship between certain characters of the novel and the forces of death and corruption. A similar and well documented point is made in Charles Ross' article 'D. H. Lawrence's Use of Greek Tragedy', which deals with the use of ritual in several of Lawrence's works. According to Ross, this fictional technique shows how 'the rituals of modern life are deathly, not life-giving'.[10] A further illustration of this point is made in the following discussion of three other incidents from *Women in Love*.

The first episode of direct relevance to this discussion is what takes place at the water-party. This highly dramatic incident is full of allusions to Gerald and the Criches as being victims of the death force. When Gerald's sister has fallen into the water, Gerald dives in to look for her. After several attempts, he climbs into the boat which Gudrun is rowing. 'He was not like a man to her, he was an incarnation, a great phase of life. She saw him press the water out of his face, and look at the bandage on his hand. And she knew it was all no good . . .' (181). A bit later, having given up the search, Gerald talks to Birkin, Ursula and Gudrun about the depth of the lake where his sister was drowned. '". . . it's curious how much room there seems, a whole universe under there; and as cold as hell, you're as helpless as if your head was cut off"' (184). Then, suddenly, switching from metaphorical to direct language: '"There is one thing about our family, you know," he continued. "Once anything goes wrong, it can never be put right again – not with us. I've noticed it all my life – you can't put a thing right, once it has gone wrong"' (ibid.). Here again we find the inevitability of approaching disaster. It is as if Gerald is foreseeing the death both of himself and the world he represents. He is caught in the grip of circumstance, just as helplessly and unwillingly as when he got his hand trapped in some machinery, crushing his fingers (163). Significantly, the general description of the Criches contains hardly any element of social bitterness. Lawrence describes them with a kind of sympathetic pity, because there is, in his view, no hope for them whatsoever.

The second relevant episode is the chapter called 'The Industrial Magnate', which is a survey of English social history from the late nineteenth and early twentieth centuries, with a typically Lawrentian bias. It describes the helplessness with which Gerald's father and afterwards Gerald himself play their tragic roles as the great representatives of their day. Deep down they are utterly useless and hollow, but they manage to retain a facade of social and personal success. The father epitomizes the ideal of the nineteenth century. He is pious, almost humble before his task in life, and full of paternal responsibility for the welfare of his workers. As his father enters the final stages of death, Gerald takes over the family business, reshaping it to the standards of modern industrial society. Baruch Hochman says about him:

> In Gerald, Lawrence diagnoses the ills of civilization in his time. Gerald is the civilization-hero of the early twentieth century: soldier, explorer, engineer, administrator, potential politician. It is suggested that, in spirit, he rules not only the mines and streets of blighted Beldover, but the entire scope of industrial England, indeed, of any analogous industrial society.[11]

Essentially Gerald is the lens through which Lawrence views the modern world. This becomes even more obvious when he turns to a more detailed description of Gerald as the successful industrial magnate:

> He found his eternal and his infinite in the pure machine-principle of perfect co-ordination into one pure, complex, infinitely repeated motion, like the spinning of a wheel. . . . And this is the God-motion, this productive repetition ad infinitum. And Gerald was the God of the machine, Deus ex Machina. And the whole productive will of man was the Godhead. He had his life-work now, to extend over the earth a great and perfect system in which the will of man ran smooth and unthwarted, timeless, a Godhead in process (228).

Here we are presented with the faltering religion of Gerald's father, a religion reduced to a pious feeling of responsibility for his workers, transformed by Gerald into a mechanised nightmare version of the idea of progress. His father 'had never lost this from his heart, that in Christ he was one with his workmen' (215), but Gerald himself takes over the role of God, as a *Deus ex Machina*. The narrator comments:

> It was the first great step in undoing, the first great phase of chaos, the substitution of the mechanical principle for the organic, the destruction of the organic purpose, the organic unity, and the subordination of every organic unit to the great mechanical purpose. It was pure organic disintegration and pure mechanical organization. This is the first and finest state of chaos. . . . The whole system was now so perfect that Gerald was hardly necessary any more (231–32).

The development of industrial technology is here intimately linked with the universal process of disintegration, a process in which even man himself becomes obsolete and irrelevant. From now on it is the cosmic forces of destruction, with their own merciless logic, which exert control.

Lawrence's description of machines and technology is a direct reminder of the fact that the novel was written in the midst of war. Michael Biddiss explains how each nation during the First World War spent its resources in a 'gigantic conversion of productive into destructive capacity', and the machine, 'so long paradigmatic of the rationalization of the world, was here central to forms of wastage partaking of the irrational, even of the insane'.[12] Thus, Gerald represents not only the mechanized and decadent world, but also the spirit of apocalyptic destruction exemplified by the war itself. Crucially, it is the universal and spiritual, rather than the political and military, significance of the war, which makes *Women in Love* a war novel.

The third episode to be dealt with is perhaps the most obscure. It takes place in the chapter significantly called 'Death and Love', concerning the death of Mr Crich and the final settling of the relationship between Gerald and Gudrun. Certainly, it is no accident that these two incidents take place at the same time, because an atmosphere of death and doom permeates both scenes. The latter event is more or less enclosed, through the narrative technique, by the former, thereby creating an atmosphere in which a normally romantic and even erotic scene is pervaded by death.

Gerald, who has just been told by the doctor that his father's pulse is weak and intermittent, leaves him to walk Gudrun home to Beldover. On the way Gerald confesses his love for her.

> They had descended the hill, and now they were coming to the square arch where the road passed under the colliery railway. The arch, Gudrun knew, had walls of squared stone, mossy on one

> side with water that trickled down, dry on the other side. She had stood under it to hear the train rumble thundering over the logs overhead. And she knew that under this dark and lonely bridge the young colliers stood in the darkness with their sweethearts, in rainy weather. . . . Her steps dragged as she drew near (330).

This whole episode is paralleled by the incident between Birkin and Ursula in the previous chapter. The two should be compared because they exemplify the fundamental duality and opposition between the fates of the two couples. The love scene between Birkin and Ursula takes place in Sherwood Forest.

> [Birkin] drove softly, watching. Then they came to a green road between the trees. They turned cautiously round, and were advancing between the oaks of the forest, down a green lane. The green lane widened into a little circle of grass, where there was a small trickle of water at the bottom of a sloping bank. The car stopped. . . . He extinguished the lamps at once, and it was pure night, with shadows of trees like realities of other, nightly being. . . . There were faint sounds from the wood, but no disturbance, no possible disturbance, the world was under a strange ban, a new mystery had supervened (320).

The two incidents, though clearly parallel, are qualitatively different. Birkin and Ursula are surrounded by an atmosphere of the Garden of Eden before the Fall, with a beautiful harmony between man and nature. Even the trees, half personified, surround the lovers with a silent blessing.[13] There was a 'little circle of grass, where there was a small trickle of water', probably intimating a primitive place of worship with a sacred spring. Gerald and Gudrun, on the other hand, confirm their love, not under the arch of the covenant – the rainbow – but under an arch of squared stone on top of which runs the thundering trains from the colliery. The description suggests an entrance to the underworld rather than to the Garden of Eden. 'They had descended the hill', and the 'arch, Gudrun knew, had walls of squared stone, mossy on one side with water that trickled down . . .'. The very trickling of water clearly has a different note than it had in Sherwood Forest. The arch is also the place where the colliers, the men of the underworld, stood with their sweethearts. This sets Gudrun thinking: 'And now, under the bridge, the master of them all pressed her to himself! And how much more powerful and terrible was his embrace, than theirs, how much more concentrated and supreme his love was, than theirs, *in the same sort*!' (330, italics added). Gerald, again, is the essence, the supreme embodiment, of the spirit of the underworld. Even his love-making reflects the spirit with which he is infected. 'His body vibrated taut and powerful as he closed upon her and crushed her, breathless and dazed and destroyed, crushed her upon his breast' (ibid.). Before they part, Gudrun 'reached up, like Eve reaching to the apples on the tree of knowledge, and she kissed him, though her passion was a transcendent fear of the thing he was . . .' (331). Their relationship is sealed with a kiss, but it is a kiss sowing the seed of destruction. Birkin and Ursula, by contrast, 'kissed and remembered the magnificence of the night' (320). The chapter ends with a sentence strikingly similar in tone to the last sentence in the gospel for Christmas Day, which announces the coming of Christ: 'They hid away the remembrance and the knowledge' (ibid.). The Biblical words are: 'But Mary kept all these things, and pondered them in her heart.'[14]

Thus Lawrence's apocalyptic vision is concealed even in the most remote corners of the novel. Birkin and Ursula carry the promise of future life and salvation, while Gerald and Gudrun, even in their love, are trapped in the maelstrom of doom and destruction. This corruption of their love is seen as Gerald reflects on his prospects of marriage: 'He was willing to condemn himself in marriage, to become like a convict condemned to the mines of the underworld. . . . He was willing to be sealed thus in the underworld, like a soul damned but living for ever in damnation' (353).

Twilight in Italy

All of Lawrence's works discussed so far were written during the First World War. Another of his books, however, *Twilight in Italy*, offers a unique opportunity to study the transformation of Lawrence's views from 1913 to 1915, that is, from the pre-war to the war period. Four of the chapters of *Twilight in Italy* – 'The Crucifix Across the Mountains', 'The Spinner and the Monks', 'The Lemon Gardens', and 'The Theatre' – were all written between September 1912 and April 1913, and the last three of them were published in *The English Review* the following September. Before the publication of *Twilight in Italy* in 1915, however, Lawrence rewrote these chapters, making major changes in the original texts and adding a fair amount of new material. A comparison of the version found in *The English Review* with that of the book version shows a radical shift in Lawrence's views during the two years from 1913 to 1915. Most critics, notably Paul Delany and Emile Delavenay, clearly prefer the earlier version, which is a peaceful and at times idyllic description of Italian people and countryside before the war. But what is more interesting for the present discussion is the way in which the second version – though perhaps artistically inferior – shows an almost obsessive preoccupation with the forces of doom and destruction. Seen against the background of other works from the same period, it is difficult to avoid the conclusion that Lawrence's interpretation of the war should be regarded as the main reason for this radical change. As in *Women in Love*, Lawrence takes a cosmic and strongly apocalyptic view of the world around him. The impending collapse of modern machine culture is clearly connected with references to the war, and compared to the almost pastoral atmosphere of the early version, the language employed in the new material is on the point of becoming hysterical. In the chapter 'The Lemon Gardens', for instance, Lawrence talks about the worship of the machine, describing it with a Blakean metaphor: 'We warlike tigers fit ourselves out with machinery, and our blazing tiger wrath is emitted through a machine. It is a horrible thing to see machines hauled about by tigers, at the mercy of tigers, forced to express the tiger. It is a still more horrible thing to see tigers caught up and entangled and torn in machinery. It is horrible, a chaos beyond chaos, an unthinkable hell' (41). It will be remembered from the discussion of *Women in Love* that the same view – and almost the very same words – were used to describe Gerald Crich in the chapter 'The Industrial Magnate'. Similarly, Biddiss's interpretation of the war industry comes to mind.

It is evident that the threat of chaos was constantly present in Lawrence at the time. As in 'The Crown', this state of disintegration is seen positively as a necessary prelude to a process of renovation. At the end of 'The Lemon Gardens', however, this faith in a new spring seems shattered and weak. Lawrence maintains that 'It is better to go forward into error than to stay fixed inextricably in the past' (53), but then the question is forced upon him: 'Yet what should become of the world?' The answer is not very encouraging:

> There was London and the industrial counties spreading like a blackness over all the world, horrible, in the end destructive. . . . And England was conquering the world with her machines and her horrible destruction of natural life. She was conquering the whole world.

> And yet, was she not herself finished in this work? She had had enough. She had conquered the natural life to the end: she was replete with the conquest of the outer world, satisfied with the destruction of the Self. She would cease, she would turn round; or else expire.
>
> If she still lived, she would begin to build her knowledge into a great structure of truth. There it lay, vast masses of rough-hewn knowledge, vast masses of machines and appliances, vast masses of ideas and methods, and nothing done with it, only teeming swarms of disintegrated human beings seething and perishing rapidly away amongst it, till it seems as if a world will be left covered with huge ruins, and scored by strange devices of industry, and quite dead, the people disappeared, swallowed up in the last efforts towards a perfect, selfless society (53–4).

This sense of helplessness and fury at the state of things is also found in passages dealing with quite different issues. In the chapter 'The Theatre', which describes a performance in Italy of Ibsen's play *Ghosts*, the early version gives a general and far from controversial evaluation of the Norwegian playwright. By the time of the revised version, however, his opinion has changed considerably:

> When one sees the perfect Ibsen, how one hates the Norwegian and Swedish nations! They are detestable. . . . There is a certain intolerable nastiness about the real Ibsen: the same thing is in Strindberg and most of the Norwegian and Swedish writings. It is with them a sort of phallic worship also, but now the worship is mental and perverted: the phallus is the real fetish, but it is the source of uncleanliness and corruption and death, it is the Moloch, worshipped in obscenity (61).[15]

Everywhere Lawrence seemed to detect sources of corruption and decay. Helplessly caught in the grip of the war, almost a prisoner in his own country, he found the forces of darkness closing in.

As has been established above, Lawrence offered a unique and highly personal expression of the view that Western civilization was rapidly entering a final and decisive crisis. Certainly, he was not the only one to claim this to be the case, but compared to most contemporary cultural critics, his was the more uncompromising stance. In his book *The World of Lawrence*, Henry Miller stands out as one of the few critics who have fully grasped the cosmic dimension of the writer's apocalyptic vision:

> Doom! Lawrence sees it written over all the universe. Even more forbidding, more devastating, more complete than Spengler sees it. Not just an Occidental culture, not just the Faustian man, the Gothic soul, and so on, *but man everywhere*. 'Our day is short and closing fast!' He returns to it eternally. He underlines it in red ink and green, in bile and vitriol. Like the Hebrew prophets, he gnashes his teeth and smears his body with dung. He runs among us naked, exposing the festering sores of the spirit. Despair, anguish – like the last man on earth seeing everything perish. Doom! Doom![16]

Lawrence, especially during the war years, seems to have anticipated a literal destruction in fire and brimstone. But the war should not be seen as the sole reason for this extreme position. There is also an intellectual background which should be taken into account. This includes a whole set of historical labels such as *fin-de-siècle*, *Kulturpessimismus*, *Angst*, disillusionment and alienation. Admittedly, these expressions do not contain the acute sense of inevitable physical disaster, which in Lawrence seems to be ultimately rooted in his Nonconformist upbringing, but they still reflect a cultural climate which is compatible with Lawrence's almost total pessimism. Also, it would be naive to assume that Lawrence would not be influenced by the largely non-religious environment in which he spent the latter part of his formative years. The following discussion – which is in no way intended to be a comprehensive survey of the intellectual history of the period – will examine a number of issues, quite different in character, but all related to the widespread feeling of crisis and cultural decay. Moreover, these issues will be related not only to the questions described in Lawrence's own writings from the period, but also to some of the literature he read during these critical years. First, I will mention a few examples of the popular sense of crisis in Edwardian Britain. Then follows an examination of the collapse of traditional, religious values. Finally, I will suggest the impact of modern science and industry.

Cultural Pessimism and Lawrence's Reading

In his book *Journey Through Despair*, an account of the intellectual history of the years 1880–1914, John A. Lester Jr. gives the following general characterization of the period: 'At the risk of imposing arbitrary categories, we may best depict the cultural mood of these years as a drift from unrest to an intense excitement, from excitement to bewilderment, and thence to a darkening disillusionment'.[17] This statement, describing the international scene, also applied to Britain. There was a strong sense of a parallel between Britain at the time and the decline and fall of Rome. There was a feeling of the old order falling apart, and the references to Gibbon were numerous. According to Esmé Wingfield-Stratford, even Britain's military power was seriously questioned: 'Never was there a more humiliating disillusionment than that which the South African War brought in its train.'[18] A Physical Deterioration Report on the physical welfare of the urban poor together with an increasing awareness of mental illness made Britain receptive to ideas suggesting an overall degeneration of the populace. One of the more peculiar consequences of this sense of crisis was Sir Robert Baden-Powell's attempt to restore not only the moral, but also the physical strength of the nation by initiating the scout movement.[19] More intensely than before, dramatic public events were interpreted as signs of an uncertain future. The fate of the Titanic, for instance, was instantly seen as an omen of what was lying in wait for modern civilization in general,[20] and the tragic failure of the Scott expedition to be the first to reach the South Pole haunted the British imagination in the last years before the war.[21]

This pessimism is clearly reflected in a passage in *Women in Love*. Birkin and Gerald, on their way to London, are discussing a newspaper article which calls for 'a man who will give new values to things, give us new truths, a new attitude to life, or else we shall be a crumbling nothingness in a few years, a country in ruin . . .' (54). There can be little doubt that Lawrence himself shared such views. Also, this passage can be seen as one of the first suggestions of his leadership ideas.

A prominent literary feature of the time was the massive wave of so-called invasion literature, which, together with a steadily growing flood of Germanophobic ideas in the popular press,[22] suggest sinister undercurrents behind the polished facade of the British empire. In this literature, which reached a climax towards the end of King Edward's nine-year-old 'Garden Party', one can discern

> what seems to be a progressive pattern: from invasion anticipated and foiled, to invasion easily defeated, to invasion defeated with difficulty and at political expense, to defeat and occupation. Such a sketch is obviously too simple to represent anything so complex as national attitudes, but it does suggest changes in the Edwardian frame of mind that are demonstrable in other terms and that

> can perhaps be best described as a loss of national self-confidence.[23]

The invasion literature was primarily a 'low' rather than 'high' literary form, but at least one figure, that of H. G. Wells, formed a link between the two camps. His novel *The War in the Air* from 1908 was both a fairly conventional invasion story, staging a German invasion of Britain, and a highly sophisticated novel which saw the war no longer as an isolated incident between two nations, but rather as an international conflict with far-reaching consequences.[24] In short, Wells was probably the first to fully realize on the practical level what a modern war would really be like. Lawrence certainly also possessed some acute sense of the significance of such an event, but being relatively ignorant about the technicalities of warfare, his knowledge was on a more intuitive level. However, considering the way Lawrence almost systematically read Wells' books – he certainly read *Tono-Bungay* in 1909 – it is also likely that he read *The War in the Air*.

But even if Lawrence was not an ardent reader of popular invasion stories, it is sufficiently documented that before and during the war he read several books whose content points to a preoccupation with ideas of crisis and disaster. One of the most striking examples of this is Lascelles Abercrombie's dramatic poem *The End of the World*, which Lawrence had read by May 1914. Lawrence, who had met Abercrombie in Italy before the war and expressed a certain admiration for some of his poems, found *The End of the World* repulsive. In a letter to Edward Marsh, he wrote that 'the spirit of the thing altogether seems mean and rather vulgar', but rather significantly goes on to say that 'the best feeling in [it] is a certain bitter gloating over the coming destruction' (*Le II*, 177). And this is exactly the context in which this work is interesting. In the poem a stranger comes to a pub and warns the regulars that the end of the world is near; a star is going to collide with the earth. First, they laugh at him, then start discussing it between them. Another regular enters and tells the rest that the whole village is talking. Fear is rising. A whole crowd enters. They have seen the star approaching. Everyone leaves, except the stranger, who is left in the pub, talking to himself:

> Oh now this life, in the brute chance of things,
> Murder'd, uselessly murder'd! And naught else
> For ever but senseless rounds of hurrying motion

That cannot glory in itself. O no!
I will not think of that; I'll blind my brain
With fancying the splendours of destruction;
When like a burr in the star's fiery mane
The crackling earth is caught and rusht along,
The forests on the mountains blazing so
That from the rocks of ore beneath them come
White-hot rivers of smelted metal pouring
Across the plains to roar into the sea. . . .[25]

From outside the pub they can see that the earth has already 'caught the heat of the star . . .'.[26] Then enters a molecatcher and tells them that the star is moving *away* from the earth, and that the stranger, who has by now disappeared, has fooled them. This is, in its essentials, the plot of the poem. The reason for giving a sketch of it is that Lawrence, about a year after mentioning it in a letter, had a dream remarkably similar to the events in the play. 'I dreamed last night that all the stars were moving out of the sky. It was awful. Orion in particular went very fast, the other stars in a disorderly fashion but all trooping out of the sky, in haste, to the left hand. And some of them, low down, took fire. I was terrified, more terrified than I have ever been. There became a smoke and a burning' (*Le II*, 346). Lawrence may of course have encountered such an incident from his reading of Norse mythology, in which, at the end of the world, 'the stars were coming adrift from the sky and falling into the gaping void', and the earth was set on fire.[27] Equally, it might derive from Revelation: in *Apocalypse*, fifteen years later, he writes of the three woes: 'A star falls to earth: Jewish figure for an angel descending. He has the keys of the abyss – Jewish counterpart of Hades' (109). Whatever the explanation, Lawrence's dream suggests a mind highly sensitive to apocalyptic imagery.

Another book Lawrence read was Vladimir Soloviev's *War, Progress, and the End of History*. Soloviev, a Russian idealist, theologian and mystic, completed the book just before he died in 1900. Lawrence said about him: 'He is interesting, very – but he never says anything he wants to say. He makes a rare mess, fiddling about with orthodox Christianity. Dostoevsky made the same mess' (*Le II*, 343). Yet Lawrence's remark is somehow not very convincing. Perhaps Soloviev is 'fiddling about with orthodox Christianity', but this is exactly what Lawrence himself is doing. Soloviev writes, for instance: 'The real victory over evil in the real resurrection. Only this, I repeat, opens the real Kingdom of God. . . . The resurrection, and not in its metaphorical, but in its literal meaning – here is the testimony of the true God'.[28] These are words which could equally well have been written by Lawrence. Furthermore, in the 'Short Story of the Anti-Christ' at the end of the book, Soloviev presents an anticipatory retrospective view of the twentieth century which is not so very remote from Lawrence's own at the time he read it in May 1915. The story begins: 'The twentieth century AD was the epoch of the last great wars and revolutions'.[29] Soloviev goes on to describe how Pan-Mongolism, having ruled Western Europe for fifty years, is fought back by a new leader, who is first seen as the Great Saviour, but who is slowly developing into the Anti-Christ. His rule of terror is finally brought to an end when he and his armies, during a mission to the Holy Land, are swallowed up by a great volcano rising from the Dead Sea. Soloviev's sense of approaching disaster, together with his vision of the millennium, with which the book ends, have many similarities with the overall pattern of destruction and renewal, which formed the basis of Lawrence's own vision. Indeed, it is tempting to regard his hostile reaction to the Russian as a tacit admittance of the fact that his own apocalypticism was no less a fiddling about with orthodox Christianity than that of Soloviev. Lawrence may have renounced the Christian God, but he always retained a fundamentally Christian view of life.

A third book which Lawrence most probably read towards the end of the war was *Harvest Moon*, a collection of poems by the American poet and playwright Josephine Preston Peabody. In a letter Lawrence asked Harriet Monroe for a copy from the author, because 'the bits you quote of her seem to me very real and valid' (*Le III*, 99). This comes as something of a surprise, Lawrence having disliked both Abercrombie and Soloviev. To a modern reader Peabody's poems may have a touch of melodrama, but Lawrence, in a poem like 'The Hunted', for instance, may have found an echo of his own visionary language:

The over-lord, he has gone his way. . . .
                                                  There
    are no shepherds now.
They have made them gods out of iron and
blood; and they plough a smoldering
path.
Blind and blinded, they follow now, the eyeless
    gods of wrath.[30]

It may even be remarked that the first phrase of this poem – 'The over-lord, he has gone his way' – is similar to an image Lawrence used in an essay from 1923, 'On Being Religious'. Here he says: 'The almighty has vacated the throne. . . . The Most High has gone out. He has climbed down' (RDP, 189). Another of Peabody's poems, 'Sea-dirge', also contains a phrase which would probably fit Lawrence's own mood in 1917: 'Now that the moon is turned to blood, and all, / All doom fulfilled'.[31]

As far as the formation of ideas during the early decades of our century is concerned, Abercrombie, Soloviev and Peabody played a minor if not insignificant role. Certainly, they are not to be counted among the forces shaping the intellectual landscape. Yet their work clearly reflects a generally held attitude. It is not unreasonable, therefore, to consider these works as 'seismographs' of a popular as well as an intellectual sentiment at the time. The fact that Lawrence read and discussed these books, while at the same time expressing views of a similar character shows how far he was part of this shared cultural environment.

A glance at a few of the major names that figured in Lawrence's reading will be sufficient to indicate the extent to which he must have been exposed to ideas of doom and fall. The decadent movement expressed a sense of cultural decay, most notably Baudelaire's *Les Fleurs du Mal*, as well as a number of Dostoevsky's novels, among them *The House of the Dead* and *Notes from Underground*. These were all books Lawrence read before or during the war. But above all in Germany, he must have met a cultural and artistic mood peculiarly receptive to ill omens. 'Max Nordau, the Jeremiah of the period, linked up his famous attack on what were called "*fin de siècle* tendencies" with certain traditional beliefs in the evil destiny of the closure of centuries'.[32] There is no definite indication that Lawrence actually read Nordau's *Degeneration*, but as the book – incredibly enough – was considered a milestone in cultural criticism both in Germany and other countries (it was translated into English as early as 1895), Lawrence would be aware of the overall message of the book. Also, as a general reader of *The New Age* during 1908 and 1909, he may have come across a lengthy article on the feud between Nordau and G.B. Shaw over Wagner.[33] William J. Brazill describes the cultural atmosphere in Germany at the time as the 'Panic terror'. 'They all experienced it: Rilke, Munch, Klee, Hofmannsthal, Kokoschka, all. It was the dread feeling that resulted from confrontation with an existence that was no longer written in fixed forms, from inhabitating a universe that could provide no standard and no value. . . . Nietzsche called it 'the death of God" . . .'.[34] Concerning Nietzsche, there should be no need to venture upon a discussion of his general influence on Lawrence; that should be sufficiently documented.[35] Let it suffice to say that Nietzsche, together with his predecessor Schopenhauer, represents a cultural force which can hardly be overestimated. Lawrence was acquainted with both thinkers from a relatively early stage, and undoubtedly he derived many ideas from both, especially from Nietzsche, who passed the most explicit, devastating and influential judgment on European culture, and who more or less set the stage for all subsequent cultural criticism.

Of the German writers, Lawrence seems to have been especially well informed about Thomas Mann, himself a representative of the sense of pessimism and decay. Robert Lucas, in his book about Frieda Lawrence, suggests that Mann's *Buddenbrooks* – a novel about the corruption and fall of a Lübeck family business – influenced the form of *The Rainbow*.[36] Furthermore, in 'German Books: Thomas Mann', Lawrence discusses several of Mann's major works, among them *Der Tod in Venedig* and *Tonio Kröger*. There is no doubt that Lawrence considered him a decadent writer: 'And so, with real suicidal intention, . . . [Mann] sits, a last too-sick disciple, reducing himself grain by grain to the statement of his own disgust, patiently, self-destructively, so that his statement at least may be perfect in a world of corruption' ('German Books: Thomas Mann', *Ph*, 312).

The above discussion has dealt primarily with popular and intellectual symptoms of crisis, showing a widespread fear for the future fate of Western civilization. But what about the values representing and supporting this ailing tradition? How did they cope with the strain and the challenge? And how did Lawrence experience this struggle?

In the study of history, it is usually taken for granted that a certain set of values or spiritual base structure is required to uphold a social and political system. Both Victorian and Edwardian Britain managed to retain – and for a long time, it seems, successfully – a popular religious commitment. But problems were mounting, as they had been for several decades, and by the turn of the century it 'seemed as if the whole historical foundation of orthodox Christianity were in process of being undermined'.[37] This process of secularization was by no means a peaceful development. The nineteenth century assumed 'that any collapse of faith would destroy the sanctions of morality; and morality gone, society would disintegrate'.[38] But which were the main forces behind this process? Alan D. Gilbert, in his book *Religion and Society in Industrial England*, gives the following answer:

> One was the popularization of what was often called 'the scientific spirit'. Already before 1850 science had begun to exercise a normative influence on most aspects of English thought, and as the century proceeded it increasingly dominated popular definitions of reality. . . . [The] second kind of societal pressure . . . was the pressure of an emerging popular materialism which undermined the religious *a priori*, not in any direct ideological sense, but by deadening what once had been a strong metaphysical element of popular consciousness. There was an obvious and important link between the Industrial Revolution and this basic secularising trend.[39]

On top of all this came the Great War, which brought 'home to the Churches the full extent of their estrangement from the "world" of modern English society'.[40]

This is a very condensed version of the position in which Lawrence, growing up at the turn of the century, found himself in relation to orthodox religion. It also provides an important background to his urgent and at times desperate attempts in later life to find an alternative spiritual foundation. During his student days, according to Jessie Chambers, 'Lawrence was interested in the question as to how the old religious ideas stood in relation to the scientific discoveries that were sweeping away the familiar landmarks'.[41] And in October 1907 he wrote a letter to the Eastwood minister, Reverend Robert Reid, in which he claimed that: 'Reading of Darwin, Herbert Spencer, Renan, J. M. Robertson, Blatchford and Vivian in his *Churches and Modern Thought* has seriously modified my religious beliefs' (*Le I*, 36–7). From this position of doubt and scepticism, caused by the influence of modern, critical science, Lawrence arrived at the view expressed in a letter to Bertrand Russell in July 1915: 'I am rid of all my Christian religiosity. It was only a muddle. . . . I have been wrong, much too Christian, in my philosophy. . . . I must drop all about God' (*Le II*, 364). The immediate background of Lawrence's farewell to Christianity at this time was his reading of John Burnet's *Early Greek Philosophy*, which obviously had a decisive influence on his thinking and which fired his interest in the pagan past.

Lawrence, then, was a typical representative of how the religious foundation seemed to be swept away from under the feet of the early twentieth-century generation. His reaction was also typical in the sense that it demonstrated the drama and the shock of the experience. To Lawrence and his contemporaries the loss of a religious framework had implications which to a later generation may seem almost melodramatic. But considering the fact that this loss had an effect on the very foundations of society, it is not surprising that this generation should have been preoccupied with corruption and decay. Only in the late twentieth century has religion become a 'subcultural phenomenon'.[42] At the turn of the century it still remained, or was thought to remain, at the core of any society. It should also be kept in mind that the 'God-is-dead' experience was primarily confined to an artistic and intellectual elite. To most people at this time the very idea of a godless universe was either unknown or too outrageous to be taken seriously. Naturally, this only served to enhance the feeling among intellectuals of possessing some terrible knowledge, some truth of which the world was as yet unaware, and it explains to a large extent the neurotic and often panic-stricken atmosphere around much of the art produced during the period. The terror of Mahler's music, and paintings such as 'The Scream' by Munch both capture this awful sense of dread. Everywhere in the arts one encounters the realization that this is the end of an era. The values of the vast wave of Western civilization are dead and gone. 'Now, as Christians, we have died. The War was the Calvary of all real Christian men' ('Resurrection', *RDP*, 233).

Turning now to the relationship between science and industry on the one hand, and the fate of Western civilization on the other, it should be remembered that the turn of the century was a period of spectacular progress for the natural sciences, and gradually these discoveries were beginning to influence the general outlook both of intellectuals and of society as a whole. 'More and more toward the close of the 1880–1914 period, literary minds sensed that science had moved into a new phase. The certainties had become uncertain; man was called on to live not so much with a world of materialistic determinism, as with a world of chance and change within which man had now to grope his way in uncertainty'.[43] The view of life offered by modern science was painfully pessimistic; most particularly since the agency of free will seemed forever lost in a whirlwind of circumstance. More and more the universe was regarded as a vast void, indifferent to human aspirations.

> No longer a machine, the universe became a thought, matter a wave, and wave a fiction. Time complicated space, which unimaginably curves. In short, the universe of the engineer-physicist, where Darwin's creatures grew, gave place, if there is place, to the universe of the mathematical physicist and he alone can think it; for he alone can multiply the time-space continuum by the square root of minus one which does not exist.[44]

William Tindall here vividly describes man's estrangement from his physical surroundings, and the feeling of losing control over the forces shaping his destiny. Naturally, there are many examples of this in the literature of the period. In one of Joseph Conrad's letters, for instance, he compares human existence to a huge knitting machine. 'And the most withering thought is that the infamous thing has made itself: made itself without thought, without conscience, without foresight, without eyes, without heart. It is a tragic accident – and it has happened.'[45]

What is important to note is the almost absolute authority ascribed to science at the time. Whereas the nineteenth century had been a period of successive blows to the defenders of traditional religion, the same period displayed an unbroken series of victories for the natural sciences, and at the turn of the century the authority of science was more firmly established than ever before, and perhaps since. Considering the painful implications of the view of life emerging from the flow of new discoveries, this undisputed authority may seem paradoxical. However, the natural sciences, like most movements on the offensive, had managed to force their opponents to accept the scientific definition of the problems in question, and consequently any discussion, whatever the topic, was confined inside the limits of scientifically established conventions.

Studying Lawrence and the literature he read, these problems acquire an interesting perspective. The point is that Lawrence did not attack the theoretical or ideological basis of the scientific view. Obviously it was presented with such enormous authority and momentum that it was next to impossible to question it. As a more manageable alternative, Lawrence instead turned to the symptoms, the practical results of science – to industrialization and the machine culture – attacking them as the principal evil of the modern age. Most explicitly, perhaps, this view is presented in the description of Gerald Crich in *Women in Love*, in Lawrence's last novel *Lady Chatterley's Lover* and, more implicitly, in 'The Crown'. In this respect Lawrence clearly takes a stand more or less identical to such precursors as William Morris and Richard Jefferies. Just like Lawrence, both of these writers saw industrialization and the machine culture in an apocalyptic perspective. According to Graham Hough the 'whole drift of [Morris'] propaganda makes it necessary for him to identify the breakdown of the capitalist system with the breakdown of the machine age'.[46] Against this background Morris wrote in a letter in 1885: 'I have no more faith than a grain of mustard seed in the future history of "civilization", which I *know* now is doomed to destruction, probably before very long . . .'.[47] Thirty years later Lawrence expressed the same view in almost identical terms. Richard Jefferies – of whom Lawrence was 'very fond' (*Le I*, 137) – similarly claimed that the growth of cities and industry would lead to a physical collapse of civilization. This idea is most dramatically expressed in his novel *After London* from 1885, which Lawrence very probably knew.

Another point to note is the scientific, or often quasi-scientific, character of much of the literature Lawrence read. This may be surprising, considering his sceptical and even hostile attitude towards science in general. It serves to prove, however, the authority of science suggested above. Any argument, once it was dressed in the garments of scientific form and vocabulary, carried such a massive claim of representing the truth that it seems almost incredible to an age whose trust in the printed word is so radically weakened. Effectively, at the turn of the century, the high priests of science had assumed the role previously played by the priests of traditional religion; a successfully popularized scientific thesis had become as influential and was as readily believed as a book of prayer or a passage from the Bible a few centuries earlier. When ideas of decline and fall, therefore, were launched in a way that conformed with the principles of science, they were treated with the utmost reverence and respect. This should be taken into account when considering a number of authors whom Lawrence read, among them Madame Blavatsky, Edward Carpenter and Ernst Haeckel. Today their works are certainly regarded as the quasi-scientific products of rather peculiar personalities, but at the time when they were published and read, they carried – to a large degree – the weight and credibility of scientific treatises.

For this reason, Madame Blavatsky's books – the holy scriptures of the spiritualists or theosophists – are highly interesting in terms of cultural history. Though equally antagonistic to both science and religion, Blavatsky claims to achieve a synthesis between them, and it is a synthesis presented in a tentatively scientific manner. An essential part of her argument is the assumption that our civilization is approaching its end, just like innumerable civilizations before us, great cultures which '*reached the culminating point of highest civilization and gradually relapsed into abject barbarism*'.[48] Later in the same book she writes: 'The cycle has almost run its course; a new one is about to begin.'[49]

In Edward Carpenter's works, whose influence on Lawrence Emile Delavenay seems to have given sufficient documentation, one also finds a multifarious body of ideas presented in a scientific vocabulary. According to Samuel Hynes, the 'inclusive eclecticism of much turn-of-the-century thought' is nowhere better exemplified than in Carpenter,[50] and among the dazzle of his ideas one also finds the sense of cultural corruption. In his essay 'Civilisation, Its Cause and Cure' from 1889, he describes the bleak prospects of our civilization: 'In order . . . at this point in his Evolution, to advance any farther, Man must first fall; in order to know, he must lose. In order to realize what Health is, . . . he must go through all the long negative experience of Disease. . . '.[51] In *The Drama of Love and Death* from 1912, he further claims that the 'negative Christian dispensation is rapidly approaching its close'.[52]

Finally, in Ernst Haeckel's book *The Riddle of the Universe* – which Lawrence read as early as 1908 – one finds a blind faith in science, coupled with the view that our civilization is only a minor and transitory incident in an eternal cosmic movement. To the modern reader, Haeckel seems a curious mixture of a cultural critic and natural scientist. While on the one hand complaining about the 'state of barbarism'[53] and corruption in political and social life, he bases his so-called Monistic philosophy on a number of:

> 'cosmological theorems', most of which, in our opinion, have already been amply demonstrated. . . . [Theorems number four and five state:] (4) The innumerable bodies which are scattered about the space-filling ether all obey the same 'law of substance'; while the rotating masses slowly move towards their destruction and dissolution in one part of space, others are springing into new life and development in other quarters of the universe. (5) Our sun is one of these unnumbered perishable bodies, and our earth is one of the countless transitory planets that encircle them.[54]

Later in the book Haeckel says that 'we have an eternal repetition in infinite time of the periodic dance of the worlds, the metamorphosis of the cosmos that ever returns to its starting point'.[55] It is a slightly more mystified version of Lawrence's message in 'The Crown': 'It is we who are carried past in the seethe of mortality. The flower is timeless and beyond condition. It is we who are swept on in the condition of time. So we shall be swept as long as time lasts' (*RDP*, 263).

An important point about Haeckel's book is that it shows, despite its pride and self-confidence on behalf of science, the background of the feeling of dread caused by the very victory of scientific ideas. Towards the end of *The Riddle of the Universe*, the author makes a statement which unintentionally implies the moral void resulting from the scientific world picture:

> It seems to me that these modern discoveries as to the periodic decay and re-birth of cosmic bodies . . . are especially important in giving us a clear insight into the universal cosmic process of evolution. In their light our earth shrinks into the slender proportions of a 'mote in the sunbeam', of which unnumbered millions chase each other through the vast depths of space. Our own 'human nature', which exalted itself into an image of God in its anthropistic illusion, sinks to the level of a placental mammal, which has no more value for the universe at large than the ant, the fly of a summer's day, the microscopic infusorium, or the smallest bacillus. Humanity is but a transitory phase of the evolution of an eternal substance, a particular phenomenal form of matter and energy. . . .[56]

In statements such as this, one discerns the motivation for Lawrence's stubborn refusal to accept a universe in which man has no more value than the 'microscopic infusorium, or the smallest bacillus'. Still, despite his struggle against it, Lawrence could not ignore the scientific affirmation of a cold and empty universe. Most probably, therefore, it contributed, along with the other phenomena mentioned, to the apocalyptic vision of doom and destruction which dominated Lawrence's writings during the war years.

This chapter has dealt exclusively with the dark side of Lawrence's message. Apocalypticism, however, also contains a powerful and consistent hope for the future, a hope which culminates in the vision of a new heaven and a new earth. This idea of the millennium and the various forms it takes in Lawrence's writings, particularly after the end of the war, will be the main topic of the following chapter.

3

A New Continent of the Soul: The Escapist Utopia

Man's longing for another and better world is a fundamental characteristic of both religion and art, and in Western culture this longing constitutes the basis of a long and winding tradition which, especially after the Renaissance, includes an intermingling of religious millenniarism and secular utopianism. Even though they cannot always be clearly distinguished, the believer in religion and the artist generally operate in slightly different ways. The former has a choice between two fairly specific historical periods in which to look for a state of perfection: the world before the fall, represented by the Garden of Eden, and the world after the great *katharsis* of the apocalypse, that is, the millennium. The artist, however, may choose from among a number of historical periods in the past which seem to offer an abundance of those very characteristics which are often so lacking in the present. Alternatively, he may turn to the future, where, free from the dogmatic bonds of traditional religion, the imagination can build new and soaring structures of happiness and perfection.

In times of crisis this attempt to transcend everyday reality becomes ever more urgent, and there is no doubt that the First World War was exactly such a period. 'It was an age of tension between father and son, an age of dreams and prophesies, an age of utopias.'[1] In intellectual history this manifestation of conflict and radical departures should be regarded first and foremost as a violent reaction against, and a deliberate movement away from, the leading values and ideas of established society. It is important to grasp the essential counter-thrust of the reaction for a later evaluation of what may be called early twentieth-century utopianism.[2] This utopianism should be seen against the same background as the apocalyptic literature discussed in the previous chapter; it was an equally desperate attempt to launch a constructive and positive alternative instead of being carried down-stream by the 'river of corruption'.

The utopianism of this period was directed against an array of ideas and institutions regarded collectively as responsible for the current state of affairs. Among intellectuals, the faculty of reason itself was brought under attack, as was the entire mental horizon connected with the natural sciences. Somewhat paradoxically, traditional religion was placed in the same category, since it represented, perhaps even more profoundly than science, the deepest and therefore most despised values of Western civilization. Religion and science epitomized the marriage of spirit and reason which was seen by many as the principal reason for the cultural and social decadence.

The utopian reaction, therefore, moved as far as possible away from the ideas and ideals which had been reigning in Europe for two thousand years. To reduce the situation to binary opposites, there was a deliberate movement from culture to nature, from reason to instinct, from consciousness to the unconscious, from mind to body, and from history to pre-history. This *Umwertung aller Werte* permeated the generation of artists and intellectuals whose experience of the war served as a brutal confirmation that the time had come for a new start. With the old world collapsing around them, the war generation was justified in feeling that it had to start from scratch, turning towards unknown territory to regain a sense of meaning and coherence.

Lawrence provides a radical and strongly personal reaction to this cultural climate. In his works the struggle between the old and the new is fought with a greater intensity than in most other works of the period. Having grown up in a strongly religious atmosphere in a heavily industrialized part of England, Lawrence's break with his background and his denial of its values was all the more decisive and uncompromising. But although Lawrence demonstrates the extent to which it is possible to change direction and pursue new courses, he was also – as he writes in a letter from November 1928 – 'somewhere still the same Bert who rushed with such joy to the Haggs' (*CL II*, 1100). Central to Lawrence's works is this survival of the very heritage he denounced, a heritage which, among other things, embodies the conflict between life as it is and life as it could be.

It may be argued that Lawrence suffers from a contradiction, an essential flaw, whose origin and existence he fiercely denies. He seeks salvation in this world and in this life, but *outside* the confines of the social and historical context into which he was born. His solution is to *move*, whether back in time, or into the future, or to distant places untouched by modern society, or into the unexplored depths of the mind. He signally refuses to act in this world, or, the moment he pretends to act for social and political change, he fails bitterly, because his interest is not primarily with the world at all. Strongly influenced by the Protestant emphasis on individual salvation in the life to come, Lawrence attempts a compromise between his proudly defended 'this-worldliness' and a search for his blessed island of perfection. Escapism underlies Lawrence's claim to offer a set of radically alternative and constructive values, which are in fact nothing but a sprawling, secular set of compromises with the religion he thought he had left permanently behind.

In the final analysis, Lawrence seems to end on a note of defiant and splendid isolation, celebrating a proud individualism which asks for nothing except 'To be alone, with one's own soul. . . . Not to be questing any more. Not to be yearning, seeking, hoping, desiring, aspiring. But to pause, and be alone' (*FU*, 137). This may seem unfair to a man whose life was one endless quest, but the point is that both the quest and the tendency towards isolation may ultimately be part of the same fundamental escapism. Admittedly, Lawrence put up a ferocious fight to avoid the Romantic flight into Elysian fields, and in his works he repeatedly attacks exactly such tendencies in others. But his Nonconformist upbringing still ensured that he retained a life-long and secret love for another and more perfect world.

Lawrence's peculiar indebtedness to a Christian view of life carries through into his use of Biblical language, which should not be considered just as a superficial or artistic means of achieving a powerful prose. Lawrence is not the man to camouflage his message. When he says that 'he who would save his life must lose it' (*SThH*, 19), or 'we shall have to sound the resurrection soon' (*Le II*, 348), then he clearly uses a terminology which can only be understood in a Christian context. Yet, he is not a traditional Nonconformist preacher, and the problem therefore remains: what exactly *does he mean* by terms such as resurrection, salvation, a new earth and a new heaven?

This is the problem underlying the following discussion of Lawrence's utopian vision: how he tries to strike a balance between his own religious background – which planted in him a vision of both a personal salvation and a social millennium – and his later views which dispensed with his childhood concepts of the omnipotent and transcendental God, of eternal salvation and a final judgment.

The closer examination of utopian/millennial elements in Lawrence will be divided into two main groups. The present chapter will discuss what I have called his 'escapist' or 'anti-social' utopia. This includes his plans for Rananim; his quest in history and pre-history for alternative life styles; his exploration of the subconscious, myth and instinct; and finally his celebration of the sexual act as the gateway to a resurrected life. The subsequent two chapters will deal with Lawrence's attempt to enter the political arena and launch a new approach to the organization of society as a whole. The final chapter will try to show how, towards the end of his life, Lawrence ended up with a heterogeneous mixture of ideas, blending elements of apocalypticism and utopianism, individualism and social involvement.

Rananim

It seems appropriate to introduce a presentation of Lawrence's utopianism with a discussion of the Rananim project, a name inspired by the words of an old Hebrew song. Obviously, it is tempting to regard the plans for Rananim as little more than a curious parenthesis within Lawrence's life, a set of rather farfetched ideas brought to a head by the hopelessness of the war and the personal despair from the suppression of *The Rainbow*. No doubt these events are important for an understanding of Lawrence's state of mind during the war years, but alone they do not explain the rather sudden appearance of almost purely utopian ideas at the time. As has been suggested above, in Lawrence the utopia and the apocalypse have a common frame of reference, and should be seen as standing in a dialectical relationship to each other. Rananim – the most naively optimistic product of Lawrence's imagination – is profoundly connected with the total despair and hopelessness which is the other main characteristic of his feelings during the war. Also, as will be shown in the following, the plans for Rananim are expressed in the same religious language as the descriptions of doom and destruction. This use of a religious vocabulary certainly points to a mental framework which always remained at the back, if not at the front, of Lawrence's mind.

The overall impression of the Rananim project is confusion, a losing touch with reality, and an escape into a world inhabited by Lawrence alone. Especially during the war years, Lawrence is subject to a conflict between levels of reality, and the acuteness of this conflict can be traced back to the problem already mentioned of

Lawrence's inability to find a tenable balance between traditional religious values and the 'anti-values' which he acquired as an adult.

At the same time, Rananim is both an introduction to and a background against which Lawrence's utopian ideas can be evaluated. It is, in a sense, a dry run for his later projects; a number of imaginative journeys, most of which took place before he actually left England and set out on his restless quest around – and to an extent beyond – the world.

As with Lawrence's apocalyptic nightmare, the most powerful and comprehensive account of Rananim is to be found in his letters. Thus, I will present Rananim basically in Lawrence's own words and in chronological order. This is perhaps the fairest and clearest way of showing how the lofty plans for a miniature heaven on earth developed and finally collapsed during a tragi-comic party at the Café Royal in London. One may ask why these plans – which for years were obviously important to Lawrence – are treated so sparingly in the novels and stories written at the same time. An answer to this question will be attempted at the end of the survey.

About six months into the war, in early January 1915, Lawrence for the first time mentions the word 'Rananim', in a letter to his friend Koteliansky: 'We are going to found an Order of the Knights of Rananim' (*Le II*, 252). Then two weeks later, in the frequently quoted letter to William Hopkin, Lawrence gave a sketch of the project: 'I want to gather together about twenty souls and sail away from this world of war and squalor and found a little colony where there shall be no money but a sort of communism as far as necessaries of life go, and some real decency' (259). It sounded all very nice, but twenty souls were hard to find, and ten days later Lawrence wrote to E. M. Forster: 'In my Island, I wanted people to come without class or money, sacrificing nothing, but each coming with all his desires. . . . I wanted a real community, not built out of abstinence or equality, but out of many fulfilled individualities seeking greater fulfilment. But I can't find anybody' (266). With renewed optimism, however, he wrote to Lady Ottoline Morrell on 1 February: 'It is communism based, not on poverty, but on riches, not on humility, but on pride, not on sacrifice but upon complete fulfilment in the flesh of all strong desire . . ., not on heaven but on earth. . . . We will found an order, and we will all be Princes, as the angels are' (273).

So far no mention had been made of where Rananim should actually be established. But writing to Koteliansky, Lawrence was expecting a visit from Lady Ottoline and Bertrand Russell, and 'they say, the island shall be England, that we shall start our new community in the midst of this old one, as a seed falls among the roots of the parent. Only wait, and we will remove mountains and set them in the midst of the sea' (277). But a fair amount of patience would have been needed for those mountains to be removed, and in late December 1915 Rananim was moved to Florida. According to a letter from Lawrence to Bertrand Russell only a few formalities remained to be sorted out before they could leave: 'We are waiting to go to Florida, for the others. We must go as a little body: it is not a personal matter – it is a bigger thing. There are several young people very anxious to come. I must wait for them. . . . Won't you come to Florida too? Do! It is hopeless to stay in England. Do you come and be president of us' (490). But only a week later, he wrote in a disillusioned letter to Koteliansky: 'Well, I am willing to believe that there isn't any Florida – assez, j'en ai soupé. I am willing to give up people altogether . . .' (498). Much the same attitude is reflected in a letter written the next day to Katherine Mansfield: 'My dear Katharine [sic], I've done bothering about the world and people – I've finished' (499).

Yet, in late February, Zennor in Cornwall had become the new Rananim – at least for the time being – and Lawrence sent Lady Ottoline an enthusiastic letter:

> When we came over the shoulder of the wild hill, above the sea, to Zennor, I felt we were coming into the Promised Land. I know there will a new heaven and a new earth take place now: we have triumphed. I feel like a Columbus who can see a shadowy America before him: only this isn't merely territory, it is a new continent of the soul. We will all be happy yet, doing a new, constructive work, sailing into a new epoch (556).

Then, towards the end of 1916, Lawrence again wanted to go to America: 'I want, immediately or at length, to transfer all my life to America. Because there, I know, the *skies* are not so old, the air is newer, the earth is not tired' (*Le III*, 25). But the dream of communal happiness seemed far away. He told Catherine Carswell: 'I am glad you are beginning to reject people. . . . They *are* a destructive force. . . . One *must* shun them' (24). And for the next months this was the main message from the cottage at Zennor. On December 23, 1916, Lawrence informed Gordon Campbell: '. . . I have *no connection* with the rest of people, I am only at war with them, at war with the whole body of mankind' (63). Two weeks later, in a letter to his American friend Robert Mountsier, Lawrence gave a rather straightforward description of his position: 'I have *finally* decided that it is only possible to live out of the world – make a sort of Garden of Eden of blameless but fulfilled souls, in some sufficiently remote spot – the Marquesas Islands, Nukuheva' (65). At this point Lawrence's proud 'this-worldliness' was seriously threatened, and though mentioned a few times later, the Marquesas remained little more than a wild suggestion. Instead he returned, four days later, in a letter to Koteliansky, with renewed vigour to America: 'I shall go to America when I can – and try to find a place – and you will come on. That is the living dream' (69). During the first two months of 1917, Lawrence repeatedly made inquiries in order to go to the United States. But in a letter to Catherine Carswell he all but admitted that he was running short of travel companions: 'Do you see Esther Andrews? And how is she? We want her to go with us to America, and to the ultimate place we call Typee or Rananim. There is indeed such an ultimate place' (87). A letter to Koteliansky showed the same desperate will to believe in his plan: 'We shall all come to our Rananim before many years are out – only believe me – an Isle of the Blest, here on earth' (90).

Then, in May 1917, in the midst of the Russian revolution, Lawrence suddenly jumped on a new bandwagon, and wrote to Koteliansky: 'I feel that our chiefest hope for the future is Russia. When I think of the young new country there, I love it inordinately. . . . We will go to Russia. Send me a Berlitz grammar book, I will begin to learn the language – religiously' (121). The tone of the letter is touching in its naiveté and childlike optimism. But two months later he was still a firm believer in the new Russia: 'Russia seems to me now the positive pole of the world's spiritual energy, and America the negative pole' (136). Only three weeks later, however, he wrote to the American novelist Waldo Frank: 'I want to come to America, bodily, as soon as the war stops and the gates are opened. I believe America is the New World. Europe is a lost name, like Ninevah and Palenque' (143–4). And things did not become much clearer when in October 1917 he introduced a new and 'certain' project to Catherine Carswell: 'We shall go to the east slope of the Andes, back of Paraguay or Colombia. . . . This plan at last *will come off*. We shall go. And we shall be happy' (173–4).

From now on there is total confusion. Towards the end of December 1917 Koteliansky received another letter about Russia: 'The war will end by the summer. Then we will really go to Russia' (193). Then, in February 1918: 'I have such a desire, that after the war, we should all go together to some nice place, and be really happy for a bit . . . – perhaps in Italy – . . . And we'll cook for ourselves, and row in a boat, and make excursions, and talk, and be quite happy for a while . . . ' (214). In March Lawrence introduced a new and short-lived project in Palestine, then again 'the thought of U.S.A. . . . sickens me' (383). In November Cecily Lambert received some rather surprising news: 'Well – I shall see you if you come to town this week – otherwise next spring, en route for Zululand' (413). Not long afterwards Lawrence sent Lambert another note: 'I still think of Africa. I hope it isn't true that Nip is losing on horses. If he seriously says he would like us to go out to Zululand, I shall certainly go . . . ' (449). In May 1920 Lawrence was 'planning next Spring to go to the ends of the earth' (516). Three days later: '. . . I should like to talk once more *South Seas*. That interests me finally . . .' (522). In January 1921 he feels that: 'Yes, when I can afford it I shall go to Spain. It is the one European country that still attracts me' (658). And the following month there is a farm in Connecticut: 'I am very serious about this. I want to come' (668). Nothing, however, materializes.

After 1921 the plans for Rananim fade into the background, and the entire project is finally buried three years later. The incident took place in the Café Royal in London, where the Lawrences, according to Harry T. Moore, were hosts for a group of prospective candidates for the Rananim, including 'the Carswells, Murry, Koteliansky, Dorothy Brett, Mary Cannan, and Gertler'.[3] The episode is vividly described in W. H. Armytage's book *Heavens Below*:

> Gertler was not at all communicative, Koteliansky was. Indeed he made a most dithyrambic speech on Lawrence, smashing wine glasses to emphasize his point. Lawrence then spoke. He asked the audience to go to New Mexico with him, to channel their separate strengths into his way of life. It was a pathetic appeal for them to support him.
>
> Mary Cannan was the first to break the silence; 'No', she said, 'I like you, Lawrence, but not as much as all that, and I think you are asking what no human being has the right to ask of another.' Gertler temporized, Koteliansky and Carswell both said that they would go but did not mean it. Only the deaf Dorothy Brett really heard the appeal. Murry went up to Lawrence and embraced him, promising never to betray him and, at that point, Lawrence fell forward with his head on the table and vomited.

The action was symbolic. Lawrence had had his last supper, and in March 1924 he sailed for Taos with Frieda and Dorothy Brett. Rananim, like Pantisocracy, was dead.[4]

As suggested above, there is not much to be found in the novels and stories that points to a preoccupation with Rananim. However, in *Women in Love*, which was written at the time when Rananim was most important to Lawrence, there *are* hints of a similar urge to go away and create something new in isolation from the world. In the chapter 'An Island', Ursula and Birkin have been – not insignificantly – to an island in the pond and are about to part, and a central question is posed:

> 'One must throw everything away – let everything go, to get the one last thing one wants,' he said.
>
> 'What thing?' she asked, in challenge.
>
> 'I don't know – freedom together', he said. She had wanted him to say 'love' (132).

This episode offers in a nutshell a brilliant portrait of Birkin, and of Lawrence: their demand for an absolute and ascetic denial of the world, combined with an uneasy evasiveness when it comes to the ultimate aim of such a radical action. Later in the book the same uncertainty occurs when Ursula and Birkin have finally settled their relationship and are wondering what to do and where to go:

> 'You see, my love,' she said, 'I'm afraid that while we are only people, we've got to take the world that's given – because there isn't any other.'
>
> 'Yes, there is,' he said. 'There's somewhere where we can be free – somewhere where one needn't wear much clothes – none even – where one meets a few people who have gone through enough, and can take things for granted – where you be yourself, without bothering. There is somewhere – there are one or two people ——'
>
> 'But where ——?' she sighed.
>
> 'Somewhere – anywhere. Let's wander off. That's the thing to do – let's wander off.'
>
> 'Yes' she said, ...
>
> 'It isn't really a locality, though,' he said. 'It's a perfected relation between you and me, and others – the perfect relation – so that we are free together' (315–16).

Unable to give an affirmative answer concerning *place*, Birkin – just as Lawrence accuses the Christian religion of doing – turns around and makes it into a state of mind, a spiritual substitute for a physical reality. The only actual consequence of their utopian vision is their decision 'to write their resignations from the world of work there and then' (316). All the rest is put on that higher and more ethereal plane which Lawrence so deeply detested.

Primarily, then, Rananim satisfied a personal need in Lawrence for some sort of a refuge during the worst mental storms of the war period, and it is to be hoped that the above presentation has brought to light the fragile and wavering nature of the project. Invariably, one is left with the feeling that Rananim was never *meant* to materialize. No doubt this essentially private aspect of Rananim helps to answer the question why it figures so prominently in Lawrence's correspondence but plays such an insignificant part in the other writings from the period. However, this does not mean that Rananim should be seen in isolation from the rest of Lawrence's life and work. On the contrary, it forms an integral part of a vision whose implications go far beyond the mere wish for a peaceful island in the sun.

History and Pre-History

The plans for Rananim reveal much of Lawrence's fluctuating temperament and sense of reality during an important period of his life. Considering the political situation at the time, one is bound to find the project something of a luxury. After all, as Anthony Burgess puts it, 'there was a war on'.[5] But Rananim is also significant in a wider context, because it illustrates the fumbling attempts of a man in the early twentieth century trying to deal with a world suddenly and greatly enlarged. Again, this should be taken into account when considering the more peculiar aspects of Lawrence's writings. Lawrence and his generation, as opposed to that of their parents, grew up with at least three revolutionary processes taking place around them: the impact of the new science was turning man's view of himself upside down; the new psychology, represented primarily by Freud and Jung, was opening up new and as yet unexplored horizons of the mind; and the improvements in communications were bringing the whole world within reach of the individual. Such a series of transformations had a decisive effect on Lawrence's view of reality, and the Rananim demonstrates this opening up of new territory. Inevitably, such an experience also created an atmosphere in which moderation and constraint were easily replaced by a naive and often greedy exploration of the newfound land: '. . . this isn't merely territory, it is a new continent of the soul' (*Le II*, 556).

This tendency is particularly evident in Lawrence's search, in history and pre-history, for peoples and places whose qualities were either unknown or regarded as inferior to those of established society. In several of these he found an innocence and a beauty which transformed them into powerful alternatives to the world in which he lived and, ultimately, into sources of salvation and renewal. This vision of a world free from the conflicts and shortcomings of the present carries a close resemblance to the Christian ideas of the Garden of Eden and the millennium, and to the Greek idea of the Golden Age. In 'Study of Thomas Hardy', finished in December 1914, Lawrence for the first time describes the beauty of the earth before the fall, or perhaps even before man: 'In the origin life must have been uniform, a great unmoved, utterly homogeneous infinity, a great not-being, at once a positive and negative infinity: the whole universe, the whole infinity, one motionless homogeneity, a something, a nothing' (42). Later in his life this interest in a time of unity and harmony turned almost into an obsession, and it became largely a utopian dream-world serving as an antidote against his rather unsuccessful attempts to find his own 'Island of the Blest'. Nowhere is this idealization of the pagan world rendered more elaborately and with greater faith than in the foreword to *Fantasia of the Unconscious*:

> I honestly think that the great pagan world of which Egypt and Greece were the last living terms, the great pagan world which preceded our own era once, had a vast and perhaps perfect science of its own, a science in terms of life. In our era this science crumbled into magic and charlatanry. But even wisdom crumbles.
>
> I believe that this great science previous to ours and quite different in constitution and nature from our science once was universal, established all over the then-existing globe. I believe it was esoteric, invested in a large priesthood. . . . Belt's suggestion of the geographical nature of this previous world seems to me most interesting. In the period which geologists call the Glacial Period, the waters of the earth must have been gathered up in a vast body on the higher places of our globe, vast worlds of ice. And the sea-beds of today must have been comparatively dry. So

> that the Azores rose up mountainous from the plain of Atlantis, where the Atlantic now washes, and the Easter Isles and the Marquesas and the rest rose lofty from the marvellous great continent of the Pacific.
>
> In that world men lived and taught and knew, and were in one complete correspondence over all the earth. Men wandered back and forth from Atlantis to the Polynesian Continent as men now sail from Europe to America. The interchange was complete, and knowledge, science was universal over the earth, cosmopolitan as it is today.
>
> Then came the melting of the glaciers, and the world flood. The refugees from the drowned continents fled to the high places of America, Europe, Asia, and the Pacific Isles. And some degenerated naturally into cave men, . . . and some, like Druids or Etruscans or Chaldeans or Amerindians or Chinese, refused to forget, but taught the old wisdom, only in its half-forgotten, symbolic forms. More or less forgotten, as knowledge: remembered as ritual, gesture and myth-story (12–13).

Similarly in *The Plumed Serpent*, Kate, the main character, compares Mexico to the world before the flood, when 'there was a mysterious, hot-blooded, soft-footed humanity with a strange civilization of its own' (414).

No doubt, this esoteric and universal science-religion was not simply Lawrence's own invention. As suggested earlier such ideas were fundamental to the whole school of comparative studies. They are clearly expressed not only by Belt – whom Lawrence mentions and whose book *The Naturalist in Nicaragua* he had read – but also by Frazer, Tylor, Jane Harrison and Blavatsky. In Lawrence, however, this vision of a glorious past is not just a source of romantic nostalgia. Rather, it is directly linked with the writer's hopes for a new and resurrected humanity. It should be remembered, for instance, that the Marquesas occur both in connection with Rananim and with the description of Lawrence's pagan paradise. Being located, both in time and place, outside the domain of Western civilization, this paradise is considered pure and unpolluted and can for that reason be used as a cornerstone in a new philosophy of life. Here we are back to the essential counter-tendency of Lawrence's message. Rejecting *in toto* the modern world, he embraces what he finds to be most strongly opposed to it. Seeing the ethereal qualities of spirit and reason as the hallmarks of European culture, he turns resolutely in the other direction. 'The promised land, if it be anywhere, lies away beneath our feet. No more prancing upwards. No more uplift' (*FU*, 19). In *Etruscan Places* he proudly announces: 'It is useless to look in Etruscan things for "uplift". If you want uplift, go to the Greek and the Gothic. But if you love the odd spontaneous forms that are never to be standardised, go to the Etruscans' (32).

It is not surprising, then, to find that he sought out parts of the world which had been only sparingly described and digested by European culture. In *Sea and Sardinia*, for instance, he makes a point of the fact that Sardinia 'lies outside; outside the circuit of civilization' (3). In *St. Mawr* the Celtic and Indian elements are consistently used, according to a well-documented article by Keith Brown, as a positive force directly opposed to the degenerate values of Western Europe.[6] In *The Plumed Serpent* Kate's being Irish connects her with the 'aboriginal Celtic or Iberian' heritage which represents something 'older, and more everlastingly potent, than our would-be fair-and-square world' (415). This tendency to glorify the pagan past and the still living remnants of it reaches a climax in Lawrence's later writings. Especially in *Apocalypse* it turns entirely away from historical fact and into an embarrassingly personal sermon drawn from Lawrence's own imagination: 'While men still lived in close physical unison, like flocks of birds on the wing, in a close physical oneness, an ancient tribal unison in which the individual was hardly separated out, then the tribe lived breast to breast, as it were, with the cosmos, in naked contact with the cosmos, the whole cosmos was alive and in contact with the flesh of man . . .' (130).

Similarly, Lawrence envisages a future state of harmony, developing out of an organic process of opposing forces. This is the note on which *Women in Love* ends:

> The game was never up. The mystery of creation was fathomless, infallible, inexhaustible forever. Races came and went, species passed away, but ever new species arose, more lovely, or equally lovely, always surpassing wonder. The fountain-head . . . could bring forth miracles, create utter new races and new species, in its own hour, new forms of consciousness, new forms of body, new units of being (479).

Normally Lawrence attacks any faith in the perfectability of man: 'Fools, vile fools! Why cannot we acknowledge and admit the horrible pulse and thresh of corruption within us' ('The Crown',

RDP, 276). But the idea still remains, and it forms the basis of his entire hope for the future. 'Out of the dragon's den of the cosmos we have wrested only the beginnings of our being, the rudiments of our Godhead' (*MM*, 89).

However, having rejected a traditional Christian faith and a personal god, Lawrence senses a paradox. The millennium and the resurrection into a new life must be explained in human, or more precisely, human-divine terms. Like the Romantics a century earlier, Lawrence tries to find a solution by means of verbal acrobatics. Towards the end of 'The Crown' – when discussing the pagan eternity of the past and the Christian eternity of the future – he attempts a difficult balancing act indeed:

> Without God, without some sort of immortality, not necessarily life-everlasting, but without *something* absolute, we are nothing. Yet now, in our spitefulness and self-frustration, we would rather be nothing than listen to our own being.
>
> God is not the one infinite, nor the other, our immortality is not in the Original eternity, neither in the Ultimate eternity. God is the utter relation between the two eternities, He is in the flowing together and the flowing apart.
>
> This utter relation is timeless, absolute and perfect. It is in the Beginning and the End, just the same. Whether it be revealed or not, it is the same. It is the Unrevealed God: what Jesus called the Holy Ghost (300).

In *Mornings in Mexico* he employs a different image: 'Only that which is utterly intangible, matters. The contact, the spark of exchange. That which can never be fastened upon, for ever gone, for ever coming, never to be detained: the spark of contact. Like the evening star, when it is neither night nor day' (52). But what all this actually means remains a mystery. Stating his theory in doctrinaire and self-confident language, Lawrence still ends up none the wiser with a conclusion similar to that of the Renaissance mystic Nicholas of Cusa, of the *Deus Absconditus*, the Unrevealed God. Yet, despite Lawrence's confusion and verbal juggle, the point is that he is dealing with categories such as immortality, eternity, the absolute, God and the Holy Ghost, and that without these categories his philosophizing would be impossible. His vision of past and future states of harmony is a fundamentally *religious* vision of the world before the fall and after the Second Coming. It is no coincidence, therefore, that Lawrence was actually interested in the exact date of the fall of man and that – according to Baruch Hochman – one of his suggestions was 'the sinking of Atlantis into the sea – that is, . . . the loss of the ancient "life-wisdom" and its dispersion within the myths and religions of various peoples'.[7] As to the idea of future glory, Lawrence makes it clear in *Studies in Classic American Literature* that the 'next era is the era of the Holy Ghost' (85). And in the above quote from 'The Crown', the Holy Ghost is described as 'timeless, absolute and perfect'. Lawrence is not only talking about an intangible spark or a moment of ecstasy; deep down he envisages a lasting state of happiness and true living – in short: a millennium. But by putting God in a place where he cannot be reached, and retaining a vision of the millennium here in this life, Lawrence's hopes were bound to be shattered. His criticism, therefore, of low church Christianity has a tendency to boomerang back on himself. In *Apocalypse* he writes: 'If you listen to the Salvation Army you will hear that they are going to be very grand, very grand indeed, once they get to heaven' (63). Lawrence never showed much interest in heaven, but his vision of a new and resurrected humanity on earth was certainly just as grand as the heaven of the Salvation Army – and also deeply indebted to it.

The Subconscious, Myth and Symbol

Closely connected with the interest in history and pre-history, is Lawrence's highly personal use of the new scientific study of the human mind and the theories concerning myth and symbol. From the turn of the century onwards, these phenomena created a widespread fascination with aspects of the human mind described by terms such as instinct, impulse, primitivism, irrationalism, blood and the unconscious. For most people these concepts remained little more than bywords in a society of essentially proper and traditional Victorian values. In *Women in Love*, for instance, Birkin draws a painfully accurate picture of Hermione's lukewarm passion for primitivism and animalism: '". . . what you want is pornography – looking at yourself in mirrors, watching your naked animal actions in mirrors, so that you can have it all in your consciousness, make it all mental"' (42). By contrast, for Birkin and Lawrence it was rather a matter of life and death, a choice between a world slowly succumbing to a process of disintegration and a world governed by forces promising a new self. '"Only there needs the pledge between us,"' Birkin tells Ursula, '"that we will both cast off everything, cast off ourselves even, and cease to be, so that that which is perfectly ourselves can take place in us"' (147). An Eastwood chapel preacher could not have put it more clearly; this pledge is a religious entry into a potentially new and resurrected life.

Fantasia of the Unconscious and 'Psychoanalysis and the Unconscious', are a good introduction to Lawrence's ideas both on psychology and the question of myth and symbol. But in order to put his position in a better perspective, it would be useful first of all to compare Lawrence briefly with three major philosophers to whom he is clearly indebted. Schopenhauer, Nietzsche and Bergson have all been described as champions of the irrational and the primitive. However, their approach is far more moderate than that of Lawrence. Both Schopenhauer and Nietzsche were well aware of the heart of darkness beating under the skin of the rational self. What Nietzsche, for instance, admired in the pre-Socratic Greek culture was the very fusion of the Dionysian and Apollonian elements, that is, a balance between free-flowing energy and rational restraint.[8] And Bergson's Intuition was similarly the product of a collaboration between intellect and instinct.

When it comes to Freud, however, the extremity of Lawrence's position becomes even more evident. In 'Psychoanalysis and the Unconscious' he puts it quite clearly: 'The Freudian unconscious is the cellar in which the mind keeps its own bastard spawn. The true unconscious is the well-head, the fountain of real motivity' (*FU*, 207). Or in William Tindall's words: 'Fulfilment comes from responsiveness to the unconscious, evil from it repression.'[9] According to Lawrence, even the most controversial and radical exponents of a more positive and tolerant view of the unconscious – possibly with the exception of Carlyle[10] – regarded it as too much of a melting pot of both positive and negative impulses. Pursuing nothing short of perfection, Lawrence ignored the dark side and settled on a view of the unconscious as a road leading to salvation and resurrection, accusing, in passing, Freud of being 'too simple' (*FU*, 167).[11] And for the rest of his life he kept clinging to this position, whose ultimate consequences are perhaps most truly expressed in *The Plumed Serpent*.

In his psychological writings, however, the ideological background is presented in rather different terms. Seeking refuge in a quasi-clinical vocabulary, he expresses himself in a tangle of lumbar, sacral and thoracic ganglions; solar, cardiac and hypogastric plexes and so on. As if Latin terminology would increase credibility, he claims: 'From the solar plexus you know that all the world is yours, and all is goodly' (29). In the chapter of *Fantasia of the Unconscious* which is suitably called 'Trees and Babies and Papas and Mamas' he says that 'since we live terribly and exhaustively from the upper centres, there is a tendency now towards phthisis and neurasthenia of the heart. The great sympathetic centre of the breast becomes exhausted, the lungs, burnt by the over-insistence of one way of life, becomes diseased, the heart, strained in one mode of dilation, retaliates' (52–3). Stressing again the solar plexus as a substitute for the brain, he takes the infallible tone of medieval religious dogma: 'At your solar plexus . . . you have the profound and pristine conscious awareness that you are you. Don't you say you haven't. I know you have' (28). Certainly inspired by a reading a couple of years earlier of *Apocalypse Unsealed* by James Pryse, who quite typically turns to a detailed description of anatomy in order to explain the mysteries of Revelation, Lawrence somehow does not sound very convincing. Still, it cannot be denied that Lawrence in these writings is expressing deep and honest convictions. Having accepted without qualification the unconscious as the very tree of life, it only remains to enjoy its fruits. This metaphor connected with the fall of man is deliberately chosen, because Lawrence actually seems to suggest the possibility of transcending the limitations of human existence by exploiting the energy of the unconscious. In *Fantasia of the Unconscious* he says: 'We've got to rip the old veil of a vision across, and find what the heart believes in after all: and what the heart really wants, for the next future. . . . Rip the veil of the old vision across, and walk through the rent' (16). As will be known, what is behind the veil is God Himself, and ripping the veil is an example of the Faustian *hybris*, by which the human attempts to enter heaven through the back door. Indeed, Lawrence's fervent religious millenniarism coupled with a romantic greed for perfection here on earth makes such tendencies inevitable. If, like the Salvation Army, he had been willing to accept the less greedy compromise of a paradise in the beyond, or the simple fact that it is not for humans to conquer the heavens, then presumably he would never have written a book like *The Plumed Serpent*. Samuel Hynes, discussing the Edwardian turn from social realism to spiritualism, quite sensibly claims that 'if you remove doctrine and dogma from the religious instinct, what you have left is a debased or sentimentalized supernaturalism, things that go bump in the night. . .'.[12] Regrettably, this was exactly the course Lawrence pursued and idealized.

But it would be incorrect to give the impression that Lawrence was entirely alone in his utopian vision of the latent powers of the unconscious. To a certain extent he represents, together with a number of others, a somewhat mystified residue of the Victorian faith in progress. As John A. Lester Jr. puts it: 'The strongest argument in the intellectual reinterpretation of Darwinism was . . . on the basis of prizing the *self-consciousness* which man had attained thus far in the evolutionary process. If acquired characteristics could be inherited, man could be called upon to widen the domain of self-consciousness. . . . The same idea occurs in Shaw's *Back to Methuselah* . . ., where he conceives of men of hundreds of years' longevity. . .'.[13] A similar idea, from Birkin's vision of the 'creative mystery' at the end of *Women in Love*, has already been mentioned. In *The Drama of Love and Death*, Edward Carpenter presents another claim on behalf of the unconscious. The endless series of scientific discoveries during the last fifty years, he wrote in 1912, 'have convinced us that . . . the world we know, is no longer now a film on the surface of an empty bubble, but a curtain concealing a vast and teeming life, reaching down endless, in layer on layer, into the very heart of the universe'.[14] Later in the same book he delivers a pantheistic sermon on the human-divine soul, which is 'destined to rise through all the circles of personal and individual life' and finally enter the 'glory of that Heaven where the All-self dwells radiant as the Sun . . .'.[15]

A similar trust in an underlying universal harmony is reflected with particular force in the occult teachings of the Theosophists and other groups which claimed to bridge the gap between religious faith and scientific truth. The Theosophists found themselves on the margins of established science, but made an efficient use of its language and credibility to put their message across. An important esoteric work like Madame Blavatsky's *Isis Unveiled* shows remarkable similarities with Lawrence's fundamental views. Both Blavatsky and Lawrence turn to a vision of a past Golden Age, which is presented more or less as a model for the renewed world of the future. And the principal means by which this former harmony is to be reinstated is an unquestioning trust in human faculties other than the rational.

Due to the fluid and largely unpredictable nature of the unconscious, it can only be properly expressed in a language and a form which give room to its true character. For Lawrence – as for many of his contemporaries – myth, legend and symbol are the principal means of entering the world of the unconscious, and he uses these elements in his dialectical scheme of destruction and construction. Their very polyvalency makes them capable of expressing both the dread of apocalyptic disaster, and the vision of resurrection and renovation. The following is a brief presentation of the most obvious uses in Lawrence of the latter kind.

The phoenix is probably the symbol most explicitly connected with the idea of physical resurrection, and it was also, of course, the symbol Lawrence chose for himself and his work. Again, the search for unity is central. In 'The Crown' Lawrence envisaged a pantheistic fusion with the universe; the dying phoenix 'was translated into the flame of eternity, she became one with the fiery Origin' (270). This is the harmonious unity from which it is later reborn, the same heaven-like unity that Lawrence claimed to find in the pre-historic ages 'before brains were invented' (*MM*, 11), and in certain remote corners of the earth yet untouched by civilization.

Other major symbols clearly related to the idea of renewal are the rainbow and the sun. The promise of a future cosmic harmony connected with the rainbow is expressed most radically in the famous passage at the end of the novel of the same name. Here it is not only a personal renewal of the individual, but also a renovation of the earth. Nowhere is Lawrence's millennial hope rendered with greater beauty and intensity, and nowhere is it more intimately related to the Christian original:

> And the rainbow stood on the earth. [Ursula] knew that the sordid people who crept hard-scaled and separate on the face of the world's corruption were living still, that the rainbow was arched in their blood and would quiver to life in their spirit, that they would cast off their horny covering of disintegration, that new, clean, naked bodies would issue to a new germination, to a new growth, rising to the light and the wind and the clean rain of heaven. She saw in the rainbow the earth's new architecture, the old, brittle corruption of houses and factories swept away, the world built up in a living fabric of Truth, fitting to the over-arching heaven (458–9).

Elsewhere in Lawrence's works the sun is endowed with much the same significance, most notably perhaps in the short story entitled 'Sun'. Juliet, a typically Lawrentian heroine suffering from the deadly burden of civilization, receives a new life from the sun. Giving herself up and thereby extinguishing her former self, she goes through a cleansing, aided by the healing rays of the sun: 'She was like another person. She was another person' (TP, 123). Significantly, her sudden primitive contact with the life-giving force of the cosmos is explicitly compared to the life of the ancient Greeks. Her husband, 'in his grey felt hat and dark grey city suit' comes to visit, and he looks 'pathetically out of place, in that resplendent sunshine, and the grace of the old Greek world . . .' (133). The symbol of the sun is like a memory of that Golden Age which Lawrence described in such detail in the foreword to *Fantasia of the Unconscious*.[16] In that book the sun is also described in what might be called a symbolic-scientific manner: 'To the sun fly the vibrations of the molecules in the great sympathy-mode of death, and in the sun they are renewed, they turn again . . . towards life, towards living. . . . [The] sun is the great fiery, vivifying pole of the inanimate universe . . .' (153). And in *The Escaped Cock* (*The Man Who Died*), in which Jesus is slowly coming back to life, the 'sun was the one thing that drew him and swayed him' (16).

Trees in Lawrence also frequently carry a memory of a past unity. In the short story just mentioned cactuses and cypresses accompany Juliet's erotic encounters with the sun, as if they were a group of angelic midwives assisting at the birth of her new being. Similarly, in *Aaron's Rod*, when Aaron goes for a walk in the countryside of Tuscany: 'In the dark, mindful silence and inflection of the cypress trees, lost races, lost language, lost human ways of feeling and of knowing. Men have known as we can no more know, have felt as we can no more feel. Great life-realities gone into the darkness. But the cypresses commemorate' (265). In *Fantasia of the Unconscious*, talking about human psychology, Lawrence suddenly and unexpectedly turns to a discussion of trees: 'I would like to be a tree for a while. The great lust of roots. Root-lust. And no mind at all. . . . I used to fear their lust, their rushing, black lust. But now I like it, I worship it. . . . I lose myself among the trees . . .' (44). This root-lust is a longing for the renewing power of the 'immense, mindless life' of the unconscious: 'tree of everything except the spirit, spirituality' (45). Furthermore, in *The Plumed Serpent* trees are even directly connected with the risen god, Quetzalcoatl. In one of the hymns, it is said that: 'Quetzalcoatl loves the shade of trees. / Give him trees! Call back the trees! / We are like trees, tall and rustling. / *Quetzalcoatl is among the trees*' (349–50).

Finally, Lawrence makes an extensive use of imagery connected with snakes and serpents. In Tylor's *Primitive Culture* he would have read about cultures in which the snake was regarded as a holy creature, 'whose change of skin has so often been associated with the thought of resurrection and immortality'.[17] In *Isis Unveiled* Madame Blavatsky sees the snake in a cosmic perspective related to the cyclical view of history: 'According to the notions of the oldest philosophers . . . the earth, serpent-like, casts off its skin and appears after every minor prayala [a geological cataclysm] in a rejuvenated state. . .'.[18] As to Lawrence's own writings, he mentions in a letter that '[I] would like to change my skin, like the serpent' (*Le IV*, 185), while the significance of the snake in Revelation is discussed in some detail in *Apocalypse*, and in *The Plumed Serpent* of course it lies at the basis of the whole novel: Quetzalcoatl is the old Mexican serpent god reborn in the person of Don Ramón. In the famous poem 'Snake', Lawrence describes the snake visiting his water-trough as a 'king in exile, uncrowned in the underworld, / now due to be crowned again' (*SP*, 139). In the chapter 'The Hopi Snake Dance' in *Mornings in Mexico* he writes at great length about the rituals in which snakes are being used, and he is struck by their 'clean, slim length of snake nudity, their beauty, like soft, quiescent lightning' (85). The snake imagery serves as an excellent example of Lawrence's tendency to give old symbols and images a new and radically different content and of his commitment to a fundamental transvaluation of all values. Thus the snake – the most striking symbol of evil in Christian thought – is turned into a source of life and rebirth.

The above examples do not in any way presume to give an exhaustive presentation of the mass of myths and symbols to be found in Lawrence's works. It is to be hoped, however, that they contribute to an understanding of the vital connection which exists between their function and Lawrence's faith in the creative power of the unconscious. Furthermore, they point to a striking similarity between his faith in the unconscious and his utopian vision of past and future states of individual and universal harmony. Naturally, it is impossible to express in a simple formula this complicated relationship between, on the one hand, the symbols and myths as they occur in the texts, and, on the other, their underlying meaning, however vague. One should not expect to find a clear-cut and allegorical meaning. Still, as shown above, Lawrence does give a fair number of hints concerning reasonable interpretations in his non-fictional, 'pollyanalytical' writings, and for that reason the conclusions I have drawn should not be too farfetched. The following passage from *Etruscan Places*, for example, sums up quite accurately the naive faith with which he stuck to his vision:

> It must have been a wonderful world, that old world where everything appeared alive and shining in the dusk of contact with all things. . . . In those days, a man riding on a red horse was not just Jack Smith on his brown nag; it was a suave-skinned creature, with death or life in its face, surging along on a surge of animal power that burned with travel, with the passionate movement of the blood . . . (68).

It is perhaps not too ridiculous to see in this a precursor of the rock'n roll dream of a powerful motorbike and a highway disappearing into a burning sunset. Both reflect the same dream of total freedom and a direct contact with the bedrock of life.

The Sexual Act

Lawrence's view of the sexual act as a source of salvation and renewal is probably acknowledged to be the most conspicuous, and the most controversial, feature of his entire work.[19] To many people – primarily because of *Lady Chatterley's Lover* – Lawrence seems to be something of a phallic freak. Although this is clearly an oversimplification, there is certainly a grain of truth in it. But before presenting a tentative picture of Lawrence's idea of sex, it is again important to have a sense of the background from which his views derived.

First of all, it should be made clear that Lawrence's generation grew up at a time when the general opinion of sex was undergoing a radical change. If his writings on the subject were frank and direct, the essential content did not necessarily come as a great surprise to the majority of people. Even before Lawrence had published anything, men like Havelock Ellis and Edward Carpenter had contributed strongly to the changing view of sex. Indeed, 'no aspect of human life changed more in the transition from Victorian England to modern England', according to Samuel Hynes, 'than the way Englishmen thought about sex'.[20] And Horace Gregory, writing about the Georgian period, remarks: 'The new freedom idealized physical well-being, young strength in the naked body, and a certain frankness concerning the purpose of women on earth and the natural union of young women with young men.'[21] Finally, the English public was not entirely unaccustomed to literary scandals for reasons of sexual libertinism. The controversy in 1909 over H. G. Wells's *Ann Veronica* was still fresh in their memory.

This growing liberalism, however, was not based entirely on a happy 'reassertion of a spring season'.[22] It can also be seen as a turning towards a new hedonism, whose immediate background, according to John A. Lester, was a sense of

> disillusionment, cynicism, and a reversion to self-centered satisfactions. . . . In our best-known expressions of the creed there is a close association between sensuous pleasure and a vivid sense of transiency. . . . The erasure of all hope for absolute truths of the spirit or the imagination brought in its wake an intensified concentration on the present, . . . on the *visible*, . . . on direct immediate impressions, on the data of the senses and on living 'in the concrete'.[23]

Thus, the general view of sex and sensual pleasure was linked with the deeper currents of thought at the turn of the century. The crucial question with regard to Lawrence, concerns whether his 'gospel of sex' is a cheap escape or the very opposite – a constructive alternative, powerful enough to support an entirely new view of life.

Undoubtedly, Lawrence's views on sex are closely related to his ideas of ancient history, the unconscious and of myth and symbol. To a considerable extent these were used as a vast and unlimited reservoir from which he constantly developed new ideas concerning the problems of salvation and renewal. But generally these ideas were not presented as direct models to be copied; they were rather suggestions – more or less tentative – of the necessity of searching in new directions. His dogmatic claim, for instance, in 'A Propos of *Lady Chatterley's Lover*', that we have to go back to 'Apollo, and Attis, Demeter, Persephone, and the halls of Dis' (120) in order to find a new footing, should obviously not be taken literally. When it comes to sex, however, Lawrence is considerably more persistent and coherent, and in my opinion it is the only one among his suggested sources of salvation which deserves to be taken more or less at its face value. From Lawrence's reservoir of ideas, sex stands out as a focal point around which his vision converges during important periods of his life. In *Fantasia of the Unconscious* sex is seen as the great manifestation of the unconscious: 'It is the basic consciousness of the blood, the nearest thing in us to pure material consciousness. . . . And this is the profound basis of my renewal, my deep blood renewal' (173–4). In *Lady Chatterley's Lover* Connie, returning a new being from the gamekeeper's cottage, says about the human body that 'with the Greeks it gave a lovely flicker' and that now once again it is 'rising from the tomb' (245).

A trust in sex as a creative force capable of transforming man – and to an extent transcending man's state as a fallen creature – is not possible without an accompanying faith in man himself. Lawrence's gospel of sex is thus a striking example of his attempt to seek salvation here in this life on earth. To a certain degree a 'this-worldly' salvation is a contradiction in terms, but it is most definitely a contradiction which Lawrence tries to remove. A religious quest which has abolished all transcendent objects of worship has to find a substitute, and in Lawrence sex has largely usurped the position previously held by God. This ties in perfectly with the writings of his anti-social period during the war and with the late period during which *Lady Chatterley's Lover* was written. Withdrawing from social participation, Lawrence sees sex as the source of salvation in the private sphere, in the isolated relationship between man and woman. It is no coincidence that in 'A Propos of *Lady Chatterley's Lover*' he makes a fierce defence of marriage and even praises the unwavering position of the Pope and the Catholic Church on the matter. During the period of his interest in social questions, however, the significance of sex fades into the background and is replaced by the equally divine aspects of the male hero.

Behind the worship of sex lay also a worship of woman, which in Lawrence had a twofold origin. First, it was a rather important part of the whole system of values which he inherited from his parents' generation. At the beginning of *The Rainbow* Lawrence discusses this Victorian idealization of woman, in a passage which is both a sermon and a beautifully condensed piece of social history:

> The woman was the symbol for that further life which comprised religion and love and morality. The men placed in her hands their own conscience, they said to her 'Be my conscience-keeper, be the angel at the doorway guarding my outgoing and my incoming.' And the woman fulfilled her trust, the men rested implicitly in her, receiving her praise or her blame with pleasure or with anger, rebelling and storming, but never for a moment really escaping in their souls from her prerogative. They depended on her for their stability. Without her, they would have felt like straws in the wind, to be blown hither and thither at random. She was the anchor and the security, she was the restraining hand of God, at times highly to be execrated (20).

Secondly, and side by side with this largely religious vision from the Victorian period, Lawrence also adopted another view. Described in great detail by Martin Green in his book *The von Richthofen Sisters*, it was an important part of the Bohemian heritage of sexual and maternal values which Frieda brought with her from her acquaintance with the intellectual milieu in Munich before she met Lawrence.[24] Expressed most strongly by Frieda's lover Dr Otto Gross, who was an early disciple of Freud, these ideas came very close to a celebration of free love. According to Green, '"Du bist Erotik" was a major ideological statement, with behind it a belief in eroticism as a philosophical and metaphysical value, as, above all, a life-creating value'.[25]

This is the twofold background against which Lawrence's views of woman and sex should be evaluated. It shows both the religious foundation which was his as well as the Brangwens', and the emphasis on physical love, which he received from Frieda. Both suggest the glorification of woman, which from *The Rainbow* onwards is a persistent theme in Lawrence. Tom Brangwen, waiting for Lydia to give birth to their first child, thinks to himself: 'Woman was immortal, whatever happened, whoever turned towards death' (71). From here Lawrence goes on, in 'Study of Thomas Hardy', to draw an even more divine picture of woman: '. . . desire is the admitting of deficiency. And the embodiment of the object of desire reveals the original defect or the defaulture. So that the attributes of God will reveal that which man lacked and yearned for in his living. And these attributes are always, in their essence, Eternality, Infinity, Immutability. And these are the qualities man feels in woman, as a principle' (58). It is no wonder that Birkin in *Women in Love* introduces the cosmic view that 'the world is only held together by the mystic conjunction . . . between man and woman' (152), and that he sees his marriage to Ursula as the 'paradisal entry', the only real alternative to the awful Northern and African ways. Having decided to propose, and drifting swiftly towards Beldover, he 'saw the town on the slope of the hill . . . and it looked like Jerusalem to his fancy' (255). Here it is woman, not God, who makes 'all things new'.[26]

Roughly speaking, *Women in Love* is the last of Lawrence's major works before the leadership novels. It is also the last novel in which woman is in the superior position of being able to offer man a touch of her own divinity. Woman is, so to speak, the divine life-giver. By contrast, in a novel like *Lady Chatterley's Lover*, which was written after the leadership novels, the roles are largely changed. Suddenly the man is the life-giver, Connie is the one who is portrayed as reborn, and the central symbol of new life is the phallus. The woman is the passive recipient and beneficiary of masculine energy: 'And now she touched him, and it was the sons of god with the daughters of men' (182).[27]

Turning now to the more specific question of the sexual act itself, it is no exaggeration to claim that in the act of copulation, the doors are flung wide open for a religious salvation and a resurrection in the flesh. In *The Rainbow*, particularly, this theme can be followed as it gradually develops. In the early part of the novel, Lydia's feelings for Tom are like 'the pain of a new birth . . . [which] strung all her veins to a new form. . . . She wanted it, this new life from him, with him, yet she must defend herself against it, for it was a destruction' (39). Tom, having proposed to Lydia at the vicarage, goes through the same experience, an extinction of his former self: 'He returned gradually, but newly created, as after a gestation, a new birth, in the womb of darkness. Aërial and light everything was, new as a morning, fresh and newly begun' (45). When the wedding is over and the guests have left, the 'time of his trial and his admittance, his Gethsemane and his Triumphal Entry in one, had come . . .' (56). Finally, two years later, there is the consummation which renews both Tom and Lydia and the world around them:

> [Tom Brangwen's] blood beat up in waves of desire. . . . If he could come really within the blazing kernel of darkness, if really he could be destroyed, burnt away till he lit with her in one consummation, that were supreme, supreme. Their coming together now . . . was the entry into another circle of existence, it was the baptism to another life, it was the complete confirmation. Their feet trod strange ground of knowledge, their footsteps were lit-up with discovery. Wherever they walked, it was well, the world re-echoed round them in discovery. They went gladly and forgetful. Everything was lost, and everything was found. The new world was discovered, it remained only to be explored. . . . it was the transfiguration, the glorification, the admission (90–1).

Whenever Lawrence makes an attempt to describe the sexual act, he has recourse to a religious vocabulary connected with the salvation of man and the world, an apocalyptic-millennial imagery of a new heaven and a new earth. When Skrebensky came to Ursula in their first 'superb consummation', she 'passed away . . . into the pristine darkness of paradise, into the original immortality' (418).

To Birkin in *Women in Love*, his marriage and union with Ursula was 'his resurrection and his life' (369). As suggested above, in *Fantasia of the Unconscious* Lawrence even tries to add to the religious dimension a scientific dimension of objective fact. After 'successful coition', as he calls it, between man and woman, 'the blood is changed and renewed, refreshed, almost re-created, like the atmosphere after thunder. Out of the newness of the living blood pass the new strange waves which beat upon the great dynamic centres of the nerves: primarily upon the hypogastric plexus and the sacral ganglion' (107). It sounds almost like a scientific travesty of the Catholic dogma of transubstantiation.

The fundamentally religious ideas underlying Lawrence's faith in the sexual act are expressed most persistently in *Lady Chatterley's Lover*. Strictly speaking, the whole novel turns on the cosmic power of the phallus. At an early stage in the book, while she is still unaware of the phallic baptism awaiting her, Connie goes to the wood to pick daffodils behind the gamekeeper's cottage. Suddenly she hears how the wind of March sweeps through her consciousness: '"Ye must be born again! I believe in the resurrection of the body! Except a grain of wheat fall into the earth and die, it shall by no means bring forth. When the crocus cometh forth I too will emerge and see the sun!"' (88). Lawrence may not have thought specifically about the Annunciation while writing this condensed declaration of faith, but the circumstances are certainly similar. First, the incident takes place in March, at the time of the Annunciation. Second, it is followed a few days later by the first sexual encounter between Connie and the gamekeeper. Furthermore, just before this happens they witness the hatching of pheasant chickens. In Christian symbolism eggs – especially with a broken shell – are closely related to the Resurrection at Easter and are frequently found in pictures of the Virgin and Child.[28]

At the very end of the novel there occurs a different and rather shocking example of Lawrence's religious view of sex. Mellors, in a letter to Connie, writes about their relationship and the child she is carrying: 'My soul softly flaps in the little Pentecost flame with you, like the peace of fucking. We fucked a flame into being' (313). Pentecost celebrates the descent of the Holy Ghost upon the apostles in the shape of a flame, and so here Lawrence endows the sexual act with a significance far exceeding a brief and transient ecstasy.

At this point an evaluation seems to be needed of Lawrence's view of the sexual act as a gateway to a resurrected humanity.

Clearly, Lawrence leaves himself open to the accusation that he uses sex not as a means of healing a shattered reality, but as a means of escaping reality altogether. Father William Tiverton, in his book *D. H. Lawrence and Human Existence*, expresses this dilemma with admirable clarity in a passage about *Lady Chatterley's Lover*:

> [Lawrence] had argued that the physical, sensual, and psychological impotence of our civilization was due to a decline in religious belief – belief in the 'dark gods'. But then he tries to restore the gods by reviving the vital phallic relation of man and woman. This is like trying to cure a cancer by prescribing gymnastic exercises: the inability to do exercises may be a symptom of cancer, and cure of the cancer may restore the ability; but the cancer cannot be cured by the exercises. If this is so, then the failure, such as it is, of *Lady Chatterley* as a novel, is symptomatic of the failure of Lawrence himself as artist and as 'prophet', or, to use Mr. Eliot's word, as 'medicine man'.[29]

Tiverton's observation can be illustrated further by a couple of passages in *Women in Love*. First, when Birkin and Gerald are on their way to London in the train, Birkin says: '"The old ideals are dead as nails – nothing there. It seems to me there remains only this perfect union with a woman – sort of ultimate marriage – and there isn't anything else"' (58). To be absolutely precise, Birkin implies that this perfect union was not a source of salvation in the first place, but having been disappointed by all the other ideals, he chooses, as a sort of emergency measure, to make it into an ideal substitute for a reality which at that very moment was being torn to pieces by the war. It is thus not an attempt to face reality, but to escape it. This same longing for the union between man and woman as a sample of another and more perfect reality is even more evident in the discussion which takes place between Birkin and Ursula after Gerald's sister has drowned in the lake. Having just said that Diana Crich is better off dead than alive, Birkin again turns to love:

> 'I want love that is like sleep, like being born again, vulnerable as a baby that just comes into the world.'
>
> . . .
>
> 'Why should love be like sleep?' she asked sadly.
>
> 'I don't know. So that it is like death – I *do* want to die from this life – and yet it is more than life itself. One is delivered over like a naked infant from the womb, all the old defences and the old

body gone, and new air around one, that has never been breathed before' (186).

This glorification of death as preferable to life – a death achieved through love – could not possibly have been regarded as anything but utopian luxury by the millions of men who – at the time when this was written – were fighting for their lives in the trenches in France. There is also an echo in it of a sentiment immortalized in Shelley's 'Adonais', written at Keats's death; a sentiment of death as a higher reality than life: 'Peace, peace! he is not dead, he doth not sleep – / He hath awakened from the dream of life –'.[30] This borderline between the real world and a Platonic sphere of other-worldly ideas is frequently the place where Lawrence seeks refuge in order to conceal the inconsistencies of his gospel.

All in all, Lawrence's celebration of the sexual act seems primarily to reflect a desperate need for something to believe in at a time when the general prospects were particularly bleak. The fact that he saw an entire world order collapse around him, also makes his turn towards a near and manifest solution more understandable. In this way the gospel of sex is closely connected with the other elements discussed in this chapter.

Before leaving the discussion of Lawrence and his view of sex, I will briefly mention an aspect which connects it with the topic of the following chapters, that is, Lawrence's social and political ideas. As suggested already, there is a period in Lawrence's life, starting roughly with the end of the war and ending with *The Plumed Serpent*, in which his views of woman and consequently of sex undergo a transformation. His opinions as they are expressed in the leadership novels will not be dealt with here, but some mention should be made of an interesting stage of transition which is evident in *Fantasia of the Unconscious*. Here the sexual act is still a source of renewal, but more important, it acts as a springboard for man into a life of social action. 'Now the new song rises, the brain tingles to a new thought, the heart craves for new activity. . . . Men, being themselves made new after the action of coition, wish to make the world new. A new, passionate polarity springs up between men who are bent on the same activity, the polarity between man and woman sinks to passivity. It is now daytime, and time to forget sex, time to be busy making a new world' (108). Suddenly, woman is relegated to a secondary position, she 'exists only in the twilight, by the camp fire, when the day has departed. Evening and night are hers' (109). He goes on to explain that sex is an affair between two isolated individuals, whereas 'man's great purposive activity' is collective and therefore more valuable. Moving away from the problem of individual salvation to questions encompassing the world at large, Lawrence's emphasis similarly shifts from woman to man, and at the same time the faith in the sexual act is reduced from a source of salvation to little more than a stimulus providing man with an extra impetus of energy for his encounter with the world outside. However, the underlying vision remained essentially the same.

4

The Background of Lawrence's Political Ideas

'Everything seems gone to pieces', Lawrence wrote in 1914, five days after the declaration of war (*Le II*, 206), and that message was to be repeated with increasing despair for the next four years. Throughout this period he never really saw any hope for reform or pragmatic solutions. From his cosmic-religious point of view, hell had been let loose and the entire social fabric was destined to collapse. Certainly, as shown in chapter 2, Lawrence lived through these years in a state of 'immediate expectation' of some all-encompassing calamity.

But the world did not come to an end, at least not quite. Somehow life continued and the social structure remained relatively intact. The war did not bring the apocalyptic finality necessary for the millennium to begin, and Lawrence's frustration and impatience forced him to look elsewhere for alternative solutions.

The view of history as an arrested organic process that Lawrence set out in 'The Crown' really left him with only two possibilities: he could leave the world behind and seek his own private Isle of the Blest, or he could look for radical political means of bringing the world out of its cul-de-sac. As it turned out he was to try both, and in doing so created a tension which is reflected in his writings, and which constitutes the main unresolved conflict of *Kangaroo*. The previous chapter dealt with Lawrence's anti-social or escapist utopia. It is now time to take a closer look at his ideas of social and political action.

There may not be an immediately obvious link between Lawrence's apocalyptic-millennial framework and the so-called leadership ideas on which his rather doubtful reputation as a political thinker is founded. In order to show a connection between this religious view of history and certain totalitarian ideas of the early twentieth century, it may be useful to quote from the conclusion of Norman Cohn's book *The Pursuit of the Millennium*. Combining political and theological terminology, Cohn uses the phrase 'revolutionary chiliasm' to denote movements whose basic ideology is religious but whose expression tends to take a political form. Revolutionary chiliasm, he says,

> thrives best . . . where history is imagined as having an inherent purpose which is preordained to be realised on this earth in a single, final consummation. It is such a view of history, at once teleological and cataclysmic, that has been presupposed and invoked alike by the medieval movements . . . and by the great totalitarian movements of our own day.[1]

Cohn then goes on to explain how both medieval and modern chiliasm generate phantasies which can function as 'dynamic social myths' and which in turn are 'collective efforts to cope with situations of strain and conflict'.[2] Lawrence's social utopia has to be seen as developing from this heritage, at once religious and secular, traditional and modern, and containing broadly the basic elements of an apocalyptic-millennial view of historical movement.

Consequently, Lawrence's political ideas have to be seen from a dual perspective. First, they were nourished by the social and religious life of his own day, and second, by the whole tradition with which he was acquainted through rather extensive reading. Thus, the following discussion will first consider some relevant aspects of the European political scene in which Lawrence lived and travelled. Then will follow an examination of Lawrence's reading in utopian and political literature. This will in turn lead, in the next chapter, to a presentation of the political ideas he himself expressed up to the completion of the so-called leadership novels, the emphasis being placed on *Kangaroo* and *The Plumed Serpent*.

European Society Around the First World War

Lawrence's formative years have already been described as a period of violent upheaval in literary and intellectual life. Turning now to the social and political background, there is in particular one socio-political conflict or source of tension which it is essential to bear in mind in order to understand Lawrence's development. On the one hand, the early twentieth century was characterized by an overall sense of pessimism, alienation and despair at the prospects of the future. On the other hand, there was an heroic vitalism which asserted itself with aggressive self-confidence. In one respect this was a conflict between social classes and between rival systems of government, a conflict of the masses versus the elite or of democracy versus aristocracy. In another respect it was a conflict between a philosophy of life which accepted man as somehow limited by natural, material or religious forces, and one which stressed man's total freedom and unlimited range of action.

Of paramount importance is that Lawrence was born a member of the anonymous working masses. According to Raymond Williams, the real significance of Lawrence's origins

> is not and cannot be a matter of retrospect from the adult life. It is, rather, that his first social responses were those, not of a man observing the processes of industrialism, but of one caught in them, at an exposed point, and destined, in the normal course, to be enlisted in their regiments. . . . Lawrence could not be certain, at the time when his fundamental social responses were forming, that he could so escape.[3]

But Lawrence's birth into the working class was only one in a series of interconnected phenomena which created a sense of being caught in a machinery in which the freedom of the human will was being slowly but surely ground to pieces. Invading the countryside, the rapidly growing cities devoured its human and natural resources. Human beings were turned into mechanical ants, tending the conveyor belts of dirty, smoky factories and producing standardized goods. A quickly expanding state bureaucracy brought a Kafka-esque sense of public authority, leaving the individual at a loss confronted with the labyrinths of power. These were some of the external forces which shaped the everyday life and the social behaviour of the early twentieth-century generation, and particularly that of the working class.

At the same time ideological and scientific ideas, connected with names such as Darwin, Einstein, Freud and Marx, contributed to and amplified the general trend. Darwinism, as it was popularly perceived, left man a helpless victim to a process of natural selection. Einstein's theory of relativity had a similar effect: 'At the beginning of the 1920s the belief began to circulate for the first time at a popular level, that there were no longer any absolutes: of time and space, of good and evil, of knowledge, above all of value. Mistakenly but perhaps inevitably, relativity became confused with relativism.'[4] Furthermore, Freudian psychology, a scientific and therefore credible examination of the human mind, forced man to look at himself in a new light, not primarily as a creature of a free and conscious will, but as one largely ruled by the irrational motivations of the unconscious. Finally, the Marxist doctrine presented man as deeply and fatally dependent upon his material surroundings.

These various phenomena undermined the fundamental principles of the whole European tradition of social and individual values. The effect was a pulverization of the Christian heritage as a basis for moral evaluation and the emergence of a new system of values based on scientific and positivist thinking. Just as common, however, was a feeling of moral anarchy, now that the old spiritual bastions had fallen and nothing had replaced them.[5] Thus by the time of the First World War, Lawrence and his generation were prepared for lines of thought radically different from those which it was claimed still ruled society at large. All that now remained was a cataclysmic confirmation on the political scene of this mental shift.

With respect to the later development of the political climate of Western Europe, the First World War had at least two decisive and far-reaching consequences which cleared the way for horrors even greater than the Somme and Verdun. First of all, the war changed the entire face of Europe. It swept away a whole tradition going back to the early Middle Ages of religious and dynastic allegiances, and replaced them, through the treaty of Versailles, by a principle of national allegiance.[6] Also, the war brought into being the Soviet Union, an event which contributed strongly to the ideological polarization of post-war Europe. Thus, the Europe of 1919 was a continent physically and mentally divided and faced with a political climate prone to move towards extreme solutions rather than pragmatism and compromise.

The second consequence of the war, which ties in with the following discussion of post-war vitalism, concerns the use of violence. The war itself is the best example of the increasing tendency to resort to violence as a means of solving problems. The German historian F. L. Carsten claims that the war 'had elevated violence to a patriotic duty: the killing of as many enemies as possible became the aim of every good soldier. After the end of the war the psychology of trench warfare could be transmitted to political life, and the "internal enemy" became the object of similar violent action'.[7] In this way the war also had an effect on the internal power structure of the countries involved. 'As the war prolonged itself, and the losses and desperation increased, the warring states became steadily more totalitarian, especially after the winter of

1916–17'.[8] No doubt Lawrence was exposed to a slight touch of this awesome power of the state during his stay in Cornwall, an experience producing the passionate 'Nightmare' chapter in *Kangaroo*.

So far those aspects of the political climate have been mentioned which reduced the individual into little more than a cogwheel in a vast machine. Seen together with the apocalyptic despair described in chapter 2, this is roughly the position from which Lawrence was eagerly searching for new and positive ideas in the political sphere. Before turning to these ideas, however, it is important to consider the political and ideological atmosphere which inspired them. That means looking at the emergence of political vitalism in Europe during the first decades of our century.

Political Vitalism

Lawrence after 1912 was not just an Englishman who kept an eye on the continental scene through books and newspapers. He spent altogether almost one year in Germany and three and a half years in Italy in the period between his elopement with Frieda and the writing of *Kangaroo* ten years later. Taking into account his alertness and intellectual appetite, the impact of these years should not be underestimated. Also, it should be remembered that Germany and Italy – more than any other countries at the time – were pregnant with ideas and political movements closely related to those later described by Lawrence.

But even from the point of view of England, which emerged from the war with at least some laurels, the world after Versailles was rather like a fleet of half-sunken battleships struggling both to keep afloat and to quench the constant threat of mutiny. It was a world in which human greatness and heroic deeds were only a subject for nostalgic dreams, and in which the mutineers would seem as apt as the captain at the task of righting the ship. 'The mood of bitterness that emerged from the First World War has no like in any other war that England has fought. . .'.[9] According to Richard Thurlow in his book *Fascism in Britain*, 'some saw fascism as a means to restore an alleged utopian past of harmonious political, economic and social relationships which had been swept away by the war and replaced by the degenerative effects of the extension of the franchise in 1918 and the emergence of political democracy'.[10] Still, it was not in England that these ideas would find the most fertile soil. Admittedly, there was a vital tradition in this country of hero worship, but as opposed to Germany and Italy it remained in the twentieth century more a cultural than political phenomenon. In much the same way revolutionary socialism never gained a sufficiently firm foothold in Britain to attempt political action.

The new and radical movements, which on the Continent came to the surface with astonishing speed after 1918, had their origins in ideas which had cut a fairly low profile in political life before the war, but which were now emerging from the ashes of a shattered Europe. These ideas included a nostalgia for certain life styles and periods of history and a powerful vision of a future harmony, elements which were already deeply ingrained in Lawrence's thinking. But there were other elements as well.

Racism, for instance, which had for decades been a relatively vague undercurrent in Western culture, found a scientific justification in post-Darwinian biology. As Thurlow says: 'The development of the understanding of the principle of heredity and the laws of genetics led to frighteningly utopian ideas of scientific breeding and pure racial types achieved through eugenic experiments.'[11] Even a socialist weekly like *The New Age*, which Lawrence read regularly during 1908 and 1909, contained in the summer of 1908 some fifteen major articles on the necessity of eugenics (the select breeding of humans) to stop the decline of the English people. Besides, the sudden appearance after Versailles of states based on national unity rather than religious or dynastic allegiance, acted as a catalyst for ideas of racial exclusion and discrimination. Thus both racism and nationalism approached their social utopia by way of an aggressive exclusion and an emphasis on qualitative differences rather than similarities between nations. Furthermore, this idea – according to Paul Johnson – was shared by both left and right on the political scale: 'Darwin's notion of the survival of the fittest was a key element both in the Marxist concept of class warfare and of the racial philosophies which shaped Hitlerism.'[12] The inevitable outcome was a sanction, even a glorification, of violence as a means of solving political problems.

Another crucial factor in early twentieth-century continental politics was the widespread circulation of elitist ideas. It was not accidental, of course, that such ideas appeared at a time when the masses were for the first time obtaining a decisive political influence, and to a large extent this dialectic is reflected in the struggle between the extreme left and the extreme right. An important exception – which shows how deeply elitist ideas had permeated politics – is the Russian Revolution, which was an elitist coup rather than a revolution of the masses. Lawrence was therefore quite right when in *Apocalypse* he described Lenin as a 'Tyrannus in shabby clothes' rather than as a humble servant of the Russian peasants (68). But elitism can also be seen as stemming from a lack of confidence in politics and the idea of social community altogether. In the modern mass society the individual had lost all sense of direct contact with the sources of authority. Even a democratic right to vote only underlined an essential anonymity. In this situation the hero offered an escape, by bringing pride and confidence back to the people. He dissolved the social glue of the masses – their sense of internal solidarity – and replaced it with a personal bond by which every member of the masses received a share in the superior being of the hero. The social network was rejected in favour of an individual one. In this way the hero, particularly in a world where people no longer felt the presence of a personal god, assumed titanic proportions. He became a substitute for a religious as well as a social point of reference. And for many the collective man-slaughter of the war only served to confirm the failure of traditional politics. But again, it was not in Britain, but in Germany and Italy, that this conflict was most explosive, and it is therefore necessary to look at these countries in some detail in order to find movements and ideas which are directly relevant to Lawrence.

Germany

The intellectual and political life of Germany in the years around the First World War contains a number of striking similarities to important aspects of Lawrence's work, and it would be tempting to see them as direct influences. The parallels, however, should be drawn with caution, since influence is not a matter of mechanical cause and effect. Moreover, our knowledge of Lawrence's relationship to Germany is still scattered and rather general. But despite such reservations there are several arguments to justify a closer examination.

First, Lawrence married a German, and there is no doubt that Frieda – who was not known for hiding her light under a bushel – had a decisive influence on her husband. Second, Lawrence was brought into contact through Frieda's family with people whose social and political position offered him an almost unique opportunity to be kept informed about political as well as cultural life in Germany. A few years earlier Frieda had found herself among the intellectual elite, of which both her sister and brother-in-law were prominent members, in both Heidelberg and Munich. The latter, according to Robert Lucas, was at that time 'the centre for intellectuals in rebellion against convention',[13] and Frieda even lived it out in a passionate affair with Dr Otto Gross, one of Sigmund Freud's disciples. Her sister Else – 'one of the first female students to be accepted at the University of Heidelberg'[14] – was a favourite pupil of the sociologist Max Weber. Furthermore, before marrying Weber's brother Alfred, Else was married to Edgar Jaffe, who worked closely with Weber and who in 1919 was briefly to become a minister in a revolutionary government in Bavaria. In *Three Faces of Fascism*, Ernst Nolte says: 'Of all the revolutionary spasms of that time, this . . . was the most haphazard, the most doomed, the most idyllic. Triggered by the senseless assassination of the Bavarian prime minister Eisner, . . . it was the revolt of part of the proletariat under the leadership of a few intellectuals, mostly Jewish and anarchist, in a completely bourgeois city in the heart of a Catholic-agrarian area.'[15] Third, Lawrence had himself a specific interest in Germany. Even before meeting Frieda he had a reasonable grasp of the language, was relatively well informed about German literature – he even reviewed a collection of German verse in 1911 – and liked to use German expressions in his personal letters. Finally, at the time of his first meeting with Frieda, he was trying, by the help of Frieda's husband, Professor Ernest Weekley, to obtain a lectureship in Germany. All in all he had a fairly intimate relationship with the country, a fact which was revealed at the beginning of the war, when he admitted: 'my chief grief and misery is for Germany . . .' (*Le II*, 209).

The Germany Lawrence encountered for the first time was a 'young and adorable country' (ibid.), and a country preparing for war. This youthful, Faustian vigour was accompanied by a self-confident pride in the Germany of a time when – as Robert Musil puts it – 'instead of death and logical mechanization, it was blood and wisdom that prevailed',[16] and a similarly naive faith in her future greatness. According to Fritz Stern, the present was a temporary impasse from which a leap was to be taken 'in order to recapture an idealized past in an imaginary future'.[17] And George L. Mosse, to whose book *The Crisis of German Ideology* this section is heavily indebted, spends an entire chapter discussing the 'significant social and ideological contribution' of the utopian movement in Germany both before and after the war.[18] Based on the idea of the *Volk*, this movement 'embodied an effort to root the Volk in the soil once more, to reconstruct surroundings that had a natural rhythm, that soothed the discord of urban life'.[19] Politically, it was a search for an alternative to the solutions suggested by capitalism and Marxism. Closed and largely self-supporting colonies – 'rural islands in a sea of industrialization'[20] – were established around the country. There were even attempts to start a similar project in Mexico. Culturally, they turned to the distant past, and one colony called Eden was to 'represent an identification with truly regenerated Germanic freedom and life. Rituals were practiced which would tend to enhance this identification; so, in addition to celebrating Christmas – with a Germanic touch, to be sure – they also paid homage to the changing of the sun and similar Germanic festivals'.[21] In another colony, designed by Hentschel, a disciple of Ernst Haeckel, 'the emphasis was clearly anti-intellectual. . . . Not the power of reasoning, but an emotional state of mind and physical prowess were the chief objectives. Germanic man should again be fused with the cosmic forces. . . .'[22] A racist tendency was never far away, and 'the belief in external beauty as the mirror of the beauty of the soul led Hentschel to praise the Aryan body and encourage the cult of the body. . . . Aryan beauty, being genuine beauty, must be nude. . . . The cult of the body grew and became so popular that just prior to the First World War the *Freibad*, nude bathing, was a more or less common phenomenon'.[23]

The cult of the body and its political implications – a question of direct relevance to Lawrence – are further illuminated by Hans Blüher in his famous book *Die deutsche Wandervogelbewegung als erotisches Phänomen*, which was published in 1912 and deals with the German youth movement.

> In his book . . . Blüher described the role played in the movement by what he called Eros. While for him Eros certainly meant a sexual attraction between men, these drives did not necessarily lead to an overt display of affection, nor did they culminate in physical sexual relations. Instead, the Eros impulse worked, socially and culturally, to deepen friendships between males and to increase the cohesion of a male group. Basing his argument on his own observations and somewhat influenced by the theories of Freud, Blüher claimed that men who stand in close relationship to one another inevitably display homosexual impulses which, however, are sublimated in the form of surplus energy. This vital force, not finding a physical or organic release, eventually finds expression in true creativity which centers on the *Männerbund*, the society of men. As evidence, Blüher listed several factors he

> observed among the Wandervögel. First, there was the *charisma* of the leaders, that captivating quality possessed by the exceptional few, the most imaginative, creative and attractive personalities. Second, there was the ideal of male beauty, which found expression in the admiration for the muscular and lithe German types. And third, there was the exclusion of women. . . .[24]

Blüher developed his ideas further in a later work, *Die Rolle der Erotik in der männlichen Gesellschaft* (1917–19), in which he gave a general description of the whole *Bund* movement, a *Bund* being defined as a rather loose 'social organization regarded by its members as the true community of man [sic] with a common soul'.[25] Influenced by Freud, Blüher thought 'that once man's sensual gratifications were sublimated his energy could be directed into the realm of cosmos and metaphysics'.[26] But Blüher's Eros was not primarily a sexual force. 'Eros had to be engaged in a situation where human relationships produced not children . . . but works of lasting cultural and social value.'[27] Under the wings of this largely male Eros there would emerge an elite of men, and these scattered individuals, who 'were the most attractive, spiritually as well as physically, would gravitate toward leadership positions'.[28] Consequently, women were turned into little more than a breeding stock, tending *Kinder* and *Küche*, and 'the modern woman, the suffragette, was a symbol of hated modernity'.[29] It should also be added that the *Wandervogel* movement had a large following for a number of years. According to Blüher there were – at the time he wrote the book – tens of thousands of members.[30]

But Blüher was not alone in expressing a longing for leadership. When after the First World War this call for authority finally came out into the open, the ground had been carefully prepared for decades, especially by people such as Paul de Lagarde, Julius Langbehn and Moeller van den Bruck, whose combination of racist, nationalist and heroic ideas 'strongly affected the sentiments, the *Lebensgefühle*, of respectable Germans for two generations before Hitler'.[31] There was a common longing 'for a Caesar, for an ultimate authority that would somehow reconcile and transcend all divisions and would realize the one common goal of all upper-class Germans, a great national future'.[32]

Philosophically, an important contribution to the leadership mythos was offered by Ernst Bertram, who, reinterpreting Nietzsche, made the philosopher into an *Überdeutscher* whose holy works were to 'lead the nation to the greatness it deserved'.[33]

However, behind Bertram, exercising a powerful influence on his activist philosophy, was an aristocratic recluse of modest background, the poet Stefan George. A homeless traveller for most of his life, George surrounded himself with a so-called *Kreis* of which he was the undisputed master. To an extent this group may be seen as George's own way of putting into practice the idea of the *Männerbund*, an idea cultivated with a more militant touch by the Youth Movement. But his elitist ideas were not confined only to the artistic sphere. Combined with a strong nationalism, they find their most radical expression towards the end of George's career, in the collection of poems called *Das neue Reich* (1928). But he had presented similar ideas well before the First World War. He was convinced that the 'coming century was to be the age of the elite, not of the masses. . . . [He] saw these new personalities as representing both godliness and manliness and possessing extraordinary powers of will'.[34] Echoing Blüher, he claimed that a cultural rebirth emerging from such an elite 'would be attained only through the sharing of Eros, through the manifestation of the beauty of both the body and the soul'.[35] Thus George represents the same exclusive attitude towards women as Blüher and the Youth Movement. Comparing him to Nietzsche, Eric Bentley says that they both 'yearned for stronger bonds than the love of women. They yearned to lead men and to be led'.[36] George was not a man of action, but according to a spokesman of his *Kreis* when the war began in 1914, soldiers '"carried his books in their packs, and after it was over, his influence grew from year to year"'.[37]

Post-war Germany was a country waiting to be awakened from the nightmare of a crushing and humiliating defeat. 'A mythos and a national leader were required. The Youth groups and the *Bünde* led the way in pressing for this demand. At the same time, they offered the ideological solution in the form of the principles of their own organizations: Eros and concepts of leadership.'[38] George's poetry contained plenty of both, and it was not wholly accidental that in 1933 the Nazis tried to use him as an artistic alibi for their own policies.

Italy

'When I think how practically seven men out of ten emigrate from the villages round about . . ., then the stability of the world seems gone', wrote Lawrence with surprising statistical accuracy in a letter from Lerici in February 1914 (*Le II*, 149). Indeed, he had reason for concern about his beloved Italy. The year before, emigration had reached a peak of more than 800,000, and the country was marred by economic problems and social unrest. Just before leaving Italy in June 1914, Lawrence even witnessed the famous and violent clashes in Turin, in which several people were killed. Against this background the war came, at least to some, as a relief. But when Lawrence returned to Italy in November 1919, things were rapidly moving from bad to worse. The struggle between fascists and socialists had taken the decisive step from verbal disagreement to street violence, the number of strikes and factory occupations gave the years 1919 and 1920 the name *biennio rosso* (the two red years), and at Versailles Italy received only a fraction of the spoils from the victory to which it had contributed.

Clearly, the years from 1918 to Mussolini's seizure of power in October 1922 are a crucial period in Italian history. In a discussion of Lawrence's own political ideas it is interesting to note that he spent two out of these four years in Italy, before sailing for Ceylon and later Australia in February 1922. Thus, during the writing of *Aaron's Rod* and right before the writing of *Kangaroo*, Lawrence was bound to have encountered political currents whose similarity to his own ideas simply cannot be coincidental. Consequently, a look at the ideological basis and political expression of Italian fascism ought to offer valuable insights concerning the development of Lawrence's political thinking.

Naturally, it is not easy to describe in a nutshell the elements that contributed to the success of Italian fascism. Ernst Nolte puts it like this: 'The springs of fascism were: the nationalists led by Enrico Corradini, the legionaries led by the D'Annunzio of the Fiume enterprise, and the former Marxists who had split off from the Socialist party and were led by Mussolini. These three groups gave Italian fascism the leaders, the ethos, and the ideas.'[39] Others would put the stress elsewhere. Still, most historians agree on two basic ingredients in Il Duce's ideological brew: a powerful dose of nationalism and a curious mixture of ideas from both extremes of the political scale.

The first element, nationalism, was based primarily on the romanticized and mythical view of two specific periods in Italian history: ancient Rome and the so-called Risorgimento or independence movement of the nineteenth century. For Mussolini, fascism was largely an attempt to resurrect or reawaken the glory and the power of ancient Rome. If not a model to be copied, Rome was nevertheless a shining symbol of past as well as future greatness.

Similarly, in the Risorgimento movement, and particularly in the writer and hero Guiseppe Mazzini (whom Lawrence discusses in some detail in *Movements in European History*), the fascists found an ideal expression of the Italian spirit. Mazzini's ideas, according to David D. Roberts, had had a 'tremendous significance . . . for disaffected Italians in the context of the war and the postwar crisis'.[40] The contribution of nationalism was therefore an attempt to bring the past – frequently a mythical past – to life in a modern setting.

The other main element of fascism, the seemingly random choice of extreme political ideas, is rather more complex. There was in Italian fascism a powerful ideological current which managed to bridge the gap between these extremes, and which functioned to a large extent as a common denominator for the adverse political development of the country. This current was syndicalism. It is no coincidence, therefore, that David Roberts' massive study *The Syndicalist Tradition and Italian Fascism* describes the way in which the syndicalists, who started out from a radically Marxist interpretation of society, finally embraced in great numbers Mussolini's fascism. Indeed, Mussolini himself was an example of just this shift. As syndicalism is a highly relevant phenomenon for Lawrence's later works, it is worth pausing to consider it in some detail.

Syndicalism started out as a splinter-group from Marxism, and by the turn of the century it constituted a powerful political movement in most industrialized countries, but particularly in France and Italy. The most well known theoretician on syndicalism was the Frenchman Georges Sorel. An intellectual eclectic, whose reading ranged from Marx to Vico and Nietzsche, Sorel saw capitalism as approaching a final collapse. Regarding himself as a revolutionary he strongly opposed any thought of compromise or softness in the coming struggle. On the contrary, he saw the need for a revolutionary catalyst, and as a result ransacked – as Manuel and Manuel put it – 'world history for heroic movements of religious, social, and political action' and claimed that 'epochs in which such movements had appeared and struggled for victory were expressions of a higher species of man'.[41] What was needed was an 'emotive breakthrough' which would bring into being an 'heroic society that might be cruel, but that created a way of life which stamped its character on a culture'.[42] Accepting violence as a necessary part of the struggle, Sorel consequently adored the primitive imagination, regarding Socrates as a traitor to the old Greek values, and insisted on the need for a new myth capable of sustaining revolutionary action. He saw world history as 'a succession of creative myths that originally possessed small, tightly knit elites; through their heroic devotion, the mythic ideal came to dominate the whole of a culture for a time. The previously enthroned myth which the new creative myth replaced had by then grown flat and stale. . . '.[43] Applying these ideas to contemporary politics, Sorel saw the syndicates or trade unions as the new elite which, with an anarchic touch, would be governed by some kind of spontaneous agreement. There is an almost cosmic dimension in Sorel's scheme, especially his vision of the general strike as an apocalyptic event. To him, this was a matter of faith – if only people believed in it, it would become a reality. 'This essentially mythic prospect of the general strike was supposed to exert upon workers the same powerful fascination as the Apocalypse, Resurrection, and Last Judgment had upon early Christians.'[44]

There is no hard evidence to show that Lawrence was actually acquainted with either syndicalism in general or Sorel in particular, but there are at least two indications that make it likely. First, Ramsay MacDonald, whom Lawrence got to know in Eastwood about 1910, published in 1912 an entire book, based on six articles in the *Daily Chronicle* from May that year, against syndicalism in general and Sorel in particular. Undoubtedly, the writing of this book shows how widespread syndicalist ideas were at the time, and it is not unreasonable to assume that these matters were discussed during the Sunday evening meetings at William Hopkin's house. Second, the man who translated Sorel (and Bergson) into English was T. E. Hulme, instigator of the Imagist movement, an intellectual closely connected with the circle around A. R. Orage and *The New Age*, and a friend of John Middleton Murry, Katherine Mansfield, Sir Edward Marsh and Richard Aldington. Indeed, it would be strange if Lawrence, himself part of this circle, was unaware of Hulme and his work.

Another figure of immense importance to the growth of Italian fascism was the poet, novelist, war-hero and popular speaker Gabriele D'Annunzio. Nolte says of him: 'D'Annunzio was in fact a Dionysian man of modern and highly original stamp, more so than almost any other man in Europe. His influence in Italy was incalculable. If the common European endeavor around the turn of the century toward rejuvenation often took on a more markedly irrational character in Italy . . . than in France and Germany, this was in great part attributable to D'Annunzio'.[45] He was a national socialist heavily influenced by Sorel's syndicalism, and during his famous occupation of Fiume in 1919 – an incident Lawrence describes in some detail in *Sea and Sardinia* – he wrote, together with the fellow syndicalist De Ambris, a constitution of Fiume which 'quickly became the most important single vehicle of syndicalist influence on the young veterans in fascism'.[46] Combining syndicalism with a fierce nationalism, D'Annunzio saw 'the dawn of a new age where life would be fuller and more beautiful. . . . This newness of life was simply the reawakening of the oldest culture'.[47]

From this bewildering maze of ideas, Mussolini built a platform for political action, taking the major part of his inspiration from D'Annunzio's startling success, which 'persuaded him that radicalism, even radical nationalism, was not enough. For fascism to succeed, it must invoke poetry, drama, mystery'.[48] And with Italian democracy crumbling fast between 1920 and 1922, the road lay open for a system of government which introduced elitism, anti-parliamentarianism and violence as integral parts of its strategy to build a new Rome. When Lawrence left Italy in February 1922 Mussolini was only eight months away from power. The political tide in Europe was turning towards the right, and so was Lawrence.

Lawrence's Reading of Utopian Literature

The above survey has shown that Lawrence's political ideas cannot be seen in isolation from the historical context in which they were conceived. Indeed, it demonstrates Lawrence's knack of being in the right place at the right time. Few people during this period had a better opportunity to keep abreast with contemporary political and ideological movements.

This view seems to be amply confirmed by an examination of Lawrence's reading of literature related to the subject in question. Again, this is not to suggest that the works discussed in the following had any direct bearing on Lawrence's ideas. They do, however, point to a certain tendency, if not a pattern, with respect to his political and ideological interests. In order not to confuse issues, it seems appropriate to divide this discussion into two sections, concerned respectively with writers seen as representatives of what may be called the 'naive utopian tradition', and with those who are to be seen as precursors of the modern totalitarian utopia. For obvious reasons, the main focus will be on the latter group.

Rose Marie Burwell's checklist of Lawrence's reading in Keith Sagar's *Handbook* includes nearly 1200 books and articles which he either read or knew. When one tries to establish connections between Lawrence's reading and his own writing, such a list obviously represents a temptation to pick and choose according to one's own liking. By any standards, however, Lawrence was comparatively well versed in the tradition of the naive utopia. Any history of this literature would count among its founders Homer, Plato, Virgil and, perhaps most importantly, Hesiod. All of these Lawrence knew, and probably Hesiod more thoroughly than any of the others. Having read about him in Burnet's *Early Greek Philosophy* during the summer of 1915, he turned back, six months later, to read the poet-philosopher's own works. The same goes for writers of the medieval and renaissance periods, including Joachim of Fiore (see chapter 1); Milton and Dante, the two greatest writers on paradise in Western culture; and Francis Bacon, author of the *New Atlantis*. Furthermore, from the literature of the eighteenth and nineteenth centuries Lawrence read some of the most important contributors to English and American utopianism. By 1909 he had read Defoe's *Robinson Crusoe*, which according to Manuel and Manuel 'launched a new utopian form with a magnetic appeal . . .';[49] and Samuel Butler's *Erewhon*. A few years later he had also explored Godwin and Richard Jefferies, together with the Americans Hawthorne and Thoreau. From his own and his parents' generations he read almost all of H. G. Wells's books, Edward Carpenter, William Morris (whose *News from Nowhere* he probably knew long before 1927 when he mentions it in a review), and most likely Bulwer-Lytton – a second-best Wells and author of *The Coming Race* – whom he refers to in *The Lost Girl*. Mention should also be made of Winwood Reade's *The Martyrdom of Man*, which Lawrence refers to in March 1919. First published in 1872, the book describes in great sweeps the course of human history. It is, according to Richard Gerber, 'the earliest and most typical post-evolutionary utopian outburst', stressing man's development from planetary dust to an immortal and godlike creature of the future.[50] With a naive and lively imagination Reade shrugs off the principles of scientific scholarship and envisages the future kingdom of reason and love: 'With one faith, with one desire [men] will labour together in the Sacred Cause – the extinction of disease, the extinction of sin, the perfection of genius, the perfection of love, the invention of immortality, the exploration of the infinite, the conquest of creation. You blessed ones who shall inherit that future age. . . .'[51]

Among continental authors, one figure of major significance is

Rousseau, who in most of his writings dealt in some way or another with the notion of an ideal world. In 1910 Lawrence read his *La Nouvelle Héloise*, a naive nature utopia whose setting is an imaginary village called Clarens at the foot of the Alps. In the *Contrat social*, on the other hand, a book Lawrence quotes from in his *Movements in European History*, Rousseau attempts a more theoretical description of political institutions designed to form the basis of a real *monde idéal*. Here the utopia of innocent escape is turned into one with a sharper edge, and it is not very difficult to find reasons why Rousseau must have appealed to Lawrence. Like Lawrence, he celebrates the life-philosophy of the powerful individual who, having abolished the nobility of birth for the nobility of soul,[52] lives according to the laws of nature and is superior to the laws of a narrow-minded society. 'As he contemplated the decadence of his own society Rousseau found the telltale symptom of its disease in the loss of any strength of passion.'[53] Very much in line with Lawrence's own cultural diagnosis of a later period, Rousseau, according to Fritz Stern, 'had fathered a new type of cultural criticism, and his followers, particularly in Germany, linked his criticism to an attack on what they called the naive rationalism and the mechanistic thought of the Enlightenment'.[54] Thus, Rousseau should be seen as a transitional figure between a traditional naive utopia and the conception of a more aggressive, power-oriented utopia which was not brought to full fruition until the early twentieth century. Certainly, Lawrence had also been exposed to this latter aspect of Rousseau's thought through Carlyle, who will be discussed later.

Maxim Gorky was another transitional figure who was deeply involved in the Russian Revolution. Lawrence must have read him with keen interest, because in a letter from March 1913 he says that he has read all the 4½ pence Gorky available (*Le I*, 524). Also, his friend Koteliansky translated a couple of Gorky's books, both of which Lawrence read, and he even polished the translation of one of them, *Reminiscences of Andreyev*, in 1923. But what was it in Gorky that appealed to Lawrence? In his book *The Cult of Violence*, Jack Roth says:

> A cataclysmic transformation of the social order was clearly implied in Gorki's vision of the revolution. Gorki too was a 'pessimist' who viewed history as a 'march toward deliverance'. The pessimist viewed society as a 'system' that could only be destroyed by a catastrophe involving the whole, while the opti-

> mist naively believed in 'progress' or 'evolution'. . . . Gorki called for the complete destruction of the present order.[55]

True to the Marxist view of history, however, Gorky did not see the catastrophe as the final word. 'Everywhere in bolshevik myths were visions of a new world in formation. . . . In Gorki's works there were visions "worthy of the Hebrew prophets".'[56] Another critic claims that according to Gorki what people lacked was a 'faith in some great cause and the spiritual valour to dedicate themselves to its fulfilment . . . '.[57] And this is where Gorky's tendencies towards a naive utopianism and his never-ending quarrel with Lenin become clear. The heart of the matter was that Gorky before the Revolution was involved with the so-called 'God-builders', socialists who, very much against Lenin's wishes, tried to create a new and 'this-worldly' vision of God, taking it for granted that the idea of God is necessary to mankind. The creation of this new God would give a 'model of perfection to which all individual men must aspire in their behaviour on earth, as in the past they had aspired to be united with the perfection of the supernatural God in heaven'.[58] On this philosophical basis Gorky started in 1909 his 'Capri school', which was to 'acquaint his worker pupils with the loftiest manifestations of human endeavour throughout the ages. . . . They would then march in the vanguard of the revolution'.[59] In short, the 'purpose of Gorky's Capri school was to unite a religious ideal with a revolutionary design'.[60] Against this background it is not very surprising to find Lawrence saying in a letter to Louie Burrows from as early as December 1910: 'Poor Gorki: I'm very much of an English equivalent of his' (*Le I*, 209).

From the group of writers who contributed to Lawrence's anti-democratic or totalitarian views, Thomas Carlyle stands out as a natural starting point. By the age of twenty Lawrence had read three of Carlyle's most influential and polemically powerful works, *The French Revolution*, *Sartor Resartus*, and *Heroes and Hero-Worship*, the latter two of which contain the germ and the flower respectively of the author's ideas on hero worship. An ardent anti-democrat, Carlyle saw the Hero as 'the messenger of the divine to the mass of mankind who cannot hear its injunctions for themselves; he [is], in fact, in a broad sense the prophet'.[61] This view was heavily indebted to his reading of Fichte, and generally 'the strong strain of élitism in the German Romantic thinkers had had a deep influence on his intellectual development'.[62] Though Lawrence never really acknowledged his debts to Carlyle, a brief glance at the latter's life and works is enough to reveal a striking number of similarities between the two, and there can be no doubt that Lawrence's early reading of Carlyle formed an ideological background of great importance to his later development. During the apocalyptic despair of the First World War, when Lawrence was frantically searching for alternative solutions, his writings echo passages from *Heroes and Hero-Worship*, which he had read a decade earlier. 'The confused wreck', Carlyle had written 75 years earlier, 'of things crumbling and even crashing and tumbling all round us in these revolutionary ages, will get down so far; *no* farther. [Hero worship] is an eternal corner-stone, from which they can begin to build themselves up again'.[63] It should also be kept in mind that Carlyle, even after the turn of the century, cast his shadow across the intellectual landscape. His influence upon his own generation had been 'so extraordinary that it has never been approached in modern British history by any other single intellectual figure',[64] and as late as after the First World War his books still had a large audience. Even for Lawrence's own generation Carlyle's message had a largely contemporary quality. It is a not entirely unjustified insult when Arnold Hauser accuses Carlyle of being 'the first and most original of the pied pipers who prepared the way for Mussolini and Hitler'.[65]

George Bernard Shaw is another writer connected with hero worship and élitism. It is interesting to note that the two books by Shaw Lawrence is known to have read – apart from *The Intelligent Woman's Guide to Socialism and Capitalism*, which, quite revealingly, he gave up – were 'the two parables of vitalism and superhumanity, *Man and Superman* and *Back to Methuselah*'.[66] The former Lawrence read in 1912, the year it was first published, and the latter he describes with disgust in *Fantasia of the Unconscious*, which was written in 1921. But even though Lawrence had nothing but contempt for Shaw, and their heroic utopias were qualitatively different, the fact remains that they both believed in the Superman or aristocrat as a unique source of social salvation, and with regard to their political ideas this stands out as a significant common denominator.

In 1916 Lawrence read, with a similarly negative attitude, Wilfred B. Trotter's book *Instincts of the Herd in Peace and War*. Its main thesis is that man possesses a number of instincts similar to those of animals; that man is in fact a gregarious animal relying on instinctual responses to his environment; and that our three main characteristics are related to those of the wolf, the sheep and the bee

– corresponding to the aggressive, defensive and social aspects of the human character. During his discussion of the ongoing war between Germany (the wolf) and England (the bee), Trotter describes man's remarkable susceptibility to leadership, and his deep and natural desire, in times of crisis, for a particular type of man: 'the strong, silent, relentless, the bold, outspoken, hard, and energetic – but at all costs he must be a "man", a "leader who can lead", a shepherd, in fact, who, by his gesticulations and his shouts, leaves his flock in no doubt as to his presence and his activity.'[67] This quality, which entails a 'conscious direction of the social unit'[68] and which is most clearly expressed in Germany, Trotter sees as an admirable attempt to cope with the apocalyptic anarchy which resulted from the 'inherent defects in the evolution of civilized life' before the war and from 'human progress being left to chance'.[69] In a vision of the future prospects of mankind, Trotter claims that this principle of an élitist direction of the social unit will create a 'biological mechanism of a wholly new type' and a 'dynamic conception of statesmanship as something active, progressive, and experimental, reaching out towards new powers for human activity and new conquests for the human will'.[70] The vision ends with a far from sober account of this new humanity which will 'sail their ships into the gulfs of the ether and lay tribute upon the sun and stars'.[71] Trotter's book, a quasi-scientific justification for a certain political view, was not the only one of its kind. Around the turn of the century a whole body of literature was produced on herd psychology and similar topics, and most of it posed the question 'whether democracy . . . could ever be more than a cloak concealing from the collectively gullible the perennial triumph of calculating elites'.[72]

Among the German writers contributing to Lawrence's political ideas, both Nietzsche and Schopenhauer have been mentioned in earlier chapters. Again, there is no reason to go into detail on either of them, since their influence on the early twentieth-century generation in general and on Lawrence in particular is indisputable and has been the subject of several studies. There is one source of Nietzschean influence, however, which does not seem to have been mentioned before. As a regular reader of the socialist magazine *The New Age* during 1908 and 1909, Lawrence was exposed to a rather astonishing number of articles and reviews – most of them enthusiastic – on Nietzsche's works. This may be due in part to the interest in Nietzsche of the editor, A. R. Orage, whose book *Nietzsche, The Dionysian Spirit of the Age* was advertised at the back of each issue for a major part of the period. Also, during this time *Thus Spake*

Zarathustra and *Ecce Homo* were presented as 'Book of the Week'. It may be assumed, therefore, that *The New Age* is a more likely source of Lawrence's first encounter with Nietzsche than the Croydon Central Library, which is referred to in Sagar's *Handbook*.

Among other philosophers, mention should also be made of Count Hermann Graf Keyserling, who is now largely forgotten but who was a major name in Germany after the First World War. Lawrence probably read his *Travel Diary of a Philosopher* in 1925, and in an essay he comments approvingly on Keyserling's views on natural aristocracy ('Aristocracy', *RDP*, 369).[73] In his book *Confessions of a European Intellectual*, Franz Schoenberner, who was the editor of the famous journals *Jugend* and *Simplicissimus* and who visited Lawrence at this time, also pays his respects to Keyserling: 'Among the treasonable intellectuals who contributed to the stage production of the ignoble horror play of Nazism were some more or less tragicomical characters like Oswald Spengler, Hermann von Keyserling, and finally the philosophical faker Alfred Rosenberg.'[74]

Belonging to the same group of infamous celebrities is Houston S. Chamberlain, a German of English descent, who was married to Richard Wagner's daughter and who contributed strongly to the ideological development of German fascism by his famous work *Foundations of the XIXth Century* (1899, English translation 1911). Emile Delavenay, who has written quite extensively on the relationship between Chamberlain and Lawrence, has shown by a comparison between Chamberlain's work and the 'Study of Thomas Hardy', that Lawrence is bound to have read *Foundations*. He even goes so far as to claim that the 'key to the resemblances noted between [Lawrence's] ideas and some of those which led to Nazism is to be found in the influence of Chamberlain. . . '.[75] This, among other things, meant 'mystic ideas of blood and race, violent reactions against humanitarian and egalitarian democracy, linked with Hegelian romanticism and theories of aesthetics of German origin'.[76] Indeed, these are all elements which assume a prominent role in Lawrence's post-war writings.

Mention should also be made of the Austrian writer Emil Lucka, whose book *Grenzen der Seele* Lawrence read in October 1921 (just after finishing *Aaron's Rod*). In this bulky metaphysical treatise, Lucka distinguishes between two types of human beings: 'der Mittelmensch' and 'der Grenzmensch'. The former 'lebt ohne entschiedene innere Spannung im Gleichgewicht'[77] – he is the man in the street, a member of the great anonymous majority. The latter, on the other hand, 'lebt in Extremen; er ist der Ekstatiker und der Heilige, der den Himmel erkämpfen will . . .',[78] and the purpose of the book is to analyse the personal characteristics of the 'Grenzmensch'. Thus *Grenzen der Seele* – with its obvious bias in favour of the exceptional individual – may at least have served as a confirmation for Lawrence of ideas which would play a crucial role in the later leadership novels.

Another German who, although regarded as one of the most important German writers of the day, was hardly known in England, was Richard Dehmel. Lawrence mentions Dehmel for the first time in his review of *The Oxford Book of German Verse* from December 1911. Here he gives a clear impression of being fairly well acquainted with the writer's work. He mentions him again in a letter to Else Jaffe from February 1913, in which he asks her to collaborate on an article about contemporary German poetry. Trusting Armin Arnold's claim that 'Lawrence always studied the literature of the country where he happened to be',[79] one can assume that Dehmel would be one of the first to catch Lawrence's attention. A closer examination of Dehmel only makes this assumption more credible. Heavily influenced by Nietzsche, Dehmel celebrated a life of physical love and natural instincts. In the introduction to *Contemporary German Poetry*, which was part of Lawrence's background reading for his review of *The Oxford Book of German Verse*, Jethro Bithell writes that 'Dehmel's ferocious masculinity rings out in the loud onflow with its shock of consonants of his lyric verse; he is the most virile, and at the same time the most ruthless, of all German poets'.[80] Dehmel's treatment of the relationship between man and woman is less relevant for Lawrence's political ideas but highly relevant for other aspects of his writings. Married to a woman who had an impact on him quite comparable to that of Frieda on Lawrence, Dehmel embraced the passionate love between man and woman as a cosmic source of salvation and liberation. This probably comes out with greatest force in the poetic novel *Zwei Menschen* (1903), in which he treats sexual themes with a frankness which shocked his contemporaries.[81] This is also the central theme in *Aber die Liebe*, a volume of poems which Lawrence appears to be familiar with in his review ('A Review of *The Oxford Book of German Verse* edited by H. G. Fiedler', *Ph II*, 270). Thus Dehmel played in German literature much the same role as Lawrence was to play in England after the ban of *The Rainbow*. Considering Dehmel's position in Germany, this parallel is bound to have come to Lawrence's attention.

Another German poet Lawrence knew as early as 1911 was a close friend of Dehmel, Detlev von Liliencron. According to R. Ensor, whose article on the poet Lawrence also read in preparation for his 1911 review, Liliencron was 'by far the foremost lyric poet of his own country' at the time.[82] Liliencron was a captain in the Prussian army – some of his poetry and stories certainly offer an interesting apropos of Lawrence's Prussian officer stories – and like Dehmel he was deeply infused by Nietzschean ideas. Ensor claims that the spiritual revolt expressed in the writings of Nietzsche and Liliencron embodies 'fundamentally and instinctively . . . two valuable ideas – the reclaiming of the individual's freedom from the pressure of modern environment, and the reassertion of the joy of life as against its burden. No doubt Liliencron's glad, strong military heroes, when you analyse them, embody with this a good deal of the Bismarckian cult of sheer force . . . '.[83]

Finally, Lawrence knew the work of Stefan George, who has already been described as a powerful exponent of certain political and cultural trends in Germany around the First World War. Admittedly, George's poetry is not easily accessible, and it is doubtful if Lawrence, with his fairly limited command of German, had a first-hand knowledge of his work. However, George and his circle were as much a cultural phenomenon as a group of individual artists, and there is furthermore a more personal link between Lawrence and George: Martin Green claims that after Else Jaffe 'moved to Munich in 1911, her house there became a social center for the disciples of Stefan George'.[84] When, therefore, Lawrence mentions George in the letter to Else in which he suggests that they collaborate on an article on German poetry, he is certainly aware of his sister-in-law's close contacts with the George circle (*Le I*, 513).

Among Italian writers, Gabriele D'Annunzio, whose 'poems, plays, and novels reflected all the worst aspects of Nietzsche's homage to instinct',[85] must have exercised a particular fascination on Lawrence. By April 1913 he was familiar with the novel *The Light Under the Bushel*, and three years later he had read *Il Fuoco*, *Il Trionfo della Morte* and *Vergine delle Rocche*, and asked in a letter for *L'Innocente*. For the present discussion, the most interesting of these works is *Vergine delle Rocche*. One of D'Annunzio's biographers, Anthony Rhodes, remarks that this book, while not being the best of the writer's novels, 'is certainly the most important, because it announces the Superman, the theme which [D'Annunzio] introduced into Italy from his reading of Nietzsche'.[86]

Another Italian Lawrence read with great interest was D'Annunzio's disciple, Filippo Tommaso Marinetti. In letters from 2 June and 5 June 1914 – only days before he witnessed the violent clashes in Turin – Lawrence goes on at great length about the 'fat book' on Futurism which he had just read in Italian, and which contained, among other things, essays and manifestoes by both Marinetti and Buzzi, a fellow Futurist poet. In *Women in Love*, the character Loerke speaks like a futurist when he claims that '"machinery and the acts of labour are extremely, maddeningly beautiful"'.[87]

Lawrence must have gone slightly out of his way to become acquainted with Futurism, because it was a movement with a fairly limited following. In his introduction to a collection of Marinetti's writings, R. W. Flint says that: 'Aside from the letters and memoirs of such men as Lawrence, Gramsci, Apollinaire, and scattered stories in biographies, the documentation of the movement is surprisingly sparse. . . .'[88] Nevertheless, Futurism was sufficiently powerful to add 'a vital strain of bluff Latin rationality to the growing cult of the irrational in art'.[89] Like D'Annunzio, Marinetti had received strong impulses from the writings of Sorel, especially his book *Reflections on Violence*, and consequently 'the need for struggle and the beauty supposed to accompany it were the main themes of Marinetti's politics'.[90] The most famous document of the Futurists was Marinetti's 'Futurist Manifesto', which was published in the French newspaper *Le Figaro* in 1909. Celebrating every form of dramatic human activity and largely ignoring traditional moral values, the eleven-point manifesto abounds with phrases such as the racer's stride, the mortal leap, the punch and the slap, the beauty of speed, the violent attack, glorification of war, militarism, beautiful ideas worth dying for, and the scorn of women.[91] From this political platform, Marinetti entered the scene of Italian politics after the First World War and remained an active politician until 1924.

It is to be hoped that the above survey will have gone some way towards clarifying at least two points. First, that the historical and cultural background of Lawrence's political ideas is mainly to be sought not in England but on the Continent, particularly in Germany and Italy. Second, that his reading, which includes both traditional utopian literature and elements pointing forward to a more militant and totalitarian millennium, reflects the political climate in which he lived. It now remains to draw a comparison between the findings of the present chapter and Lawrence's own views as they are expressed in his writings.

5

The Mystery of Lordship: The Leadership Utopia

The previous chapter sketched out the continental background against which Lawrence's political ideas become more comprehensible. It did not, however, deal with Lawrence himself in any great detail and his personal reasons for renouncing salvation through the love of woman. This change is by no means easily explained, but Martin Green's study *The von Richthofen Sisters* offers some interesting suggestions. Green describes the strong impression made on Lawrence by the intellectual and artistic milieu in Schwabing – a kind of Greenwich Village of Munich – to which the Richthofen sisters were significant contributors. During the first and second decades of the century Schwabing was the centre of opposition against the Prussian patriarchal society represented above all by Bismarck. The Schwabing alternative, as suggested earlier, was a celebration of woman and of maternal values. According to Green, these were the ideas Lawrence hoarded from the very first day of his acquaintance with Frieda. The significance of this experience for Lawrence's fiction is beyond dispute, as Green makes abundantly clear. What he largely fails to discuss is the relationship between Lawrence's German experience and his leadership ideas. This I hope to do by adding to the general background of the previous chapter the personal and psychological elements which contributed to Lawrence's overall view of politics.

It is obvious that novels like *Kangaroo* and *The Plumed Serpent* reflect the marital conflicts of Lawrence and Frieda. What does not seem to have been noted is that the ideas discussed in these novels go back several years, and that their rising to prominence after ten years of marriage can be seen as an indication of Lawrence's need to claim independence from the ideas that Frieda had so powerfully exposed him to – ideas which he had at first accepted as a gospel of salvation, and which made up the basic philosophy of *The Rainbow* and *Women in Love*. But this does not mean that Lawrence abandoned Frieda's cultural background as a source of inspiration. On the contrary, his leadership ideas are probably more German than anything else, but they are in deliberate opposition to the maternalistic philosophy of Frieda's Schwabing. Without doubt, Green is right in regarding the erotic maternalism of Schwabing as a clearly profiled subgroup of *Lebensphilosophie*. Thus, by embracing the fundamentals of this philosophy Lawrence never had to stray very far from Frieda's path in order to vent his dissatisfaction with the rule of women.

The relationship between Lawrence's social background and the later leadership ideas is another element which was briefly mentioned in the previous chapter and which bears more heavily on the experience of his adolescence. Like many other working class youths at the time, he started out instinctively sympathetic to the socialist cause. 'In the flush of youth, I believed in Socialism, because I thought it would be thrilling and delightful' ('Red Trousers', *Ph II*, 563). By the time he met Frieda, however, he had written two novels, caused some stir in literary circles because of his working class background, and had finally entered those very circles which had been a closed world to him. Lawrence, by the age of 27, had climbed the social ladder from the bottom to the position of artists and intellectuals. This rise through society explains his contempt for the Fabians' pitying condescension towards the working class. Having himself risen from this class, Lawrence naturally objected to this patting on the head by people who were secure in their superior position, who had never had to fight to obtain it, and whose concern for the working masses, therefore, did nothing but put him back into place as a representative of the working masses. Quite rightly, Lawrence must have regarded himself as one of a chosen few who had made a narrow escape from the iron grip of material and social forces. It is not surprising, therefore, to find this escape reflected in political ideas which stress the importance of the élite and the heroic deed. It also explains why Lawrence tends to turn the socialist gospel upside down and call it a form of bullying. In the essay 'Nobody Loves Me', he describes this 'nasty pronounced benevolence, which wants to do good to all mankind, and is only a form of self-assertion and of bullying. From this sort of love of humanity, good Lord deliver us! and deliver poor humanity' (*Ph*, 205).

A third element which served to strengthen Lawrence's anti-democratic attitude, was his gross and fatal oversimplification of regarding the England of the war years as a true example of democracy in practice. As has been suggested earlier, the Western democracies turned more and more totalitarian as the crisis of the war deepened. To make matters worse, this was exactly the time when Lawrence – because of conscription, the suppression of *The Rainbow* and the allegations of spying – was exposed to the heavy hand of the state. Characteristically, his response was based more on violent emotions and subjective experience than on political analysis. He clearly embraced a set of ideas which, if applied to the England of the First World War, would undoubtedly have exercised an even more rigorous rule of public authority. When reading Lawrence's political writings, it is important to remember that his idea of democracy is largely based on his personal experience from the war years. Furthermore, it explains why he considered both Socialism and democracy as a form of bullying.

Finally, the end of the war offered Lawrence yet another argument against democracy, for in his opinion the peace made it evident that the whole war had been a bloody venture from which nothing had been gained. The 'apocalypse' had not had the cathartic effect which could have justified the four years of death and destruction. Rather the war was only 'another rent in the old ship's bottom' (*Le II*, 611–12), proving for all to see that the democratic ideals by which Britain had conducted the war were beyond repair. Significantly, Lawrence's leadership ideas began to take form during the war but did not gain momentum until after the outcome was clear and the futility of the war had become apparent.

The following is a chronological survey of Lawrence's political ideas up to the completion of *The Plumed Serpent* in 1925. Naturally, this does not mean that his thinking ever developed into a coherent system of political philosophy, rather it should be seen as a continuous exploration of possibilities. There is no conclusion or *finis*, no clearcut ideology in which he comes to rest.[1] Nevertheless, his ideas are worth examining. First because there has been a general reservation among Lawrence's critics against accepting the presence of proto-fascist ideas in his works. Second, these ideas dominated Lawrence's writings during an important period of his career and are therefore crucial for an understanding of the continuity of his thought. Third, they show the conseqences of a religious quest which is content with nothing short of heaven on earth. And finally, they reflect in a fascinating way an entire generation's tentative search for harbour among the coral reefs of totalitarian ideologies.

The Leadership Ideas Before Aaron's Rod

The first obvious appearance in Lawrence's works of ideas directly relevant to the leadership ideas of the 1920s, is in the 'Study of Thomas Hardy', which was finished in December 1914. Throughout this essay, Lawrence's discussion focuses on two closely connected issues. First, the role of the hero or aristocrat and the way in which 'Hardy, like Tolstoi, is forced in the issue always to stand with the community in condemnation of the aristocrat' (*SThH*, 49). Second, the struggle through history between the principles of the male and the female. The connection and friction in Lawrence's own life between these two elements has already been touched upon, and the 'Study' can be regarded as initiating this discussion, which was brought to a climax in the leadership novels. It is interesting to note that the 'Study' clearly states how the male and the female are mutually dependent and equally important, thus echoing strongly the love philosophy of Frieda's Schwabing: 'The clear, full inevitable need in me is that I, the male, meet the female stream which shall carry mine so that the two run to the fullest flood, to furthest motion. It is no primary need of the begetting of children. It is the arriving at my highest mark of activity, of being; it is her arrival at her intensest self' (54). However, the reference to the begetting of children carries not only the voice of Frieda and Otto Gross, but also that of Hans Blüher, and a few pages later Lawrence turns to ideas which imply a qualitative difference between the male and the female. He starts out rather vaguely by introducing certain racial theories and connecting them to the religious tradition of the West: 'According to the race-conception of God, we can see whether in that race the male or the female element triumphs, becomes predominant' (60). This approach concerning sexual characteristics in different races was close to common currency in Germany at the time. Otto Weininger, who was a disciple of both Blüher and Chamberlain, developed this dichotomy into a set of racist ideas according to which the Jews were seen as representing the female principle and the Aryan race the male. One of Weininger's own followers, Georg Lomer, an advocate of Germanic sun worship, saw 'the Aryan male symbolized by the sun, while the Jew, like the female, represented only reflected light in the form of the moon'.[2] Emile Delavenay argues very convincingly that Lawrence actually read Weininger (his book *Sex and Character* was very widely read at the time, and was translated into English as early as 1906), and the 'Study' goes a long way to confirm this connection.[3] 'The male in the

Jew', Lawrence says, 'was too weak, the female overbore him. He remained in the grip of the female. . . . In the whole of the ten commandments, it is the female who speaks' (*SThH*, 62). In opposition to this rule of the female, both Weininger and Lawrence, according to Delavenay, launch the notion of the aristocrat. Throughout the 'Study', however, Lawrence maintains a less radical stance than Weininger: the aristocrat 'is, by virtue of breed and long training, a perfect instrument. He knows, as every pure-bred thing knows, that his root and source is in his female' (99). Still, the 'Study' sets the scene for future confrontation.

During the year that followed, 1915, Lawrence completed three major works. In June he finished *The Rainbow*, in the course of the summer he wrote 'The Crown', and in October he rewrote major parts of *Twilight in Italy*. In none of these works does he bring to the fore ideas which are radically different from those of the 'Study'. Still, *Twilight in Italy* contains strong indications of Lawrence's reading of Houston Chamberlain, and Delavenay is not surprised that Rolf Gardiner

> should have loved and admired *Twilight in Italy* and found in it 'all the germ' of Lawrence's thought. The 1915 views 'on leadership and community, on discipline and power', which Gardiner found 'remarkably akin to those exemplified by the German *Buende* after the war' and to the Spirit of National Socialism, did indeed constitute a platform for a corporatist, authoritarian and mystic State, not exempt from latent philo-Teutonic racialism.[4]

However, this seems to be going a bit far. In fact the references to aristocratic ideas in *Twilight in Italy* are not as explicit as Delavenay claims. Only in his condemnation of Cromwell's celebration of utilitarianism and the average does Lawrence turn with a nostalgic look to the reign of Charles I, who still represented the proud 'supremacy of the Me who am the image of God, the Me of the flesh, of the senses, Me, the tiger burning bright, me the king, the Lord, the aristocrat, me who am divine because I am the body of God' (39).

The discussion about aristocracy and democracy between Ursula and Skrebensky towards the end of *The Rainbow* also deserves some attention, because here the aristocratic values are expressed not by the male, but by the female. It is Ursula, in the process of breaking loose from her bonds to Skrebensky, who asserts her independence and individuality in terms of political ideas. Denouncing democracy as symptomatic of 'degenerate races' (427) and preferring an aristocracy of birth to one of money, she cries: '"I hate it, that anybody is my equal who has the same amount of money as I have. I *know* I am better than all of them. . . . I hate equality on a money-basis. It is the equality of dirt"' (ibid.). At this point, in other words, Lawrence's aristocratic ideas – since there can be no doubt that Ursula is here echoing Lawrence's own views – were not connected exclusively to the role of the male, as they were to be later. In 'The Crown' Lawrence even talks consistently about the phoenix as a female creature: 'Sitting upon her tree, she was the only one of her kind in all creation, supreme, the zenith, the perfect aristocrat' (*RDP*, 270).

An interesting context to these statements is offered by Lawrence's letters from the same period. The difference is quite astonishing the moment he turns to the reality of wartime England. In February 1915 he wrote to Bertrand Russell: 'There must be a revolution in the state. It shall begin by the nationalising of all industries and means of communication, and of the land – in one fell blow' (*Le II*, 282). A few days later he suggested the forming of a revolutionary party. In June, however, he suddenly pleaded with Russell 'not to get into trouble now, at this juncture. I do beg you to save yourself for the great attack, later on, when the opportunity comes. . . . Let us wait a little while, till we can assemble the nucleus of a new belief, get a new centre of attack . . .' (357). In July, in another letter to Russell, he returned safely to his own world of political fantasy, suggesting an idea which he was to try out ten years later in *The Plumed Serpent*: 'In your lecture on the State, you must criticise the extant democracy, the young idea. That is our enemy. This existing phase is now in its collapse. . . . The whole must culminate in an absolute *Dictator*, and an equivalent *Dictatrix*' (365). Thus, in the course of a few months, Lawrence spanned the whole political landscape, from a traditional Marxist revolution to a pseudo-religious vision of a joint dictatorship between man and woman.

Moving to 1916 and *Women in Love*, one is faced with a renewed and more outspoken tension between the sexes. Furthermore, Lawrence obviously drew more heavily on his German experience in this novel than in *The Rainbow*. A document of the greatest interest in connection with this is the 'Prologue to *Women in Love*', which has not been properly dated, but which must have been written between December 1915 and October 1917 (*WL*, Expl. Notes, 587).

In the previous chapter the German idea of the *Männerbund* was described in some detail. Another and related phenomenon is the *Blutbrüderschaft*.[5] Together they form an explanatory key to the political implications of *Women in Love*, and they clearly point forward to Lawrence's later works.

The vaguely homo-erotic aspects of *Women in Love* have generally been seen as simply a reflection of Lawrence's own personality, and when he speaks out strongly against homosexuality this has again been regarded either as a deliberate attempt to hide his own sexual ambivalence or as an unconscious psychological projection. This may well be the case to a considerable extent. However, if one considers the *Männerbund* ideas outlined above, a different picture emerges. In the 'Prologue' the relationship between the three men, especially that between Birkin and Gerald, is expressed only ostensibly in direct and unambiguous language, because although the author uses the word 'love' quite freely, he seems at pains to convey a meaning different from what a modern reader would take more or less for granted. On a climbing trip in the Alps, the three friends are literally on another and higher plane:

> The three men were very close together, and lifted into an abstract isolation, among the upper rocks and the snow. The world that lay below, the whole field of human activity, was sunk and subordinated, they had trespassed into the upper silence and loneliness. The three of them had reached another state of being, they were enkindled in the upper silences into a rare, unspoken intimacy, an intimacy that took no expression, but which was between them like a transfiguration (*WL*, 489).

As to Birkin and Gerald, they 'knew they loved each other, that each would die for the other' (490). Thus Lawrence includes in his description important aspects of the *Männerbund*: an Eros which surpasses the relationship between man and woman, together with a noble willingness to sacrifice one's own life. There is also a distinct flavour of medieval chivalry, whose ideals formed the ideological basis of the German Youth Movement. Finally, the 'Prologue', like the idea of the *Männerbund*, stresses the exclusion of women. Hermione is pushed aside by Birkin and Gerald's relationship, and it is evident that the author regards the bond between the two men as deeper and more valuable than that between Birkin and Hermione.

In *Women in Love* Lawrence develops the idea of the *Männerbund* to its crystallized form, the *Blutbrüderschaft*. He tries, however, to have his cake and eat it, because what Birkin is searching for all through the novel is an ideal relationship with a man and a woman at the same time. It begins with Birkin's suggestion that he and Gerald swear a *Blutbrüderschaft*: '"You know how the old German knights used to swear a Blutbrüderschaft. . . . We will swear to stand by each other – be true to each other – ultimately – infallibly – given to each other, organically – without possibility of taking back"' (206–7). Gerald shrugs it off, but the relationship between them reaches a climax some time later, in the famous wrestling scene in 'Gladiatorial'.

There are several elements in this chapter which testify to a German influence. First, wrestling, like fencing, was a popular sport in German universities and in the Youth Movement at the time, and Birkin admits that he learnt some Japanese wrestling during his student days in Heidelberg. This connection is confirmed by a passage in the essay 'Education of the People', written a couple of years later. Here Lawrence describes how boys should learn to fight: 'Egg them on, and look on the black eye and the bloody nose as insignia of honour, like the Germans of old. Bring out the foils and teach fencing' (*RDP*, 159).

Second, Lawrence stresses the men's nakedness and describes in detail how Gerald has a 'northern kind of beauty, like light refracted from snow – and a beautiful plastic form' (273). As mentioned before, the beauty of the blond, Germanic type was a key feature of the primitive life philosophy of the period.

Third, these elements are directly linked with Birkin's previous suggestion of a *Blutbrüderschaft*. When the wrestling match is over, Gerald asks: '"Is this the Brüderschaft you wanted?" "Perhaps"', Birkin replies (ibid.).[6]

An essential aspect of this whole chapter is that it takes place the same night as Birkin's unsuccessful proposal to Ursula. Thus even the structure of the story underlines the theme already mentioned: Birkin's search for two ideal relationships at the same time. Indeed, this is the conflicting note on which the novel ends. After Gerald has died, Birkin tells Ursula: '"You are enough for me, as far as woman is concerned. You are all women to me. But I wanted a man friend, as eternal as you and I are eternal"'. Ursula objects: '"You can't have it, because it's false, impossible", she said. "I don't believe that," he answered' (481).

Similar matters – from Lawrence's own personal life – occur in the letters. As early as July 1915 he wrote to Lady Ottoline that he and Russell 'have almost sworn Blutbruderschaft. We will set out together, he and I. We shall really be doing something, in the autumn. I want you to believe always' (*Le II*, 363). The following year, however, the whole idea takes on a less convincing tone as Lawrence is settling a quarrel with Murry: 'Good, all is well between us all. No more quarrels and quibbles. Let it be agreed for ever. I am Blutbruder: a Blutbruderschaft between us all. Tell K[atherine] *not* to be so queasy' (570)! Still, despite this slight incommensurability between theory and practice, the idea of a holy pact between men recurs quite frequently and in varying forms in later works.

The last work to be dealt with before *Aaron's Rod* is the collection of essays entitled 'Education of the People', which Lawrence wrote during a period of two years, from 1918 to 1920. Lawrence's point of departure is a head-on attack on the values of the present system of education. Probably inspired by Marinetti's 'Futurist Manifesto', whose tenth point called for the destruction of 'museums, libraries [and] academies of every kind',[7] Lawrence says: 'We should be wise if by decree we shut up all elementary schools at once, and kept them shut' (*RDP*, 100). As an alternative Lawrence outlines a more rigorous and hierarchical system, which, he claims:

> will inevitably produce distinct classes of society. The basis is the great class of workers. From this class will rise also the masters of industry, and probably, the leading soldiers. Second comes the clerkly caste. . . . Thirdly we have the class of the higher professions. . . . Finally, there is the small class of the supreme judges: not merely legal judges, but judges of the destiny of the nation. . . . all the professionals in our new world are not mere technical experts: they are life-directors (107–8).

Clearly, Lawrence's ideal is the Platonic utopia of the *Republic*, mixed with a powerful dose of Nietzsche. The latter aspect is most evident in an hysterical passage on the upbringing of babies: 'Send the volts of fierce anger and severing force violently into the child. . . . It is not too late. Quick, quick, mothers of England, spank your wistful babies' (140). This, in turn, creates in the boys a true spirit of the male, who 'is always a fighter. The human male is a superb and godlike fighter. . . . In fighting to the death he has one great crisis of his being' (159). Rounding off, in a passage which deserves to be quoted at length, Lawrence puts woman in her place (ref. *Kinder, Küche und Kirche*) and returns to his precious vision of the *Männerbund*:

> . . . let the men scout ahead. Let them go always ahead of their women, in the endless trek across life. Central, with the wagons, travels the woman, with the children and the whole responsibility of immediate, personal living. And on ahead, scouting, fighting, gathering provision, running on the brink of death and at the tip of the life advance, all the time hovering at the tip of life and on the verge of death, the men, the leaders, the outriders.
>
> And between men let there be a new, spontaneous relationship, a new fidelity. . . . Let them realize that they must go beyond their women, projected into a region of greater abstraction, more inhuman activity.
>
> There . . . let men have a new attitude to one another. Let them have a new reverence for their heroes, a new regard for their comrades: deep, deep as life and death.
>
> Let there be again the old passion of deathless friendship between man and man. . . .
>
> Friendship should be a rare, choice, immortal thing, sacred and inviolable as marriage. Marriage and deathless friendship, both should be inviolable and sacred: two great creative passions, separate, apart, but complementary: the one pivotal, the other adventurous: the one, marriage, the centre of human life; and the other the leap ahead (165–6).

Aaron's Rod

Though *Aaron's Rod* is the first of Lawrence's novels to develop leadership ideas as a major motif, it is a bitterly disappointing introduction to the cult of male superiority. Having read Lawrence's earlier philosophizing on the subject, one would expect someone more heroic than Aaron, who, fed up with his wife and children, wanders off on Christmas Eve without as much as a word of explanation. The book conveys very clearly, however, the fact that the real background of Lawrence's theories is not a deeply felt social commitment, but rather – as has been suggested already – the lack of a religious fulfilment in his relationship to the other sex. In *Aaron's Rod* and particularly in Lilly's homespun system of philosophy, the word 'Love' is used to denote the values represented by woman, whereas 'Power' covers the opposite principle, the idea of male leadership. For the first time in Lawrence's fiction, Love is most definitely brought on the defensive. Both *The Rainbow* and *Women in Love* are novels of marriage and sexual consummation, whereas *Aaron's Rod* sees this scheme turned upside down. Aaron finds his marriage destructive to his inner being, and when later in the novel he becomes the lover of the Marchesa, he feels 'blasted – as if blighted by some electricity' (262). Love no longer brings resurrection to a new life. Only 'one fact remained unbroken in the debris of his consciousness: that in the town was Lilly: and that when he needed, he could go to Lilly . . .' (264).

Again, we are faced with the *Blutbrüderschaft*, the idea of a marriage-like relationship between men, and in *Aaron's Rod* this is expressed in a nearly literal way. Several critics have noted that Aaron and Lilly are a sort of Dr Jekyll and Mr Hyde, two characters who both carry the traits of Lawrence himself. The connection between these two men is emphasized by the fact that Lilly is a form of Elizabeth, or – in the Hebrew original – Elisheba, who was the wife of the Aaron of the Old Testament. Lawrence has thus established exactly the kind of relationship which he had described in such detail a year before, in 'Education of the People': a friendship 'sacred and inviolable as marriage'. In the chapters 'Low-Water Mark' and 'The War Again', which are said to be based on Lawrence's own experience from nursing his blood brother Murry, this analogy to marriage is obvious. Here Lilly shows 'skilful housewifery' (106), he washes and darns Aaron's socks, and does all the cooking. Significantly, however, the two men have 'an almost uncanny understanding of one another – like brothers' (ibid.). And equally important, the reason for Aaron's illness is not primarily the flu, but the fact that he was seduced by Josephine. Finally, the scene in which Lilly rubs Aaron's body with oil, echoes the passage in the Bible where Moses 'poured of the anointing oil upon Aaron's head, and anointed him, to sanctify him'.[8] Thus Lawrence underlines the exclusion of women in favour of a holy communion between men, as was seen in the 'Prologue to *Women in Love*'.

In fact *Aaron's Rod* does not go much further than this; it never really tries to formulate a programme of political action. The only hint of it is Lilly's remarks a few minutes before the bomb goes off: '"You've got to have a sort of slavery again. People are not *men*: they are insects and instruments, and their destiny is slavery"' (281). He adds that '"after sufficient extermination"' people will come to their senses. However, in *Fantasia of the Unconscious*, which was written only a couple of months after the completion of

Aaron's Rod, Lawrence offers a less emotional expression of his political views. He still operates with the main principles of Love and Power, but he distinguishes between them by claiming that Love (or sex) is purely individual, whereas Power (or 'man's great purposive activity') is collective: 'The great collective passion of belief which brings men together, comrades and co-workers, passionately obeying their soul-chosen leader or leaders, this is not a sex passion. Not in any sense. Sex holds any two people together, but it tends to disintegrate society, unless it is subordinated to the great dominating male passion of collective *purpose*' (110).

This conflict between the love of woman and the attractions of the *Männerbund* had pursued Lawrence since the war, and steadily his sympathy tended towards the latter. In the spring of 1922 he and Frieda left a chaotic Italy and set out for Ceylon, to go on a few months later to Australia.

Kangaroo

Aaron's Rod is a novel of limited scope and quality, and the gulf between the politico-philosophical speculation and the violent background of political chaos in post-war Italy is embarrassingly wide.

However, *Kangaroo*, the product of Lawrence's brief stay in Australia during the summer (in Australia, the winter) of 1922, returns to the universal, all-encompassing perspective of *The Rainbow* and *Women in Love*. Attempting the difficult task of exploring the dialectical interaction between ideology and reality much more intimately than its predecessor, *Kangaroo* emerges as a considerably more complex novel. Furthermore, there is the vastness of the Australian landscape infusing events with a cosmic significance.

Although four years had passed since the war and he was thousands of miles from Europe, Lawrence's point of departure is still the war and the sense of apocalyptic finality that went with it. There is in Richard Somers's escape from a war-ridden Europe a strong element of the naive utopian who has had enough of the world: 'In Europe, he had made up his mind that everything was done for, played out, finished, and he must go to a new country. The newest country: young Australia' (18). Australia is a new frontier, a virgin territory of hope and promise. Its potentiality, however, is still not brought to realization; it is a seed which has yet to break the crust of the soil, a country capable – as opposed to the rest of the world – of a new start. For this reason Australia is the ideal testing-ground for a new and radical political endeavour. Somers/ Lawrence, then, brings with him to the country two important ideas: the destruction of the old world and the vision of Australia as a potentially new world. Together these two elements form the basis of almost any utopian vision.

The topic of the present chapter is Lawrence's political utopia. In the works leading up to *Kangaroo*, this utopia has only reached a half-way stage in the notion of a small but perfect community of men: the *Blutbrüderschaft* and the *Männerbund*. In *Kangaroo* this idea is both retained and expanded, but also seriously questioned, and the following discussion will examine the various forms Lawrence's utopian vision takes in the novel.

Kangaroo revolves around a wish persistently expressed by Somers from the very beginning: '"I intend to move with men and get men to move with me before I die . . ."' (77). But equally it deals with Somers's ambivalence with regard to active involvement, and his inability to choose among the opportunities that arise. In the course of the novel, he is faced with two such major challenges: the Diggers, led by Kangaroo, and the Socialists, represented by Struthers. Eventually, Somers turns down both of these offers and sticks instead to his own path. As a result, *Kangaroo* provides three suggestions for an answer to the question of political involvement, and each of them contains an underlying vision of utopia, coupled – at least in two of them – with the idea of a leader, a semi-divine spirit capable of making the vision come true.

A para-military, vaguely nationalistic group of secret cells, the Diggers' Club is presented to the reader from two different perspectives. Jack Callcott, Somers's neighbour and a war veteran, represents the grass roots level of the organization, the unsophisticated longing for a powerful leader, '"a boss like a father who gets up first in the morning, and locks up at night"' (208), and for a simple but absolute bond of friendship or 'mateship' between men. For Jack the latter almost amounts to a vision. In a scene strikingly similar to the one in *Women in Love* where Birkin suggests a *Blutbrüderschaft* with Gerald, Jack says to Somers: '"I'd stick to you through hell fire and back, and we'd clear some land between us. I *know* if you and me was mates, we could put any blooming thing through. There'd be nothing to stop us"' (118).

R. P. Draper, in an article on *Kangaroo*, claims that 'mateship is an idea that Lawrence would . . . frequently have met [in the *Bulletin*]', an Australian newspaper which he read regularly during his stay.[9] It should be abundantly clear, however, from Lawrence's earlier works, that he had cultivated this idea for years before coming to Australia. When it comes to the organization of the Diggers, however, Lawrence must have gathered significant information from native sources. In a rather astonishing book, *D. H. Lawrence in Australia*, Robert Darroch argues quite convincingly that *Kangaroo* is a considerably more autobiographical novel than previously assumed, and that Lawrence was directly involved with the movement portrayed as the Diggers. Certainly this would account for the surprisingly detailed description of the organization itself. But granted that Darroch's hypothesis holds water, it still fails to explain the obvious continuity between earlier works and *Kangaroo*. This discussion, however, is of minor interest; the fact remains that Jack's account of the Diggers pictures an organization remarkably similar to movements connected with the growth of fascism in the early 1920s. The parallels to the German Youth Movement are particularly obvious. The Diggers, according to Jack, started out like a social club:

> [G]ames, athletics, lectures, readings, discussions, debates. No gambling, no drink, no class or party distinction. The clubs were still chiefly athletics, but not *sporting*. They went in for boxing, wrestling, fencing, and knife-throwing, and revolver practice. . . . The men were grouped in little squads of twenty, each with sergeant and corporal. . . . the squad worked in absolute unison among themselves, and were pledged to absolute obedience of higher commands (204).

The Diggers are organized around isolated cells, small male societies which not only serve a military purpose but also offer the men a social point of reference, a sense of belonging, or – as Eric Bentley puts it – a *Kameradschaft*.

Benjamin Cooley, or Kangaroo, offers a rather different view of the Diggers. Being their leader or 'First', he represents a broader mental horizon than Jack, and his links with the European scene are underlined by the fact that he has been 'a student at Munich' (131), just as Birkin had been at Heidelberg. Kangaroo's vision of a new Australia, which he reveals during his and Somers's first meeting, is a Rousseauesque blend of power politics and religion. To Somers's question whether he wants a benevolent tyranny, Kangaroo replies:

> Not exactly. You see my tyrant would be so much circumscribed by the constitution I should establish. But in a sense, he would be

> a tyrant. Perhaps it would be nearer to say he would be a patriarch, or a pope: representing as near as possible the wise, subtle spirit of life. I should try to establish my state of Australia as a kind of Church, with the profound reverence for life, for life's deepest urges, as the motive power (125).

Later on in the novel it becomes clear that Kangaroo bases his philosophy on the principle of Love. Exactly what meaning is ascribed to this word never becomes clear. There is, for instance, at the same time a strong element of élitism in his ideas. He claims both that '"in ninety per cent of the people [education] is useless"' (ibid.), and that he will be '"absolutely stern against anti-life"' (126). Despite this inconsistency, many critics regard Kangaroo as representing the Christian tradition, which 'sees love as the motive power of the Universe. He is almost a symbol of the Saviour'.[10] Kangaroo's concern, however, is not with 'sin and repentance and redemption' (125). He is most definitely a secular saviour, whose utopia is firmly based in this world. Though he is less blood-thirsty than Jack, he is still the leader of a movement which is entirely based on violence as a means of achieving its goals. Thus the major difference between Kangaroo and any other vulgar supporter of heavy-handed politics is that the former's leadership role has been expanded into quasi-religious proportions, thereby making him seem more respectable. His saviour quality could also be compared to the leader of the original Diggers from the English Civil War, Gerrard Winstanley, who – according to Manuel and Manuel – stressed the 'sudden discovery of God within [oneself], accompanied by a depreciation of all exterior sources of divine knowledge, no matter how eminent the preachers or hallowed the book'.[11] Similarly, Kangaroo says about himself: '"I offer no creed. I offer myself, my heart of wisdom, strange warm cavern where the voice of the oracle streams in from the unknown . . ."' (126). All in all, we are back to Lawrence's natural aristocrat, a leader at once human and divine.

Finally, the historical mission of Kangaroo and the Diggers is particularly evident in Jaz's enthusiastic description of the way they will enter the political stage when the revolution of the Socialists has failed. Then '"Kangaroo steps in like a redeeming angel, and reminds us that it's God's Own Country, so we're God's Own People, and makes us feel good again"' (179). The secular utopia and the religious millennium merge into one.

Somers's second offer of an active role in Australian politics comes from Struthers and the Socialists. He is brought to their headquarters, Canberra House, by Jaz, who is also involved with the Diggers. To a large extent this meeting is little more than a repetition of Somers's encounter with Kangaroo. Like Kangaroo, Struthers has read Somers's book on democracy, is well informed about events in Europe, and asks 'questions concerning the Fascisti and Socialisti in Italy, the appropriation of the land by peasants, and so on; then about Germany, the actual temper of the working people, the quality of their patriotism since the war, and so on. . . . They talked about Europe for some time' (215). Struthers, again like Kangaroo, wants to found a new spirit on the principle of Love between men, or in Socialist terminology, solidarity. Once more this links directly with a Socialist version of the *Männerbund*. It reminds Somers of Whitman: 'Whitman said the next, broader, more unselfish rock should be the Love of Comrades. The sacred relation of a man to his mate, his fellow-man' (219).[12] So far the Socialists are presented as disappointingly similar to the Diggers, and the one real difference only emerges when Struthers's offer to Somers is brought up. It then becomes clear that while Kangaroo and the Diggers concentrate on the all-important role of the leader, Struthers – following the recipe of Sorel's syndicalist revolution – sees Socialism as too weak and in need of a myth, a '"real unifying principle among us. . . . [Australians] need to be touched emotionally . . .' (221). In Struthers's opinion, a newspaper is the ideal means of communicating this new gospel, and Somers is just the man for the job: '". . . You've got to give [the Australians] something to appeal to the deeper man in them. . . . And we're waiting for the right individual to come along to put the appeal to them"' (222). The newspaper should appeal to the Australian's '"heart, for his heart is the right place to appeal to"' (222–3). Thus, all the quasi-religious ingredients of Sorel's utopian myth are present. Somers, tempted to accept the offer, even thinks of it as the building up of a 'great Church of Christ' (223). But there is even more direct connection to syndicalism. Explaining that the Canberra House of the novel is actually Sydney Trades Hall, Darroch remarks that Lawrence was aware that 'it was under militant control, being the headquarters of the "industrialists" – the syndicalist radicals of the New South Wales labour movement'.[13] He even goes on to claim that 'Struthers is really the image of Jock Garden, the Scottish lay preacher and militant syndicalist, and boss of Trades Hall'.[14]

As mentioned already, Somers declines both of these offers in favour of his own philosophy of the dark god. First, and most important, this means a rejection of social or collective action and a return to the small world of himself and Harriet. If one regards Somers as Lawrence's self-portrait, it is even a rejection of Lawrence's only serious alternative to the love of woman as a source of salvation – the society of men, or the *Männerbund*.

In different ways three men offer Somers a man-to-man relationship: Jack, Kangaroo and Struthers. In Jack's case, Somers admits that he wants 'some living fellowship with other men. . . . Maybe a living fellowship! – but not affection, not love, not comradeship. Not mates and equality and mingling. Not blood-brotherhood. None of that' (120). In Kangaroo it is the more intangible kind of love, what Somers calls the 'hateful will-to-love', which proves too much for him (233). With Struthers it is almost the same. In Somers's view, solidarity is only another word for a self-defeating love: 'Human love, human trust, are always perilous, because they break down. The greater the love, the greater the trust, and the greater the peril, the greater the disaster' (220). In all three instances, Somers's rejection is based on a fear of responsibility and commitment, as well as an ultimate lack of interest. Leaving Canberra House with Jaz, he confesses: '"I try to kid myself that I care about mankind and its destiny. . . . But at the bottom I'm as hard as a mango nut. . . . I don't really care about anything, no I don't"' (225).

For Lawrence himself, however, the motives are more complex. What becomes clear from a reading of *Kangaroo* is that Lawrence – more than anything – is looking, not for a good reason to *join* the real world, but rather an excuse for *rejecting* it. This excuse he finds in the highly dubious attempt at portraying both Kangaroo and Struthers – representatives, to a large extent, of the two main revolutionary ideologies of the early twentieth century – as Christians in disguise. Having already rejected Christianity as a religion of the spineless and 'vengeful mob', a religion inherently opposed to the great and heroic individual, he can also safely escape the challenge posed by Kangaroo and Struthers. They do not stand up to Lawrence's/Somers's radical ideal of the aristocrat; they compromise themselves by including in their ideologies a certain concern for the ordinary man in the street.

The lack of logical consistency in Somers's position is fully revealed in his attempt to state an alternative creed. Having rejected Jack's proposal of a mateship and wondering what else there is to turn to, he thinks to himself:

> Perhaps the thing that the dark races know: that one can still feel in India: the mystery of lordship. . . . The other mystic relationship between men, which democracy and equality try to deny and obliterate. Not any arbitrary caste or birth aristocracy. But the mystic recognition of difference and innate priority, the joy of obedience and the sacred responsibility of authority (120).

Some time later, he broods over a dressing-table tray which Harriet had bought in Baden-Baden. On it there is engraved a heart with the inscription: '*Dem Mutigen gehört die Welt*. That was the motto to have on one's red heart: not Love or Hope or any of those aspiring emotions. . . . *Mut! Mut!* A good word. Better even than *courage*. Virtue, *virtus*, manliness. . . . It was *Mut*, profound manliness, that is not afraid of anything except of being cowardly or barren' (167). Then, turning down Struthers's offer, he ponders how it 'all seemed so far from the dark God he wished to serve, the God from whom the dark, sensual passion of love emanates, not only the spiritual love of Christ. He wanted men once more to refer the sensual passion of love sacredly to the great dark God, the ithyphallic, of the first dark religions' (224). This, then, is Somers's alternative to political action, an alternative with which he is far from satisfied himself; an escape to the past, and an escape from human contact. '"I neither want love nor power. I like the world. And I like to be alone in it, by myself"' (226).

And so he leaves Australia, retaining the vision at once élitist and monastic of denying 'the world's "outwardness"' and of following one's sacred, inner voice (172). As so often in Lawrence, courage and escapism are hard to distinguish.

The Plumed Serpent

Lawrence's arrival in America did little to alter the fundamental questions and conflicts which he brought with him from Europe and Australia. In many respects, the only full-blown novel he wrote in America, *The Plumed Serpent*, is ideologically the final and extended version of the hastily written draft called *Kangaroo*. The differences, however, are equally obvious. *The Plumed Serpent* was written in a different continent, Lawrence plunging wholeheartedly into the cultural and religious heritage of his new surroundings, and it took him nearly two years to complete, not six weeks, as with *Kangaroo*. It is an ambitious and considerably researched novel, which should be regarded as one of the high points of Lawrence's career. Moreover, this is the way Lawrence himself regarded it, at least for some time after it was finished. Just as *Women in Love* can be seen as the culmination of his first major period, *The Plumed Serpent* can be seen as the climax of the second.

Kangaroo is a novel primarily concerned with the comparatively straightforward question of political involvement. Its cast of characters consists on the one hand of a group of men who are all involved in political action, and on the other hand of a visitor whose ultimate withdrawal and departure gives the story a fairly clean ending. Also, the novel is relatively simple when it comes to establishing the attitude of the author; *Kangaroo* is clearly the most autobiographical of Lawrence's novels. In *The Plumed Serpent*, by contrast, the picture is far more complex. There is no character who consistently speaks on behalf of the author, the whole atmosphere is considerably more foreign than in earlier novels, and the plot is entangled in a maze of myth, religion and politics. Indeed it cannot be discussed as a purely political novel – the political content is only a by-product of the religious-mythical framework from which the action of the novel initially springs.

In spite of these complicating factors, however, it is possible to discern Lawrence's political thinking in *The Plumed Serpent*. First, it has an ideological content which is undoubtedly developed from views expressed in earlier fictional and non-fictional works. Second, it is characterized by the underlying apocalyptic framework which dominates Lawrence's writings from the war onwards. By keeping these two elements in mind, it should be possible to separate the opinions of Lawrence himself and those of his fictional characters.

The whole of *The Plumed Serpent* revolves around the unresolved conflict of *Kangaroo* – the problem of isolation versus action, or escape versus involvement. In both novels the main character is a European who, having fled from a shattered continent, finds himself stranded in a new world. Here he is faced with an opportunity to take part in political action. In *Kangaroo* the main character finally decides to decline the offer and to return to a life of isolation. In *The Plumed Serpent*, Kate eventually becomes involved, but she is slow and hesitant in her decision, and this lack of enthusiasm is an important characteristic of the book. Thus throughout *The Plumed Serpent* there are echoes of Lawrence's tendency to withdraw from the world, or at least to make his world as small and managable as possible. But the novel also takes the important step from political and religious theorizing to the world of action, and this is what really makes it particularly interesting from the point of view of the present discussion. In *Women in Love* the world of action was limited to Birkin's and Ursula's letters of resignation from their jobs; in *Aaron's Rod* it was limited to little more than a broken flute; and in *Kangaroo* the climax was the 'Row in Town', to which Somers was a passive spectator. As will be shown, *The Plumed Serpent* goes considerably further.

In order to show the connection between *The Plumed Serpent* and the more naive, escapist utopianism of earlier works, the presence of these latter elements in the novel will be dealt with first. After all, they form the background from which the real drama ultimately unfolds. They also bring into focus one of the great inconsistencies in Lawrence: the insistence on a this-worldly universe, coupled with a deep-rooted tendency to search for a transcendent state of perfection.

First, the two most important characters, Kate and Ramón, are both seeking refuge from the painful challenges of the external world in a meditative introspection. In a passage full of references to 'the only reality' and to the 'soft bloom of being', Kate knows only one thing for certain: 'she must preserve herself from worldly contacts' (59). Somewhat later, she sees Ramón and Cipriano as representatives of the beyond: 'She would believe in them. Anything, anything rather than this sterility of nothingness which was the world . . .' (103). And having rented a house for herself, she intends to retain her monastic isolation: 'Now I am alone. And now I have only one thing to do: not to get caught up into the world's cog-wheels any more, and not to lose my hold of the hidden greater thing' (109).

Ramón achieves a similar state of mind in his prayers. 'He had broken the cords of the world, and was free in the other strength' (169). Typically, he finds it painful to turn back to the world. 'It was hard to have to bear the contact of commonplace daily things, when his soul and body were naked to the cosmos' (181). When Cipriano wants him to enter politics, Ramón replies firmly: '"I must stand in another world, and act in another world. – Politics must go their own way, and society must do as it will"' (191).

This isolationism, however, also extends beyond single individuals. In the earlier works discussed in this chapter, the close and exclusive relationships between men, the so-called *Männerbund* or *Blutbrüderschaft* have been emphasized. The first reference to such a man-to-man relationship in *The Plumed Serpent* occurs during the dinner at Tlalpam, where both Ramón and Cipriano are present. Here, very much 'in the presence of men', Kate notices that

'Cipriano looked at Ramón with a curious intimacy, glittering, steady, warrior-like, and at the same time betraying an almost menacing trust in the other man' (67). Later, when Cipriano visits Ramón at Jamiltepec, the 'two men embraced, breast to breast, and for a moment Cipriano laid his little blackish hands on the naked shoulders of the bigger man, and for a moment was perfectly still on his breast. Then very softly, he stood back and looked at him, saying not a word' (181–2). Cipriano even goes so far as to tell Kate: '"To me Ramón is *more*, than life. *More* than life"'. And when she asks if he means more than anything, Cipriano replies: '"Yes!"' (309–10). Furthermore, the sacredness of the relationship is emphasized by the colours of their serapes. Cipriano tells Kate that Ramón's colours are '"blue, and white and natural black"'. And: '"Those are my colours: scarlet and black. But I myself have white as well, just as Ramón has a fringe of my scarlet"' (322–3). The use of scarlet may well be Lawrence's vague hint of a *Blutbrüderschaft*. Finally, the ritual by which Cipriano becomes the god Huitzilopochtli, contains homo-erotic elements closely related to the wrestling-scene in *Women in Love* and the nursing-scene in *Aaron's Rod*. They even 'rub oil in their limbs' (369).

But *The Plumed Serpent* goes even further. Since *Women in Love* Lawrence had repeatedly stressed the need for a kind of double marriage: a deep blood relationship between man and man, and man and woman, at the same time. In *The Plumed Serpent* both of the main male characters eventually achieve this: Cipriano through his friendship with Ramón and his marriage to Kate; Ramón through his friendship with Cipriano and his marriage to Teresa. The divine significance of these relationships is highlighted by the fact that all four of them are members of the new pantheon – at least, Ramón wants Teresa to become his goddess. But between the women there is no suggestion of divine relationships. On the contrary, when Ramón and Teresa invite Kate to stay with them at Jamiltepec, Ramón says bluntly about his new wife: '"She needs a woman-friend"' (402). The deeper blood contact is clearly reserved for the men.

The third point which connects *The Plumed Serpent* to ideas expressed in earlier works – particularly, perhaps, to Rananim – deals with the description of Ramón's hacienda, Jamiltepec. Taking the reader on a guided tour of the hacienda, Lawrence portrays it as a closed but happy community with an old-fashioned, William Morris-like reverence for quality handicrafts. 'Within the courtyard there was the sharp ringing of metal hammered on an anvil. It came from a corner where was a smithy, where a man and a boy were working. In another shed, a carpenter was planing wood. Don Ramón stood a moment to look around. This was his own world' (170). The workers show him a kind of humble, grateful respect. They 'worked the quicker for having seen him, as if it gave them new life' (ibid.). The hacienda is almost like a medieval village. Besides the smith and the carpenter, there are people spinning and weaving, and an artist who is busy making an iron symbol for the new cult. Later in the novel, the village of Jaramay is described in a similar manner. The element of rural utopianism present in these descriptions is confirmed by a remark by Ramón in an open letter to the clergy: '". . . if the old communal system comes back, and the village and the land are one, it will be very good. For truly, no man can possess lands"' (361). Certainly, the rural utopia was an essential element of the German *Volk*-movement at the time, and German settlers at one stage actually tried to establish a community in Mexico. Most likely, therefore, this idea stems from Lawrence's German experience. At least, it is not very likely that he was in touch with such naive projects during his stay in Mexico. The land reforms following the Mexican revolution were definitely more down-to-earth than what Ramón suggests.

The gradual development in *The Plumed Serpent* from a religious awakening to political action is marked by a series of closely related conflicts. As is so often the case in Lawrence, it is the dialectic between these rival forces which sets the plot in motion. These conflicts can be regarded first as a struggle between the values of the new cult of Quetzalcoatl, on the one hand, and the traditional values represented by Christianity, Americanism and Bolshevism, on the other (Lawrence clearly groups these three together); second as a struggle between the two main principles in *Aaron's Rod*, Love and Power; and third as an example of the perennial conflict between the sexes. The following discussion will attempt to show that *The Plumed Serpent* deals with all of these problems, but that they are ultimately reduced to the one overall conflict between the male and the female, and that the female is the decisive loser in the battle. Just as Lawrence in *Sons and Lovers* 'handed his mother the laurels of victory',[15] in *The Plumed Serpent* he gives them to himself and to the male. (A rather humiliating counterpart to Lawrence's literary show of male power, however, was that while writing the book, he had to give in to Frieda and humbly leave for England, just as Kate finally decides to return to Cipriano.) Thus, as will be shown in the following, there is in *The Plumed Serpent* a losing side, which is everywhere connected with the female principle and sharply contrasted with the victorious male.

The Plumed Serpent is primarily a religious novel, and in Lawrence's framework such political and economic phenomena as Bolshevism and Americanism are consistently and intimately related to Christianity. As in *Kangaroo* Christianity represents all the values that ought to be subdued or abandoned, and one finds all through *The Plumed Serpent* a chain of interconnected elements which all point to Christianity as both a religion of the weak and a religion of women.

In chapter 1 it was shown how Lawrence makes use of Joachite ideas in order to present Christianity as a dying religion, and it is obvious from his description that Joachim, Kate's second husband, was by no means a man on a par with Ramón and Cipriano. The essentially feminine character of Christianity, however, is reflected more strongly in Ramón's first wife, Doña Carlota. Apart from the bishop, she is its only living representative, and Lawrence shows her little mercy. She is a little, nervous thing, 'pure European in extraction', 'pale' and 'faded' (155), and just as Joachim was compared to Christ, so is Carlota compared to Mary the Virgin. In fact, Lawrence emphasizes very strongly the role of Mary in the Christian religion. In the hymns of Quetzalcoatl she is portrayed as of equal importance to Christ. This, I think, cannot be attributed only to the fact that Mary has always been a central figure in Catholic worship. Rather, it is a deliberate attempt on Lawrence's part to give the impression of Christianity as a religion of women. In one of Carlota's outbursts against Ramón, this female priority is evident. She tells Kate: '"Ah, Señora, as if a woman who had ever known the Blessed Virgin could ever part from her again. Ah, Señora, what woman would have the heart to put Christ back on the Cross to crucify him twice! But men, men!"' (189). Furthermore, Carlota is the symbol of Christian love and charity. She runs a Cuna, a foundlings home, in Mexico City, and is 'an intense, almost exalted Catholic' (156). Thus, the Christian virtues are brought to something approaching a caricature in one and the same female character. Finally, Carlota is carried lifeless out of the church by the members of the new cult, just like the statue of Mary some time earlier.

Another interesting aspect is the relationship Lawrence develops between Christianity and the female, on the one hand, and the symbolism of the moon, on the other. Mary and the moon are already connected in the Revelation of St. John, and in addition the moon had a number of maleficent attributes in ancient Mexican mythology (Expl. Notes, 468). But Lawrence makes more of it than this. His position is more that of the German racist, Georg Lomer, who, as mentioned above, saw the Aryan male as connected with the sun, and the Jew and the female with the moon. Lawrence, similarly, draws a direct line between the moon and Christianity, and an important symbol for the cult of Quetzalcoatl is of course the sun, which stands for the male: 'For man is the Morning Star / And woman is the Star of Evening' (340). In one of the hymns Jesus tells Quetzalcoatl: '*My mother the moon is dark. / Brother, Quetzalcoatl, / Hold back the wild hot sun. / Bind him with shadow while I pass*. . . . Quetzalcoatl, Sir, my mother went even before me, to her still white bed in the moon' (226–7). Even in Juana, Kate's rather simple-minded servant, one gets the impression that Quetzalcoatl is superior to Jesus because the latter is infected with the weakness of the female. She says: '"The Santísima is leaving us, and this Quetzalcoatl is coming! He has no mother, he!"' (225).

By linking Christianity so closely to the female, Lawrence has achieved two things: to present it as a weak and exhausted religion, and also to predict a new era, a new religion, where the female qualities of weakness and pity are subdued, while the qualities of the male are finally let free to start afresh with other and radically different values. In the novel this final turning point is the death of Carlota. It is Nietzsche's God-is-dead experience expressed in literal terms. Love is replaced by Power.

The death of Christianity raises once again the whole question of the function of religion. Having discarded all the idealism and spirituality of the old creed, Lawrence cannot accept a divine and transcendent god. His only alternative is to create a new faith and a new *vicarius dei*, both containing a sufficient amount of earthly sensuality to satisfy the author's desires. The result is a quasi-religious version of *Lebensphilosophie*, a combination of ideas far beyond logical coherence. By this Lawrence attempts to combine two main elements: first, the nineteenth and early twentieth century Western idea of the hero, the superman or the aristocrat, which replaces the former god; second, a revival of a long since dead Mexican mythology, which replaces the former religion. Lawrence's experiment thus also poses the question whether a deliberately constructed faith can become a living faith which moves the hearts of people.

The first element, the semi-divine superman, is found everywhere in the novel. The cult of Quetzalcoatl is based on an élitist group of superior men, which even Kate – the sceptical Westerner – acknowledges. Overwhelmed by Cipriano's personality, she wonders what a life with him would be like: 'She could conceive now her marriage with Cipriano: the supreme passivity, like the earth below the twilight, consummate in living lifelessness, the sheer solid mystery of passivity.' It would be a 'submission absolute, . . . beneath an over-arching absolute' (311). During the marriage ceremony Kate kisses Cipriano's feet, while Cipriano kisses her brow and breast (329).

Both Ramón and Cipriano are men touched with divinity. There are numerous references to Jesus in connection with Ramón. During a meeting of the new cult at Jamiltepec, he masters the wind and the rain just as Jesus did on the lake of Gennesaret; Ramón's servant, Martin, is described as 'the man who loved him' (193), just as John was the disciple Jesus loved (only here, to comply with Lawrence's aristocratic principles, it is the disciple who loves the master); and as Jesus wept over the fate of Jerusalem, so 'Ramón watched [his sons] as they stood in their black clothes and bare knees upon the jetty, and his heart yearned over them' (357). In another passage he more resembles the furious Zeus. In the presence of Kate and Cipriano, he suddenly 'rose with sudden volcanic violence, and rushed away' (255). Later in the novel the new pantheon is actually called the 'Mexican Olympus', of which Ramón, of course, is Zeus himself.

Cipriano, besides being the god Huitzlopochtli, is compared to Pan. 'He was once more the old dominant male, shadowy, intangible, looming suddenly tall, and covering the sky, making a darkness that was himself and nothing but himself, the Pan male. . . . The Master. The everlasting Pan' (311–12).

Drawing divine strength from the depth of the cosmos, Ramón and Cipriano are also natural leaders, born aristocrats, fit to rule over lesser men and – naturally – women. Cipriano in particular is rendered as a man of superior leadership. He tells his soldiers: '"Of yourselves you are nothing. You are of me, my men"' (365). Again, there is in these passages a powerful echo of a Germanic nostalgia for the primitive past. Cipriano would 'motion other men to fight, giving his spear and shield to another officer or soldier, going himself to sit down on the ground and watch, by the firelight' (ibid.). Fencing, spear and shield: this is not a twentieth-century revolutionary army. Furthermore, he

> had got his own small, picked body of men out of the ignominious drab uniform, dressed in white with the scarlet sash and the scarlet ankle cords, and carrying the good, red and black sarape. And his men must be clean. On the march they would stop by some river, with the order for every man to strip and wash, and wash his clothing. Then the men, dark and ruddy, moved about naked, while the white clothing of strong white cotton dried on the earth. . . .
>
> He divided his regiment up into little companies of a hundred each, with a centurion and a sergeant in command. Each company of a hundred must learn to act in perfect unison, freely and flexibly (366).

The similarity to the *hird*, the chosen 'security force' of the Viking kings, to the German Youth Movement, and to the description of the Diggers in *Kangaroo*, is evident. Another embarrassing detail is the raising of the right arm, which was adopted as the way of saluting fellow cult members.

But even supermen need a gospel to sustain their position, and in *The Plumed Serpent* this gospel is the revived mythology of ancient Mexico, the cult of Quetzalcoatl. For the present discussion, the actual content of the old mythology is of secondary importance to the manner in which Lawrence makes use of it for his own purposes.

But before dealing with this, it is necessary to emphasize that *The Plumed Serpent* is more of a European than a Mexican novel. It would be naive to assume that Lawrence, despite his artistic qualities, would be able to see his characters through Mexican eyes and in a purely Mexican context. He may well capture with amazing accuracy the scenery and the atmosphere, but the problems and the conflicts tackled in the novel are still almost exclusively European, or at least Western. It should be noted, for instance, that Cipriano and Ramón are educated at Oxford and Columbia University respectively. The Mexicanness of *The Plumed Serpent*, in other words, is a cleverly constructed facade which, to some extent, successfully conceals the European structure behind it. From the point of view of political ideas, therefore, a detailed study of Mexican history would only cast light on relatively insignificant details. This position is borne out by the new and carefully annotated Cambridge edition of the novel. On the other hand, it seems obvious that Lawrence himself was suffering from just such a naiveté. Generally, his idea of leaving behind his European heritage to embrace a new culture contributes strongly to the ultimate failure of the novel.

Viewed in this light, the cult of Quetzalcoatl becomes a fake, a religion acted out like a play. Explaining his new faith to his sceptical son, Ramón says: '"I only pretend that the Aztec god Quezalcoatl is coming back to the Mexicans"' (269). Talking to Kate, he says: '"Why not you as the First Woman of – say Itzpapalotl, just for the sound of the name?"' (316). Thus, the cult is a deliberately created myth, rather than a religion in the traditional sense, and consequently it functions as a political ideology. The close relationship to religious revelation, however, recalls the myth of the French syndicalist Georges Sorel mentioned in the discussion of *Kangaroo*. While arguing the death of religion, Sorel clearly saw the need for a substitute, a constructed myth whose function was to take over the role of religion. Indeed, this is what the cult of Quetzalcoatl provides – a vision of a past Golden Age, i.e. the primitive culture of ancient Mexico, lifted out of its pre-historic context and transplanted into the present to function as a model for the future millennium. This is a deliberate human act far removed from traditional, spontaneous revelation. Precisely because it is void of an inherent religious energy, it has to be enforced – like other totalitarian ideologies – by political means. The German hotel owner in Orilla virtually expresses Lawrence's own conclusion when he claims: '"They thought socialism needed a god, so they're going to fish him out of this lake. He'll do for another pious catchword in another revolution"' (102). The only difference is that for Lawrence socialism is a dead letter and Lenin a 'Tyrannus in shabby clothes', so he dresses his own political experiment in another garment.

However, before pursuing this any further, it should be noted how Lawrence develops his narrative to make the introduction of the new cult as credible as possible.

First of all, he presents Christianity as implausibly weak and lifeless. Carlota is a vicious caricature, as is the bishop. Furthermore, there is no sign of opposition to the drastic removal of the holy images from the church. Public and spiritual authorities seem entirely absent from the scene, and the crowd only 'murmured and swayed on its knees' (282). Particularly, as there has been no mention of popular opposition to the Church earlier in the novel, the improbability of this event shows that Lawrence is forcibly conveying the impression that the new cult is actively welcomed by the people.

Second, Lawrence eases the introduction of the cult by allowing the moral framework of the novel to collapse. Here the use of violence – an essential element in the Sorelian myth – needs to be considered. It is an element which has been vaguely present in Lawrence's work for a long time. The difficulty is in knowing how seriously to take these outbursts. When, for instance, during the war, he exclaims in a letter: 'I don't care if sixty million individuals die: the seed is not in the masses, it is elsewhere' (*Le II*, 529) – how should it be interpreted? A somewhat more sober – and remarkably prophetic – account is found in 'A Letter from Germany', which was written at the same time as *The Plumed Serpent*, in February 1924:

> The hope in peace-and-production is broken. The old flow, the old adherence is ruptured. And a still older flow has set in. Back, back to the savage polarity of Tartary, and away from the polarity of civilized Christian Europe. This, it seems to me, has already happened. And it is a happening of far more profound import than any actual *event*. It is the father of the next phase of events. . . . The ancient spirit of pre-historic Germany coming back, at the end of history (*Ph*, 109).

In this essay Lawrence does not reveal his own position on the subject, but if one takes into account the development of his ideas as described so far in this chapter, together with the unfolding of the story in *The Plumed Serpent*, it is difficult to avoid the conclusion that he went a long way towards sanctioning this revival of the primitive spirit. This is partly confirmed by a statement in 'Paris Letter', written only a month before the above letter from Germany: 'What I believe in is the old Homeric aristocracy, when the grandeur was inside the man, and he lived in a simple wooden house' (*Ph*, 121).

The outright use of violence is only made explicit in *The Plumed Serpent*, and it is present on the mental as well as on the physical level. Also, unless one claims that the novel was written as a study in barbarism and moral degeneration, one is bound to assume that Lawrence himself had no stronger objections to the events described than those expressed by the main characters themselves. When it is suggested, therefore, that *The Plumed Serpent* shows a collapse in moral values, it is also implied that this goes for Lawrence himself. The novel is thus an experiment in the transvaluation of values. Violence appears as necessary and acceptable, because the end justifies the means. Which is also the logic behind Sorel's defence of violence.

But again Lawrence goes further by not only defending the use of violence. He also glorifies it – as did the Futurists – and shows admiration for the men responsible. The novel draws a disturbing equation between violence and purity. Having killed several of the bandits who attacked Jamiltepec, Ramón is, in a sense, newly baptized. His brow was 'like a boy's, very pure and primitive, and the eyes underneath had a certain primitive, gleaming look of virginity. As men must have been, in the first awful days, with that strange beauty that goes with pristine rudimentariness' (296). Kate, having witnessed the attack and shot one of the bandits, has the same look: 'She had the face of one waking from the dead, curiously dipped in death, with a tenderness far more new and vulnerable than a child's' (312). Finally, Cipriano, having just stabbed the three prisoners to death during the ritual in the church, comes to Kate's room and asks her to be his bride as the goddess Malintzi: 'He stood before her flickering and flashing and strangely young, vulnerable, as young and boyish as flame. She saw that when the fire came free in him, he would be like this always, flickering, flashing with a flame of virgin youth' (391).

The development of Kate's personality is another indication of Lawrence's moral transvaluation. During the bullfight in the first chapter, she is outraged at the cruel treatment of the bull and the old horse. Then, in the scene in which Carlota is dying, she has already become accustomed to the new moral code. Carrying the lifeless Carlota out of the church, both Kate and Cipriano linger in the doorway 'to hear the end of [the] hymn' (345), clearly regarding the gospel as more important than the dying patient. The same evening, while Carlota is moaning for the sacrament and Ramón, condemning his wife, is delivering a furious sermon about his new faith, 'Kate sat by the window, and laughed a little' (347). As if this were not enough, there is the famous passage later in the book, in which Kate is thinking about Cipriano:

> Let him be a general, an executioner, what he liked, in the world. The flame of their united lives was a naked bud of flame. Their marriage was a young, vulnerable flame. . . . So, when she thought of him and his soldiers, tales of swift cruelty she had heard of him: when she remembered his stabbing the three helpless peons, she thought: Why should I judge him? He is of the

gods. . . . What do I care if he kills people? His flame is young and clean (394).

Even the guru himself, Ramón, descends into barbarism, despite Lawrence's attempts to let Cipriano do the dirty work. Not long before the executions of the bandits, the two men are discussing whether the cult should be declared the official religion of Mexico. Cipriano is all in favour of it, and wants to use the army to back up the declaration. 'But no! no! said Ramón. Let it spread of itself' (359). However, shortly afterwards he presides as Quetzalcoatl over the executions in the church, apparently without any objections.

In *The Plumed Serpent* Lawrence is clearly blinded by the light (or in his own terminology: the darkness) of the world he envisaged, a world which, he thought, could only be brought about by godlike men capable of an historical *salto mortale* back to the Golden Age of a primitive sensuality. It is a demonstration of the *hybris* of Faust, Manfred and Peer Gynt, a refusal to acknowledge human life as limited, and an attempt to enter heaven by the back door. It is much the same blindness from which Sorel and the progenitors of German fascism suffered: it is 'a rejection of reality to a glorification of ideology'.[16]

But what kind of ideology? What becomes clear from a close reading of *The Plumed Serpent* is that the novel is based on two related visions: the one transcendent, religious and millennial, the other earthly, political and utopian. Thus, the novel exemplifies both the Christian and the secular views of history, and Lawrence found himself caught between the two, desperately trying to create a synthesis. In no other novel is this failure expressed with greater despair than in *The Plumed Serpent*. Like other 'revolutionary chiliasts' he tried every imaginable means: the suppression of women, the exaltation of the leader, the creation of a myth, and the sanctioning of violence. All to no avail; the gap remained. But being caught between the two visions, he still drew nourishment from both and made use of them in his fierce exploration of what – for lack of a better word – he called the 'unknown'. But as was explained in chapter 1, the two visions also have a considerable area of common ground, and this common ground makes up the structural framework of the novel.

First, the novel starts out by stating the need for rebirth and renewal, on an individual as well as a collective level. Kate has just turned forty, and 'the first half of her life was over. The bright page, with its flowers and its love and its stations of the Cross ended with a grave. Now she must turn over . . .' (50–1). Mexico is in a similar state. It is marred by revolutions and civil war, and there is everywhere an atmosphere of hopelessness and despair, like a country locked inside a tomb. Gradually, a resurrection takes place, and it is remarkable to note just how closely Lawrence adheres to the message of the Christian gospel while managing to include in it elements from the new faith. The starting point is the newspaper article, which Kate reads immediately after brooding over her grave-like existence. It is worth noting that Lawrence only makes use of those elements from Mexican mythology which are compatible with the Christian frame of mind and the Christian imagery. As a matter of fact, the whole story is based on the Easter gospel. The man of Quetzalcoatl rises from the lake and says to the frightened women: '"Why are you crying?"' Jesus, having risen from the tomb, similarly says to Mary Magdalene: 'Woman, why weepest thou?'[17] Furthermore, the man of Quetzalcoatl asks a labourer to walk with him to his house, where he performs a ritual of the resurrected god. In the same way Jesus walked to Emmaus, unrecognized by his two apostles. On arriving he 'took bread, and blessed it, and brake, and gave to them' as a sign of his resurrection from the dead.[18]

The pattern established in this episode is then repeated throughout *The Plumed Serpent*. During a sermon at Jamiltepec, Ramón says: Quetzalcoatl '"has risen, and pushed the stone from the mouth of the tomb, and has stretched himself. And now he is striding across the horizons even quicker than the great stone from the tomb is tumbling back to the earth to crush those that rolled it up"' (200). Here, the apocalyptic framework is made evident. The resurrection of Quetzalcoatl parallels Christ's Second Coming, and the executions in the church, the Day of Judgment. Indeed, the latter has already been anticipated by Ramón's Fourth Hymn, in which he condemns all second-rate men: '"Prepare for doom. . . . I tell you, sorrow upon you: you shall all die. And being dead, you shall not be refreshed"' (258). Then, before stabbing the three prisoners, Cipriano says: '"Men that are less than men are not good enough for the light of the sun"' (379). Again, Lawrence has used elements from Mexican mythology which parallel the Christian apocalypse. The Day of Judgment, when the wheat is distinguished from the tares, marks the beginning of a new and perfect age, and in Aztec mythology a human sacrifice was needed in order to start a new age or 'sun' (Appendix, 553).

Another set of parallels to Christian tradition is offered by the vision of the period before the Flood as a true Golden Age. This vision, frequently expressed by Lawrence, has been described in earlier chapters, but in *The Plumed Serpent* it is not only a source of nostalgia. Here the whole point is to bring about a physical revival of it in the present and use it as a model for a future millennium. Thus, there is in Ramón's and Cipriano's political adventure, a vision of a perfect state, which places them in the tradition of Cohn's revolutionary chiliasts. But true to Lawrence's moral transvaluation, it is a state of radically different values. Even the pleasure of sex is denied Kate, and as is the case in most charismatic movements, she 'understands' that the pleasure she had previously found in it, was not a true pleasure, and slowly 'came the knowledge that she did not really want it, that it was really nauseous to her' (422). She is lucky to be saved, though the *katharsis* of the conversion is a painful one. 'She could feel it, the terrible katabolism and metabolism in her blood, changing her even as a creature, changing her to another creature' (421). Thus a somewhat modified version of the chapel experience in Eastwood is transferred to the cult of Quetzalcoatl.

Finally, to show how firmly Lawrence remained inside the Biblical framework, one may compare a passage from *The Rainbow* with one from *The Plumed Serpent*. In the former, Lawrence refers directly to the story from Genesis while describing how Ursula watches the rainbow:

> . . . in the blowing clouds, she saw a band of faint iridescence colouring in faint colours a portion of the hill. And forgetting, startled, she looked for the hovering colour and saw a rainbow forming itself. . . . The arc bended and strengthened itself till it arched indomitable, making great architecture of light and colour and the space of heaven, its pedestals luminous in the corruption of new houses on the low hill, its arch the top of heaven.
>
> And the rainbow stood on the earth (458).

The corresponding symbol in *The Plumed Serpent* is the star, now turned into a symbol of power. Lawrence's description, however, is clearly based on the image of the rainbow, so that the whole passage has a hollow ring. Kate, thinking about Ramón's 'supremacy, his godhead', concludes that it is found in

> a star within him, an inexplicable star which rose out of the dark sea and shone between the flood and the great sky. . . . For this,

> the only thing which is supreme above all power in man, and at the same time, is power; which far transcends knowledge; the strange star between the sky and the waters of the first cosmos: this is man's divinity. And some men are not divine at all. They have only faculties. They are slaves, or they should be slaves (417–18).

The symbol of the covenant between god and man has been reduced to a vulgar symbol of the right of some men to bully others. Thus the reader is also left with something of a symbol – of Lawrence's failure to create a synthesis in this world between religion and politics, between heaven and earth.

6

A Tragic Age and a Hopeful Heart: The Double Vision of the Final Years

So far, the examination of apocalyptic and utopian elements in Lawrence has been primarily concerned with the period from 1914 to the completion of *The Plumed Serpent* in 1925. The war years were mostly dominated by an apocalyptic mood, whereas the post-war period up until 1925 was characterized by Lawrence's search for social and political solutions other than those offered by the democracies of Western Europe. Moving now to the last five years of Lawrence's life, one finds that 1925 marks a new turning point in his development.

First, it is a period of returns. Towards the end of 1925 Lawrence left America and came back to Europe, never to leave it again. Similarly, with the completion of *The Plumed Serpent*, he left behind his social and political concerns of universal renewal, to return to the less ambitious hope of the pre-*Aaron's Rod* years for a rebirth of the individual. Furthermore, in the only novel from the period, *Lady Chatterley's Lover*, Lawrence returned to the England of his childhood, while in *Apocalypse*, he returned to the religious world of his early years in Eastwood.

Second, the sense of doom and despair reappeared with greater intensity, particularly when compared to the period of the leadership novels. But now this apocalyptic sentiment had a new dimension. Lawrence still saw a disaster coming, but could now look back on the war as an event of a similar kind. Both the immediate past and the immediate future were sealed by major catastrophes. No doubt this feeling contributed to the growing despair discernible in the three versions of *Lady Chatterley's Lover* and in *Apocalypse*. There is a stark contrast in these works between the hopelessness of the outside world and the almost desperate will to believe in a return to another sphere of reality. The relationship between apocalypse and utopia, despair and hope, becomes ever more tense, without being reconciled into a greater whole, which a traditional religious world picture would succeed in doing.

Third, the writings from this period suggest an uneasy compromise in the relationship between the sexes. '"There are only two great dynamic urges in *life*: love and power"', said Lilly in *Aaron's Rod* (293). To a large extent Lawrence had been grappling with the ebbing and flowing of these forces for major periods of his life up to 1925. It is often claimed that *The Plumed Serpent* marks the end of Lawrence's obsession with male superiority, and that *Lady Chatterley's Lover* is a return to the idea of woman as the messenger of salvation. The present chapter will take a closer look at this view and argue that the latter novel rather subtly ensures the essential superiority of the male.

Thus, Lawrence's last five years are characterized by a resurfacing of old questions, together with a steadily increasing tension and impatience in the way in which he dealt with them.

The following discussion of the post-1925 period will be divided into three major sections: the interplay of apocalypse and utopia in *Lady Chatterley's Lover* and related works; the development of political ideas during the period, with special reference to the three versions of *Lady Chatterley's Lover*; and an evaluation of *Apocalypse* as Lawrence's final word.

Lady Chatterley's Lover

In no other novel by Lawrence is the contrast sharper between the naive and rustic utopia, on the one hand, and the apocalyptic nightmare of modern industrialized society, on the other, than in *Lady Chatterley's Lover*. From the very opening of the book, the space in which the characters move is physically split in two between the wood and the world outside. There is no neutral ground; no room for a diplomatic compromise. This clear-cut distinction is a direct reflection of Lawrence's deeply religious frame of mind, which regarded contemporary reality as part of an historical process torn between the cosmic extremes of the millennium and the apocalypse. To Lawrence, both worlds were manifest realities, existing side by side in a perennial battle between rival cosmic forces. And again, it is the dialectic of this rivalry that sets the action of the novel in motion. Thus, *Lady Chatterley's Lover* is a consistent expression of the darkest cultural pessimism, while at the same time preaching the most tender and heartfelt hope for the future. It describes a 'tragic age' and a 'hopeful heart', to quote from the first and the last lines of the book.

As suggested already, in *Lady Chatterley's Lover* Lawrence describes events of apocalyptic character both in the past and in the future. Both Connie and the narrator repeatedly look back on the First World War as a watershed of universal significance from which a renewal of life is urgently needed. 'The cataclysm has happened, we are among the ruins, we start to build up new little habitats, to have new little hopes' (*LCL*, 5).[1] In the second version, *John Thomas and Lady Jane*, there is a long passage which describes, in clearly Biblical terms, the effects of the war:

> Those that had never died, who had, in a way, dodged, like Olive and Jack and so many second-rate people, were utterly out of touch with those who had died and were walking now in the dim, grey days before ascending unto the Father. There was no touch with that which lay behind. The new body could not touch the old. . . . Clifford, at least, could never rise to a new body: no, nor even hope for it. Lately, since the excitement at the rolling back of the gates of the tomb had died down in him, he had known. . . . He thought she could be connected with the old body of life, like Jack – men who had got the old body, which had dodged the descent into hell (*JTLJ*, 69).

However, the sense of *approaching* doom is expressed more frequently and consistently in the novel. During a party at Wragby, Tommy Dukes says: '"Our old show will come flop; our civilization is going to fall. It's going down the bottomless pit, down the chasm". But he adds: '"And believe me, the only bridge across the chasm will be the phallus"' (*LCL*, 78). In the second version, the narrator states that 'it is useless to talk of the future of our society. Our society is insane. . . . Insanity can only be cured by death' (*JTLJ*, 106–7). While Connie is on her way to the gamekeeper with Clifford's message, the 'air was soft and dead, as if all the world were slowly dying. . . . The end of all things!' (*LCL*, 68). Perhaps even the trees, she thinks,

> were only waiting for the end; to be cut down, cleared away, the end of the forest, for them the end of all things' (ibid.). Over everything there is 'a sense of doom. Doom, doom, impending, inevitable doom! This she saw in the Midlands' sky, and on the

> Midlands' earth. It looked at her out of all the faces, Clifford's, Mrs. Bolton's, the colliers', the rector's, they all walked with unconscious and impending doom upon them (*JTLJ*, 338–9).

Furthermore, there are references of a more obscure, but related character. In the third version Clifford is reading a book about the wasting of the universe, while in the second version, the musician Archie Blood is convinced that the white race will be extinct in sixty years: 'because by that time, the last warm-souled man will be dead, and the last gentle, warm-bodied woman"' (*JTLJ*, 293–4).

But Lawrence does not only render the approaching disaster as a dreaded and inevitable event. In *John Thomas and Lady Jane*, Connie – just like the Salvation Army in *Apocalypse* – actively welcomes it, as if out of a hatred for the world as it is:

> The Romans sowed salt on the place that was accursed, but she, with deeper hate, would sow nettles. And the park! – if one could set fire to all the trees, so that it was a bare desert, save for a few black stumps! And burn down the colliery works, and destroy Tevershall, and wipe out all the people! Ah a grand, grand destruction! How her soul gloated on the thought! If something would happen that would *really* destroy the world and make it into a desert, with a few charred remains and the salty bitterness of ashes blowing on its surface! If *that* could happen, then, then at last one would feel relieved. Even if one were dead oneself in the holocaust, it would still be a relief (*JTLJ*, 42).

And in the final version, Mellors gives the following Beckettian statement: '"To contemplate the extermination of the human species and the long pause that follows before some other species crops up, it calms you more than anything else"' (*LCL*, 227).

Everywhere the apocalyptic sentiment is implicated with the modern mass society in which the voice of the individual cannot be heard. Invoking images of purgatorial heat and blazing dragons, Lawrence describes with horrifying effect the mechanized world:

> There, in the world of the mechanical greedy, greedy mechanism and mechanized greed, sparkling with lights and gushing hot metal and roaring with traffic, there lay the vast evil thing, ready to destroy whatever did not conform. Soon it would destroy the

wood, and the bluebells would spring no more. All vulnerable things must perish under the rolling and running of iron (*LCL*, 124).

Moreover, in the second version, Archie Blood redefines the proletariat – no doubt in line with Lawrence's own views – to include the haves as well as the have-nots. 'It was a polarized homogeneous proletariat. It was all Robot. And it was the suicide of the human race' (*JTLJ*, 293). Thus, the apocalypse is not just a passing crisis which affects only a section of society. Rather, it is the cosmic, all-encompassing event as seen by traditional religious apocalypticism. As Tommy Dukes puts it: '"We're all as cold as crétins, we're all as passionless as idiots. We're all of us, Bolshevists, only we give it another name"' (*LCL*, 41).

The traditional aristocracy of heroism and true leadership is slowly becoming extinct. The paralysed and impotent Sir Clifford is its last and degenerated representative. A cripple and a traitor to the true qualities of his class, he has embraced the noise and nonsense of the modern world.[2] Worse still: he is a personal success, a lord and master, a captain of the proud Titanic; he is a leader of modern industry and a successful author whose writings give 'a wonderful display of nothingness' (*LCL*, 54). For Lawrence, culture and business have become rats in the same sewer. 'He realised now that the bitch-goddess of Success had two main appetites: one for flattery, adulation, stroking and tickling such as writers and artists gave her; but the other a grimmer appetite for meat and bones. And the meat and bones for the bitch-goddess were provided by the men who made money in industry' (*LCL*, 111). Clifford's energy, directed with increasing efficiency towards the underworld of the mines, is thus an active contribution to the ultimate destruction of the modern world.

This broader historical process can be seen at work in at least two seemingly insignificant references in the novel. First, in both the first and the second versions of *Lady Chatterley's Lover*, it is mentioned that 'by the time the *Untergang des Abendlands* [sic] appeared, Clifford was a smashed man . . .' (*JTLJ*, 11). This work by Oswald Spengler, which has been mentioned earlier, is characterized by a heavily apocalyptic approach to historical movement, and describes how the two thousand year cycle of Western civilization is rapidly coming to an end. Thus, Clifford is not just symbolic of the England of the First World War, but also of the greater tide of European culture to which he belongs. Second, Lawrence appears to view Christianity itself as a dying religion. In *The First Lady Chatterley*, in a passage similar to the descriptions of Christianity in *The Plumed Serpent*, Lawrence compares Clifford to Jesus: 'He was the god that had fallen and become an idol. [Connie] could still make offerings to the idol in respect of its old godhead. . . . But it only carried him further away from any deep bodily interchange and left him, as it were, high and dry, as a man who had already died to everything except nervous appreciation or irritation' (*TFLC*, 54–5). Later on in the same version it is even stated explicitly that 'the cross . . . is an evil symbol and carries evil wherever it goes' (157). In *John Thomas and Lady Jane*, 'Christmas always inspired [Connie] with indefinable dread, as if something bad were going to happen' (*JTLJ*, 58). Furthermore, 'Clifford had been wounded on Christmas day' (ibid.), and according to Mrs Bolton, her husband had been killed in the mines 'twenty-two years [ago] last Christmas' (*JTLJ*, 83). The suggestion is that both the horrors of the war and the fatal underworld activity of the mines are somehow linked to the overall quality and character of the Christian religion.

A study of apocalyptic themes across the three versions of *Lady Chatterley's Lover* shows significant differences, some of which have been pointed out by Stephen Gill in an article on the first and the final versions. The first version is a soft-spoken and well-balanced story; it is not 'a statement about industrialisation to be taken without question. The validity of its statements is no stronger than the degree of conviction carried at the moment by its spokesmen – that is, by the characters in the ever-changing rainbow of their relationships'.[3] In the third version the sense of impending doom and its intimate connection with business and industry is not only integral to the story, but also strongly stressed in a number of authorial interventions. For instance, as Connie drives through Tevershall in the car, Lawrence obtrudes himself into the narrative, which takes on a considerably more hysterical tone than the same passage in *John Thomas and Lady Jane*. Everything is infected with the rot of decadence: the soap in the grocers' shop, the rhubarb and lemons in the greengrocers, the cinema announcement, the windowpanes in the new chapel, the song of the schoolgirls. Thus, the third version reads as both a novel and a piece of cultural criticism, the latter presented in a series of violent outbursts interspersed throughout the story. Consequently, as a literary work, the book clearly suffers, but as an expression of Lawrence's growing despair over the world in which he lived, *Lady Chatterley's Lover* is a powerful and radical statement of contemporary relevance.

At the other extreme of Lawrence's dramatic vision of reality, there is the wood, which is a world almost untouched by the forces of evil and an image of natural harmony and renewal of life. In a somewhat cryptic comment on the novel in a letter from 12 September 1929 to D. V. Lederhandler, Lawrence said: 'The wood is of course unconscious symbolism – perhaps even the mines – even Mrs. Bolton' (*CL II*, 1214). And just as the tree of knowledge cast its shadow of temptation on the perfect harmony in the Garden of Eden, there is in *Lady Chatterley's Lover* a shadow falling on the wood from the world outside. During the war, Clifford's father had cut part of the wood for trench timber, so that now it 'let in the world'. As a result, this 'remnant of the great forest where Robin Hood hunted' had been spoilt by contributing to the collective suicide of the war (*LCL*, 44). Also, 'there was no game; no pheasants. They had been killed off during the war . . .' (*LCL*, 45). Thus, the wood has been invaded and damaged – a Garden of Eden after the Fall. But as it says at the beginning of the novel, despite the cataclysm of the war, 'we start to build up new little habitats, to have new little hopes' (*LCL*, 5), and even Clifford wants to retain this piece of paradise. 'He wanted this place inviolate, shut off from the world' (*LCL*, 45). For this purpose, he employs the gamekeeper Mellors, who takes a personal satisfaction in protecting the wood and breeding the pheasants. Through Mellors' efforts to re-establish the natural balance of the wood, it retains a sense of being a sacred place apart from the world. Yet, in the end it is too good to be true, and Mellors and Connie – like Adam and Eve – are driven out of paradise. As Parkin, the gamekeeper in *John Thomas and Lady Jane*, puts it: '"I always knowed I should get chucked out o' this wood. It couldn't last"' (*JTLJ*, 331). These parallels to the story in Genesis clearly should not be carried too far, but the imagery connected with the Fall is certainly used to create an apropos to Genesis. During one of Connie's visits to the cottage, Mellors' 'curious hiss of passion, sudden indrawn, when he touched her naked body, was far back almost as the snake itself' (*JTLJ*, 174).

In all three versions of *Lady Chatterley's Lover* there is one reference to classical mythology which deserves close examination since it contributes to a clearer understanding of Lawrence's intentions with his book. This concerns Mellors as a Pan figure. First, however, it will be useful to raise the question of which *qualities* the wood and the character Mellors embody. In the wider context of Lawrentian ideas – which main connotations do they carry? As suggested already, Mellors and the wood are part of a vision of a resurrected humanity. The main component of this vision is – with respect to history – a deliberate return to a primitive, pre-historic culture, in which Lawrence found the kind of natural harmony he was looking for. As to the chances of modern man to succeed in this enterprise, Lawrence claimed man's unconscious to be a direct reflection of the primitive state of mind, and that an access to the hidden resources of the unconscious would make man capable of this return to a pre-spiritual and pre-intellectual state. Furthermore, he envisaged an aristocracy of individuals, a world of strong and separate beings who lived in bodily contact with the forces of the cosmos. Finally, he regarded the phallus as the well-head from which the new richness of life would flow, or – to use a different metaphor – as the spearhead which would break open the gates to a new, or rather old, sphere of reality.

All of these themes are focused in the references to Mellors as a Pan figure and the wood as his domain. Indeed, to a large extent Lawrence's sylvan utopia is built around Pan. This is evident both from the numerous references to the classical Pan myth and from the way in which Lawrence included another and more modern version of the myth in his novel.

As so often in Lawrence, the name of a character is not chosen at random. In the first two versions of the book, the gamekeeper is called Oliver Parkin. The name Oliver is etymologically connected with the 'olive-tree', and in Greek mythology Pan is the protector 'particularly of the vine and olive'.[4] In Parkin's family background, there is further evidence of this connection. In *John Thomas and Lady Jane* there is a rather curious piece of information about Parkin's father. Talking to Connie about the gamekeeper's family, Mrs Bolton says: '"His father was Dicky Seivers, a cricketer, who went off all summer professional cricketing. Mrs. Seiver was only married to him a year . . .' (*JTLJ*, 198). According to the Pan myth, Hermes is generally considered to be Pan's father, and 'the classic aspect of Hermes is that of an athlete-god', and he had 'the epithet *Agonios*, "who presides over contests"'.[5] Moreover, Pan was in the retinue of Dionysos, as were the Bacchantes, and in *John Thomas and Lady Jane*, Clifford, looking at Connie's flashing beauty as she returns from the wood, says to her: '"You look like a Bacchante just off to the hill, with the Iacchos! cry ready in your throat"' (*JTLJ*, 266). And Iacchos, to complete the picture, is a mystic name for Dionysos.

Connie's first reaction to Mellors also suggests that Lawrence had Pan in mind while writing the book. While at the beginning of the novel Connie and Clifford are out in the wood, Mellors suddenly appears. 'A man with a gun strode swiftly, softly out after the dog, facing their way as if about to attack them; then stopped instead, saluted, and was turning downhill. It was only the new gamekeeper, but he had frightened Connie, he seemed to emerge with such a swift menace. That was how she had seen him, like the sudden rush of a threat out of nowhere' (*LCL*, 49). Of Pan it is said that he 'amused himself by giving the lonely traveller sudden frights, called for this reason panics'.[6]

In the final version, the most obvious references to Pan are slightly played down. The gamekeeper is called Mellors, and his father is given the rather more likely occupation of a miner. But in one passage Pan is explicitly mentioned, which he is not in the earlier versions. In Mellors' final letter to Connie, which marks the end of the novel, he writes that people 'are all one-track minds nowadays. . . . They should be alive and frisky, and acknowledge the great god Pan' (*LCL*, 312).

Lady Chatterley's Lover is not the only Lawrence text which makes use of the Pan myth. In *The Plumed Serpent*, Cipriano was both Huitzlopochtli and Pan at the same time. In the essay 'Pan in America', which Lawrence wrote in 1924 and which provides an excellent introduction to a reading of *Lady Chatterley's Lover*, Lawrence pays an enthusiastic tribute to the great god which, in the Christian tradition, was reduced to a devil, 'with the cloven hoofs and the horns, the tail, and the laugh of derision' (*Ph*, 23). Thus, Pan is a natural ingredient in Lawrence's transvaluation of values: the god, which had been made into a devil, is again made into a god. In this essay Lawrence also goes on at some length about Pan and trees, and claims that 'I am conscious that [the contact with the tree] helps to change me, vitally. I am even conscious that shivers of energy cross my living plasm, from the tree, and I become a degree more like unto the tree, more bristling and turpentiney, in Pan' (25). Similarly, in *John Thomas and Lady Jane*, 'Constance sat down with her back to a young pine-tree, that swayed against her like a animate creature, so subtly rubbing itself against her, the great, alive thing with its top in the wind' (*JTLJ*, 91). And Lawrence himself, of course, while writing the novel in the country outside Florence, frequently sat with his back to a trunk in 'a little wood of umbrella pines'.[7]

However, before turning to the role of Pan in *Lady Chatterley's Lover*, it seems appropriate to mention another literary use of the Pan myth, which may well have influenced Lawrence. This is Knut

Hamsun's novel *Pan*, which was published for the first time in 1894 and translated into English in 1920. According to the Danish painter Knut Merrild, who stayed with Lawrence in New Mexico, Lawrence liked *Pan* the best of Hamsun's works,[8] though in 'The Novel', written at roughly the same time, Lawrence puts *Pan* in among other 'pathetic or sympathetic or antipathetic little Jesuses . . .' (*SThH*, 182).[9] The fact remains, however, that *Lady Chatterley's Lover* – which Lawrence wrote just a few years after he read *Pan* – contains an unusual number of parallels to Hamsun's novel. First, the settings are almost identical.

The action of *Pan* takes place in a small fishing village in the north of Norway during the summer of 1855. The local Tevershall is called Sirilund, where Herr Mack, the financially somewhat weather-beaten merchant on whom the entire village depends, lives in a modest counterpart to Wragby. Herr Mack has a daughter, Edvarda, and she is courted by the Doctor, who – with a typical Hamsun touch – is limping, using a walking stick, and is taken in a carriage to spare his foot. Another suitor, brought to Sirilund by Edvarda's father, is a scientist from Finland, a thin and sickly baron, who quite effectively sums up Hamsun's heartfelt contempt for the men of his class and occupation. It is into this quiet village that Lieutenant Glahn arrives, the narrator of the main part of the book. He rents a little cottage owned by Mack in the wood on the edge of the village, in which he lives in deliberate isolation from the outside world. A hunter, he wears a rough leather dress and a gun slung over his shoulder, and roams the big forest shooting game together with his faithful companion, the dog Æsop. Glahn is a mysterious character, and very little is revealed about him apart from his military rank and the fact that – at the end of his story – he is thinking about going to India or Africa. So far, the general outline of Hamsun's and Lawrence's stories are remarkably similar. When it comes to the passionate relationship between Glahn and Edvarda things take a rather different turn. But in both novels, the woman is drawn as if by a magnet to erotic encounters with the strange man in the wood. And on the more detailed level, there are several points that suggest an intimate connection between the two novels.

First, Mellors in *Lady Chatterley's Lover* has the same military rank as Glahn, and he has previously been in India and Egypt. Second, in *Pan*, Edvarda tells Glahn: '"Do you know what my friend says about you?' she began. 'Your eyes are like an animal's, she says, and when you look at her, it makes her mad"'.[10] In *The First Lady Chatterley*, Parkin 'stared down at Constance with his small-pupilled eyes like some animal that hunts' (*TFLC*, 73). Third, when Glahn is leaving Sirilund, Edvarda asks him if she can keep his dog as a remembrance, and Glahn agrees. In *John Thomas and Lady Jane*, when Connie and Parkin are parting for the last time in the wood, the same question arises. Though the new gamekeeper is supposed to have Flossie, Connie wants to '"have her for a friend". . . . "And if she's not happy, *I'll* take her". He pondered this for a time. 'Ay!' he said. 'If yer'd have her"' (*JTLJ*, 329). Fourth, between Herr Mack and Clifford there is another parallel. The former shows an almost childish admiration for modern inventions. He proudly shows Glahn 'his new lamps; the first paraffin lamps to be seen so far north. They were splendid things, with a heavy leaden foot', and he talks enthusiastically about railways and the telegraph.[11] Clifford, likewise, is obsessed, particularly in the second version, with modern things. 'He bought a new car, and gave Connie the old one', and 'he would sit for hours vacant as an empty whelk-shell, listening to the radio' (*JTLJ*, 341).

Finally, to give an impression of how closely the two novels resemble each other in their general atmosphere, compare the following passages, the first of them from *Pan*:

> Often in the evening, when I came back to the hut after being out shooting all day, I could feel that kindly, homely feeling trickling through me from head to foot; a pleasant little inward shivering. And I would talk to Æsop about it, saying how comfortable we were. . . . And when . . . we had both fed, Æsop would slip away to his place behind the hearth, while I lit a pipe and lay down on the bench for a while, listening to the dead soughing of the trees. There was a slight breeze bearing down towards the hut, and I could hear quite clearly the clutter of a grouse far away on the ridge behind. Save for that, all was still.[12]

> He went home with his gun and his dog, to the dark cottage, lit the lamp, started the fire, and ate his supper of bread and cheese, young onions and beer. He was alone, in a silence he loved. His room was clean and tidy, but rather stark. Yet the fire was bright, the hearth white, the petroleum lamp hung bright over the table, with its white oil-cloth. . . . He sat by the fire in his shirt-sleeves, not smoking, but with a mug of beer in reach (*LCL*, 125).

As has been suggested already, the relationships between the lovers differ quite considerably in the two novels. In *Pan* the match is a relatively even one. At one moment Glahn shows Edvarda an air of arrogant superiority, while the next he licks 'a few blades of grass by the roadside' in humility and despair.[13] Edvarda is a similarly unstable character. Consequently, there is a violent clash of personalities between the two, a clash which is too volcanic to result in a lasting relationship.

This brings the discussion back to *Lady Chatterley's Lover* and the relationship between Mellors and Connie. Given the association of Mellors with Pan, the aspect of male superiority is brought more effectively into focus. First of all, the wood is almost exclusively Mellors's domain, and all the references to fertility – they are all connected with the wood – ultimately point back to the old Pan as a god of fertility and virility. Rabbits – the very symbols of lust and procreation – 'bobbed and nibbled' at the wood's edge (*LCL*, 44). Then there are new trees being planted, pheasants being hatched, and most important, a child is conceived. The gamekeeper is the protector and the lifegiving force behind all this new life. His domain is 'a sacred place, silent and healing, . . . one of the unravished places of old stillness' (*JTLJ*, 101). But the very symbol of the gamekeeper's divine fertility is his phallus, which 'came with a strange slow thrust of peace, the dark thrust of peace and a ponderous, primordial tenderness, such as made the world in the beginning' (*LCL*, 181). It possesses, in truth, the creative power of the Old Testament Jehovah, or as Mellors says on its behalf: '"Lift up your heads o' ye gates, that the king of glory may come in"' (*LCL*, 218). Indeed, the phallus takes on a separate and godlike being: 'Between the two hesitating, baffled creatures, himself and her, [Connie] had seen the third creature, erect, alert, overweening, utterly unhesitating, stand there in a queer new assertion, rising from the roots of his body. It was like some primitive, grotesque god . . . ' (*JTLJ*, 238). The phallus resurrects not only the body of man, but it also restores man's relationship to the universe. Having herself experienced the awesome power of the phallus, Connie knew that

> the penis is the column of blood, the living fountain of fullness in life. . . . 'There is a fountain filled with blood', said the hymn. And it is eternally true. And every man is such a fountain. . . . And the symbol of the rush of the living blood is the phallus, and the penis is the fountain of life filled with blood. And with the mystery of the phallus goes all the beauty of the world, and beauty is more than knowledge. . . . The knowledge of the movement of the stars and the laws of celestial gravitation is wonderful,

> but the beauty of the stars in their motions is still more wonderful, and it is the penis which connects us sensually with the planets. But for the penis we should never know the loveliness of Sirius or the categorical difference between a pomegranate and an india-rubber ball (*TFLC*, 156).

As part of this vision, the phallus is also a key back to the primitive culture of Pan himself, in which Lawrence found his own world of perfection. Mellors 'seemed to slide through centuries, thousands of years of human culture, in this hour with her. . . . when his eyes began to dilate and flash, he began to slide back through the centuries' (*JTLJ*, 174). It is this twofold view of phallicism and primitivism which gives Lawrence's vision its character of a utopian escape from everyday reality: 'What did it matter who he was, in the daytime world! Now he was the silent man who enclosed her in the phallic circle, and she was like the yolk of the egg, enclosed. She wanted only, only to be perfectly enclosed, to be perfectly comforted, to be put perfectly to sleep' (*JTLJ*, 239). Certainly, this passage evokes an echo of *The Plumed Serpent*, in which Kate finds an excuse for Cipriano's cruelty: 'Let him be a general, an executioner, what he liked, in the world. The flame of their united lives was a naked bud of flame' (*TPS*, 394).

Thus the superior male of the leadership novels resurfaces in *Lady Chatterley's Lover*, and the tendency becomes gradually more pronounced in the three versions. Admittedly, in the first version the problem of female submission or male superiority hardly occurs. Here Parkin is himself too much of a harassed victim – though a proud one – of his social surroundings to assume such a position in relation to Connie. In the second version, however, Connie appears as a more humble recipient of male divinity: 'She had really touched him at last, like the woman who touched Jesus, and who found the world changed. . . . The man had caused her soul to turn, to become aware in a different way. . . . And now, she felt, with a dim inward knowledge, he had impregnated her body as well as her soul' (*JTLJ*, 176). In the final version, Connie's total submission to Mellors is described as her own deliberate choice after a long argument with herself. She is tempted to claim the phallus for herself and use it for her own satisfaction, as the 'pure god-servant to the woman!' (*LCL*, 141). But she soon realizes that she 'did not want it, it was known and barren, birthless; the adoration was her treasure. . . . No, no, she would give up her hard bright female power; she was weary of it, stiffened with it; she would sink in the new bath of life, in the depths of her womb and her bowels that sang the voiceless song of adoration' (*LCL*, 141–2). Later in the book, her total submission is presented as an essential requirement for the following death and resurrection through sex. 'She had to be a passive, consenting thing, like a slave, a physical slave. Yet the passion licked round her, consuming, and when the sensual flame of it pressed through her bowels and breast, she really thought she was dying: yet a poignant, marvellous death' (*LCL*, 257).

As in *The Plumed Serpent* Lawrence gets his own way, and the result is a Mellors who – running away from the world – can only show his manhood in a phallic hunt to which the female is bound to submit. The Parkin of the first version, who despite his beating is too proud to accept Connie's money, and whom some critics regard as a comical figure, appears in the final version as a tragic specimen of Lawrence's new aristocracy of individuals. He is a gymnast on the ladder of the social classes, a man who despises the world, who accepts his lover's money, and who seeks refuge in the claim to a superior phallic power. As it turns out, this is the real content of Lawrence's phallic utopia in the final version of *Lady Chatterley's Lover*. It carries not only the weakness, discussed in chapter 3, of investing the sexual act with the Sisyphean task of resurrecting the body to a new and fuller life, but it also singles out the male as the only creature capable of bringing about this divine transformation. Consequently, Lawrence creates in Mellors his own vision of a phallic *Übermensch*, thus forcing him to develop a character more in line with his idea of a true aristocrat than the Parkin of the earlier versions, who had his teeth knocked out, who could not speak the King's English, and who at the end of the tale ended up where he came from – as a simple footman among the proletarian legions. But as has been suggested already, Mellors is a split character without a social anchorage, a kind of solitary rider whose individual utopia can only be an escape. As such he becomes himself a symbol of Lawrence's own failure to infuse his vision with the amount of realism necessary to give the story a real edge.

Lawrence and Politics After The Plumed Serpent

So far this chapter has dealt almost exclusively with non-political issues of the post-1925 period. The topic of the following section will be Lawrence's political utopia after the completion of *The Plumed Serpent*, and, like the previous chapter, it will deal with the period in a chronological order. Thus it will be necessary to consider briefly some of Lawrence's essays from the period immediately after *The Plumed Serpent* before returning to the three versions of *Lady Chatterley's Lover* and the other writings that lead up to his final statement in *Apocalypse*.

Having just finished *The Plumed Serpent* in June 1925, Lawrence wrote a series of mystical-political essays collected under the title of *Reflections on the Death of a Porcupine*.[14] They make far from easy reading, and the distinction between mysticism and politics is difficult to work out. Still, one finds in them an overall resemblance to themes dealt with in *The Plumed Serpent*. In 'Blessed Are the Powerful', he says: 'The reign of love is passing, and the reign of power is coming again. The day of popular democracy is nearly done. Already we are entering the twilight, towards the night that is at hand' (*RDP*, 321). This is confirmed in a letter to Martin Secker from the October of the same year: 'Tell the man, very nice man, in your office, I *do* mean what Ramón means – for all of us' (*Le V*, 318). But Lawrence's own lack of conviction is never far off, for later on in the essay just quoted, his wavering position is obvious: 'Myself I want Power. But I don't want to boss anybody. I want Honour. But I don't see any existing nation or government that could give it me. I want Glory. But heaven save me from mankind. I want Might. But perhaps I've got it' (*RDP*, 324–5). Similarly, in the essay 'Aristocracy', the true aristocrat is described not as a person involved in his social surroundings. Instead, Lawrence retreats to safer territory, to the relationship between the sexes and their relationship to the cosmos, comparing, as in earlier works, the woman to the moon and the man to the sun. 'The sun makes man a lord: an aristocrat: almost a deity. But in his consummation with night and the moon, man knows for ever his own passing away' (*RDP*, 375). After a series of rather esoteric statements like this, he arrives at a conclusion which may, or may not, carry a political message: 'Bah! Enough of the squalor of democratic humanity. It is time to begin to recognize the aristocracy of the sun. The children of the sun shall be lords of the earth' (376).

However, after his visit in the summer of 1926 to an England still marred by the General Strike, Lawrence seems to have regained a taste for political matters, though the strike itself does not figure very prominently in his letters from the period. In 'Return to Bestwood', probably written just before going back to Italy at the end of September, he claims that 'we could, if we would, establish little by little a true democracy in England: we could nationalise the land and industries and means of transport, and make the whole thing work infinitely better than at present, *if we would*. . . . I know we are on the brink of a class war. . . . But beyond the fight must lie a new hope, a new beginning' (*Ph II*, 265). Again, it is difficult to judge exactly how serious Lawrence is being, and in the context of his other writings from the same period, this remark stands out as curiously positive to the socialist cause. In a letter to Koteliansky, for instance, written in May the same year, he described the Bolshevists as 'loutish or common. I don't believe in them, except as disruptive and nihilistic agents' (*Le V*, 455). Still, in *Lady Chatterley's Lover*, the first version of which he began a few months later, Bolshevism plays a fairly prominent part, and it is to this work one must turn in order to get a more coherent impression of the extent to which political questions concerned Lawrence after *The Plumed Serpent* and before *Apocalypse*.

Kenneth Muir claims in his article 'The Three Lady Chatterleys', that the 'first version of the book is Lawrence's only serious attempt to deal with the class structure of English society'.[15] Yet, *The First Lady Chatterley* is not a political novel in the sense of taking up a position in the ideological landscape and defending it against rival views. When it comes to ideas of political action, Lawrence is not particularly sophisticated. Also, there is no thorough description of the social forces at work. Stephen Gill, therefore, is probably closer to the mark than Muir, when he says that the 'full complexity of actual political realities in the nineteen-twenties are [sic] conveniently sidestepped'.[16] Even so, political matters are constantly being discussed. Clifford, for instance, goes on at great length about the equality of man being 'all bunk' (*TFLC*, 104) and about the necessity of a 'higher type of life' (105), of which he – presumably – is himself a representative. In direct contrast to this, Parkin is described as an active Communist who shows a considerable amount of solidarity with his mates when offered Connie's money: '"An' t' other chaps? Would they all find women wi' money to pick 'em up an' start 'em on their own? They've got to ding at it till Doomsday, and their children after them, with no more hope in it than if they was dead"' (224). Towards the end of the book, of course, there is the long discussion on class differences during Connie's visit to the Tewsons'. But despite the fact that Connie and Parkin are presented as belonging to two different worlds which are engaged in a deathly struggle, there is no serious attempt on Lawrence's part to suggest an alternative social framework which would make their relationship socially acceptable. Instead, he takes the easy way out by giving Duncan, Connie's friend, a prominent role towards the end of the story. Duncan is a character who becomes gradually more sympathetic and more Lawrentian as the novel develops. He and Parkin strike up a sort of man to man friendship, and Duncan – who very significantly belongs to the classless world of artists – thus bridges the gap between Connie and Parkin. He even shows a certain sympathy for Communism, and – in a highly Lawrentian perspective – sees the revolution as an opportunity for an apocalyptic entry into the millennium. During a discussion with Connie, he says: '". . . perhaps if the Communists *did* smash the famous 'system' there might emerge a new relationship between men: *really* not caring about money, *really* caring for life, and the life-flow with one another"' (242). Thus Duncan, regarding both democracy and aristocracy as blind alleys (243), rounds off the book with Lawrence's own bland escape into the world of the isolated individual. Clearly, *The First Lady Chatterley* is a far cry from a political manifesto, but all the same it is the most realistic of the three versions. In a highly ironical passage on the last page, Lawrence even seems to admit that the common life-flow between Connie and Parkin may not be quite sufficient to sustain a relationship across the class barriers. Connie thinks about the future:

> . . . to live in an ordinary house in some suburb! What bliss! To be out in the cold air of life, not stifled in the lifelessness of Wragby. No, she needn't go into a workman's dwelling! But some farm-house, or some suburban villa with nine or ten rooms – she didn't care! Anything, to be in contact with life. And if she could possibly be in contact with the working people, well and good. It would be nonsense to try to pretend to be one of them (252).

As one would expect, the second version, *John Thomas and Lady Jane*, represents a half-way stage between the first and the final versions, and as such it shows very clearly the shift in Lawrence's development. The tension in *The First Lady Chatterley* between the wood and the outside world is sharpened, and Lawrence uses an increasingly religious vocabulary to put his message across. The threat of a class war, for instance, is closely related to the apocalyptic visions discussed above. Connie senses:

> a gathering sense of doom. . . . Dimly she could feel some new sort of disaster accumulating: accumulating slowly, with awful,

> serpentine slowness, but with peculiar cold dread. It was something she dreaded coldly and fatally, the working-out of this new, unconscious, cold, reptilian sort of hate that was rising between the colliers of the under-earth, the iron-workers of the great furnaces, and the educated, owning class to which she belonged, by the accident of destiny (*JTLJ*, 112).

However, this description comes immediately after a similar description of the 'keen, tingling, subtle hate' (ibid.) of the working classes, which is the driving force behind Clifford's new lease of life. There is, then, on both sides a letting loose of the forces of evil and destruction. Both parties are possessed by hatred of the other, and both are waiting for the apocalyptic moment of crisis – the revolution, which Lawrence himself thought inevitable. Clifford already envisages what it will be like. '"They'll burst through every barrier, by mere weight of numbers, and it will be a swamp of common people, profane vulgarity. Thank God, I don't think I shall live to see the worst of it. I wish we had enough strong men to form a small aristocracy, and put the rest back into slavery, where they belong"' (27). As a way out of this impasse of a hopeless present and a hopeless future, Clifford is 'harping, with an insistency that Constance felt was purely destructive, on the problem of immortality, and on the reality of mystical experiences' (86–7). Lawrence obviously regards Clifford's *idée fixe* as an example of the latter's failure to get in touch with the deeper realities of sensual living. But before accepting this condemnation of Clifford, one ought to consider Parkin and Connie from a similar perspective. Are they really – as opposed to Clifford – in touch with reality?

If by a sense of reality one means an awareness of the world outside oneself and one's lover, then the answer is surely no. As in the first version, Lawrence provides the two lovers with an exit from an imprisoning society in general and the problem of class conflicts in particular. Admittedly, Parkin is still a secretary for his trade union, but in connection with his Bolshevist sympathies, there is a strange discussion between him and Connie the night before she leaves for the Continent. Connie's sister Hilda has just left the cottage after a rather cool encounter with Parkin, when Parkin exclaims:

> 'It strikes me the Bolshevists was about right, to smash 'em up. What good are they?'
>
> 'Who?' she said.

'Folks!' she was silent, feeling her heart sink. Then at last she asked: 'But didn't you like Hilda?'

'Ay – ay – all right!'

'Then why do you talk about Bolshevists?'

'Eh well! I don't!'

'I think Bolshevists are such dreary, uninspired people, just smashing things and creating nothing.'

He received this in silence. But as he pushed off his boot with his other foot, he said:

'It's us or them. One or t'other's got to go smash.'

'Who? Us or who?'

'Folks! Other folks!' he said.

'But that's everybody except you and me!' she said, laughing at the idea.

''Appen so!' he said complacently (275).

This passage seems to imply that Parkin is actually siding with the Bolshevists against Hilda and the upper classes in general – Connie included – and that there can be no true human contact across the class barriers. However, face to face with Connie, he shrinks from admitting it, and the action quickly switches to more pleasant matters. This creates an interlude of uncertainty for Parkin, in which he is torn between his love for Connie and a sense of solidarity with his class. But it is only an interlude. At the end of the book, he quits his job and accepts Connie's helping hand. He writes to her: 'I don't really care about money, though I'll earn my living somehow. But if you can set me up, next year, so that I can be my own boss, and keep to myself, I'll take it from you, and be thankful, and I know there won't be anything lost, because I trust you, and I'll work for it' (370). He accepts the money he was too proud to take in the first version. Not only this, but the whole question is actually done away with even more effectively than in the first version, through Archie Blood's redefinition of the term 'proletariat'. '". . . we are really all proletarian", he said. "A German once made that plain to me. The proletariat is a state of mind, it's not really a class at all. You're proletarian when you are cold like a crab, greedy like a crab, lustful with the ricketty egoism of a crab, and shambling like a crab"' (293). Connie immediately accepts this view, which removes all the social complications of her relationship with Parkin. – 'Parkin wasn't [proletarian]. He was hot blooded and single, and he wasn't at all absorbed in himself. . . . Now the barrier broke, and her soul flooded free. Class is an anachronism. It finished in 1914'

(294). Parkin, then, is one of 'a few individuals who have not been proletarianised' (ibid.), he is, in fact, a true aristocrat. Thus, Lawrence has gone full circle and managed to include the vulgar gamekeeper into the aristocracy, Connie's own class. Cinderellus has found his princess, and with it, his political involvement is definitely ended: '"I shouldn't care if the bolshevists blew up one half of the world, and the capitalists blew up the other half, to spite them, so long as they left me and you a rabbit-hole apiece to creep in, and meet underground like the rabbits do"' (369).[17] Connie heartily agrees: '"I was so afraid you were just going to deteriorate into a socialist or a fascist, or something dreary and political"' (ibid.). And that is the end of *John Thomas and Lady Jane*. Instead of burying their heads in the sand to avoid the revolutionary hurricane, Parkin and Connie prefer the ruttings of the rabbit-hole.

Lawrence finished the final version of *Lady Chatterley's Lover* in February 1928, only a few months after *John Thomas and Lady Jane*. There are few clues from both his life and other writings of the period to explain the steadily growing sense of despair discernible in the three versions. Of course, Lawrence was approaching the end of his life, and there was no longer any hiding the fact that he was seriously ill. But whatever the reason, in *Lady Chatterley's Lover* this increasing pessimism takes the form of a turn towards broader and, so to speak, more universal topics than he had been grappling with in the previous versions. His political interests are now nearly insignificant to the story. The entire discussion with the Tewsons on class differences, which had played a quite dominant role in both the earlier versions, is completely removed. Moreover, Mellors (the former Parkin) is associated with neither socialism nor trade unions. Whereas in the earlier versions he was a worker of working class background, he is now turned into a natural aristocrat, but with the same social background as before. He is a lieutenant – the same rank, incidentally, as Clifford – and once had a fair chance of becoming a captain; he has a pension; has travelled widely; speaks the King's English when he feels like it; and in his bookshelves Connie finds a variety of books. 'So! He was a reader after all' (*LCL*, 221). He is, in fact, Clifford's equal, and for this reason his position as a gamekeeper carries little conviction.

However, as the importance of politics is reduced, two themes of the former versions receive increased attention. First, as has been suggested earlier, the wood and the phallic power of Mellors become the only possibilities of hope and renewal. Second, both narrator and characters see the world around them as caught in a universal and inevitable chain of events. As Mellors says in his final letter to Connie: 'If things go on as they are, there's nothing lies in the future but death and destruction, for these industrial masses' (312). What was once a concern with social and political questions, is now expanded into a deeply pessimistic cultural criticism which views politics as just one element in a larger picture. For instance, Bolshevism is no longer seen as a political movement, rather it is regarded as a symptom of all the evils contained in the modern, industrialized world. According to Tommy Dukes, who to some degree is Lawrence's spokesman, '"we drive ourselves with a formula, like a machine. The logical mind pretends to rule the roost, and the roost turns into pure hate. We're all Bolshevists, only we are hypocrites"' (41).

Perhaps it was as he came towards the end of the final version that Lawrence began to realize that he had placed too great a trust in the redeeming power of the phallus. Faced with the massive forces of doom and destruction, his scheme was simply out of balance, and too escapist to carry any conviction. It may have been for this reason that at the very end of his novel Lawrence included another and rather different utopia, one which is closely related to the political realities of post-war Europe. This is the rural utopia described in Mellors's final letter to Connie, and it will need some explanation.

In 1925 Lawrence became acquainted with Rolf Gardiner, a young Cambridge graduate who was heavily involved with conservative youth movements in England and on the Continent, especially with the so-called *Bünde* in Germany. Gardiner's view of Western civilization was not very different from that of Lawrence, as when he writes: 'I believed that the *Untergang des Abendlandes* was an immediate process. A new Dark Ages was descending on Europe and the world'.[18] During a visit to the Lawrences in London in 1925, he and Lawrence had 'an animated talk about the approaching doom of civilization',[19] and Lawrence admitted that he felt England 'to be doomed, finished . . .'.[20] Despite Lawrence's usual scepticism, the friendship with Gardiner brought out in him his profound sympathy for the rural utopias of the German youth movements described in chapter 4. In a letter to Gardiner, he wrote:

> I am sure you are doing the right thing, with hikes and dances and songs. But somehow it needs a central clue, or it will fizzle away again. . . . I will try to come to England and make a place – some quiet house in the country – where one can begin – and from

> which the hikes, maybe, can branch out. Some place with a big barn and a bit of land – if one has enough money. Don't you think that is what it needs? And then one must set out and learn a deep discipline – and learn dances from all the world, and take whatsoever we can make into our own. . . . I tell you, we'd better buck up and do something for the England to come, for they've pushed the spear through the side of my England (*Le V*, 591–2).

And some time later: 'The German *Bünde* has the sound of a real thing . . .' (*CL II*, 1030). In November 1927 Gardiner bought Gore Farm in Dorset, with Lawrence's enthusiastic approval. According to W. J. Keith's article on the relationship between Gardiner and Lawrence, the rural utopia at the end of *Lady Chatterley's Lover* is clearly indebted to Gardiner's ideas and his convincing attempt at putting them into practice.[21] A quote from Mellors's letter should be sufficient to confirm this influence:

> . . . if [the men] could dance and hop and skip, and sing and swagger and be handsome, they could do with very little cash. And amuse the women themselves, and be amused by the women. They ought to learn to be naked and handsome, and to sing in a mass and dance the old group dances, and carve the stools they sit on, and embroider their own emblems. Then they wouldn't need money (*LCL*, 312).

But Lawrence's acquaintance with Gardiner is also interesting beyond merely the context of *Lady Chatterley's Lover*. Without doubt, his sudden interest in the *Wandervögel* during 1927 can be traced back to his discussions with Gardiner. In April that year Lawrence wrote two articles, 'Germans and Latins' and 'Germans and English', both of which discuss this German youth movement, and both of which reveal a quite extensive knowledge of the topic. These articles also suggest that Lawrence had grasped the essentially utopian character of the German *Bünde*. The *Wandervögel* boys, he writes in 'Germans and Latins', 'bring with them such a strong feeling of *somewhere else*, of an unknown country, an unknown race, a powerful, still unknown northland. . . . [To the Romans they were] creatures from the beyond, presaging another world of men. So it was then. So it is, to a certain extent, even now. Strange wanderers towards the sun, forerunners of another world of men' (*Ph*, 130). Also, in 'Germans and English', he shows an acute understanding of the currents of thought in Germany at the time, and he finds support for his views in a book by Karl Scheffler, *Zeit und Stunde*.[22] Asking where the *Wandervögel*] are going and what they are making for, he answers with a quote from Scheffler: '"Weil sie – eine Welt der reinen Idee brauchen"' (*Ph II*, 246). This is an implicit criticism of the *Wandervögel*, because in Lawrence's opinion it is exactly the pure idea, the ideal, which is 'the beast we have to fight and to kill . . .' (247). According to Lawrence, the source of redemption is rather to be found outside the sphere of intellect, reason and idea. Consequently, he claims, along with Scheffler, that it was certainly 'for the lack of [instinct, intuition and imagination] that Germany lost the war' (ibid.).

This points to a central flaw in Lawrence's view of reality. Conceiving of the unconscious as 'the well-head, the fountain of real motivity' (*FU*, 207), he ignored the possibility – which in German nationalism became a reality – that the irrational qualities themselves can also be turned into a pure idea and a programme for political action. Thus Lawrence glorified certain aspects of human nature which he regarded as pure and good, but which turned out to have the same destructive effects as the qualities he found to dominate the Christian culture of the West. As Mosse remarks on the German youth movement, he went from 'a rejection of reality to a glorification of ideology';[23] an ideology, that is, celebrating the instincts and an anti-ideological irrationalism. In 'Germans and Latins' Lawrence clearly detects this disintegration of the intellect in the *Wandervögel* movement. In it, he says, 'thought altogether falls into chaos – and then into discredit. The young don't choose to think any more. Blindly, they turn to the sun. Because the sun is anti-thought' (*Ph*, 131). In this essay Lawrence does not take a clear stand on the issue, merely claiming that the northern nations are 'buttoned and choked up. Then comes a revulsion. They cast off the clothes and turn to the sun, as the *Wandervögel* do, strange harbingers' (132). Similarly, in a letter to Gardiner, he stated, with remarkable clairvoyance: 'Even the German *Bünde*, I am afraid, will drift into nationalistic, and ultimately, fighting bodies: a new, and necessary form of militarism. It may be the right way for them. But not for the English' (*CL II*, 1031). With keen intuition, Lawrence sensed the dangers of the German movement, but he was still hesitant about distancing himself from it. However, against the background of his other writings, particularly the leadership novels and his enthusiasm for Gardiner's involvement in the right-wing youth movements, there can be little doubt that he saw in them certain qualities that he was himself propagating.

To give further weight to the utopian ideas in Lawrence's later works, it seems appropriate to consider an unfinished short story written in October 1927, only a couple of months before starting the final version of *Lady Chatterley's Lover*. 'A Dream of Life' is a perfect example of the way in which Lawrence's utopia is indebted both to the religious millenniarism of his childhood and to the popular, naive utopia of the early twentieth century. Despite its unpolitical plot, it also marks a phase in Lawrence's political development. The story is both strange and un-Lawrentian, first of all because it is set partly in the future. Second, it lacks the kind of realism which normally characterizes Lawrence's writing. The final part definitely reminds the reader more of H. G. Wells than of Lawrence.

However, the story starts – in the manner of *Lady Chatterley's Lover* – with a description of 'the poor, grimy, mean' Midlands (*TP*, 155), drawn, surely, from Lawrence's visit to the strike-ridden area in 1926. After this introduction follows a long, essay-like account of the relationship between the sexes in a modern, industrial society, with the men standing 'at the street corners, pale, shrunken, well-dressed, decent, and *under*. The drunken colliers of my father's generation were not got under' (156). The lifeless and materialistic vulgarity of the modern world is painted in garish colours, and the narrator concludes that 'my home place is more depressing to me than death . . .' (160–1). Suddenly, the whole atmosphere changes. The narrator is going for a walk, out of the old town, past the new and monstrous buildings surrounding the coal pits, and up to an old quarry, full of 'awful rocky caves. . . . There was a legend that these little caves or niches in the rocks were "everlasting wells", like the everlasting wells at Matlock. At Matlock the water drips in caves, and if you put an apple in there, or a bunch of grapes, or even if you cut your hand off and put it in, it won't decay, it will turn everlasting' (164). The narrator clambers into a little cave: '"Now", I thought, "for a little while I am safe and sound, and the vulgar world doesn't exist for me"' (166). Then he goes to sleep, and wakes up a thousand years later.

From this point, the story enters the world of the pure utopia. Two naked men are washing him, as if baptising him into a new life. They have 'formal, peaceful faces and trimmed beards, like old Egyptians' (169), and he comprehends their language, which faintly reminds him of the local dialect, 'as a dog understands, from the voice, not from the words' (ibid.). The men help him out of the cave, and he sees a new world. 'This place was bare, like a new working. And when we came out, it was another place altogether. Below was a hollow of trees, like parkland. There was no colliery, no railways, no hedges, no square, shut-in fields. And yet the land looked tended' (170). Risen from the dead, the narrator is clearly compared to Lazarus. He is filled with a new and curious strength, his feet hardly touch the ground. On their way they meet a cart 'drawn by two oxen and led by a man who was entirely naked' (171), and all around the fields are being ploughed. Then the narrator looks ahead at the steep hill in front of him:

> And at the top of the hill was a town, all yellow in the late afternoon light, with yellow, curved walls rising massive from the yellow-leaved orchards, and above, buildings swerving in a long, oval curve, and round, faintly conical towers rearing up. It had something at once soft and majestical about it, with its soft yet powerful curves, and no sharp angles or edges, the whole substance seeming soft and golden like the golden flesh of a city. And I knew, even while I looked at it, that it was the place where I was born, the ugly colliery townlet of dirty red brick. Even as a child, coming home from Moorgreen, I had looked up and seen the squares of miners' dwellings, built by the Company, rising from the hill-top in the afternoon light like the walls of Jerusalem, and I had wished it were a golden city, as in the hymns we sang in the Congregational Chapel. Now it had come true (171–2).

The narrator is taken up the hill to the town, where he is given a tunic and shown to his room, and in the evening he watches in the town square a dance of the setting sun, a swift, instinctive performance to the 'queer squeal' of bagpipes. 'The crowd had gathered in order, a cluster of men on the left, in grey, grey-and-scarlet, and pure scarlet, and a cluster of women on the right, in tunics of all shades of blue and crocus lilac' (175). In the living quarters men and women seem to be living separately, and there is obviously some kind of a guard or army present in the town. Just before the story breaks off, the narrator is taken to the leader, whose palace is where the Congregational Chapel used to stand.

The story has been recapitulated in some detail in order to show, first, the perfect combination of a religious millennium and a popular utopia. Second, to demonstrate the unbroken line from the rural utopias of the German youth movements, which were described in chapter 4, via the power utopia of the leadership novels, particularly *The Plumed Serpent*, and finally back again to the rural utopia of *Lady Chatterley's Lover* and 'A Dream of Life'. Thus Germany, more so than England, provides a kind of common reference for these various works, and Lawrence's friendship with Rolf Gardiner only serves to emphasize the connection.

To complete the discussion of political ideas, one finds in 'Matriarchy', an essay written a few months after *Lady Chatterley's Lover*, a vision somewhat related to that in 'A Dream of Life'. It takes the form of a call for the introduction of matriarchy, which sounds like a total surrender of male authority, but in fact turns out to be the very opposite. It is a diplomatic but shrewd move to ensure, once again, the man's freedom to pursue his natural longing for great deeds. Using the Mexican *khiva* – 'the great underground religious meeting-house where only the males assemble' (*Ph II*, 551) – as a primitive model, Lawrence pays tribute to such male institutions as the clubs and the pubs. It is here that 'men have really educated one another, by immediate contact, discussed politics and ideas, and made history. . . . To satisfy his deeper social instincts and intuitions, a man must be able to get away from his family, and from women altogether, and foregather in the communion of men' (552).

In the discussion of Lawrence's political ideas after 1925, two main points have been emphasized. First, the gradual substitution of explicitly political issues by a search for more private and frequently nostalgic solutions. Second, the continuing presence of a thinly disguised ideological content which is primarily connected with the leadership novels. Thus the main concern has been to show that the post-1925 period is marked by a non-social and naive utopianism which also contains important elements from the power utopia of the leadership years. In both cases the importance of Lawrence's German experience has been stressed. It is now time to turn to Lawrence's last statement, the strange and powerful *Apocalypse*, and examine how it relates to the main themes discussed in the preceding chapters.

Apocalypse

Apocalypse is a small but surprisingly complex work, containing a bewildering mixture of violent rejections and passionate visions. It is loud, self-contradictory, and generally unbalanced. Even so, it is a book to be reckoned with, and a work which quite effectively sums up the major concerns of Lawrence's artistic career.

Lawrence's immediate motivation for spending his remaining energy on a topic as obscure as the Revelation of St. John, was twofold. He very clearly felt this last book in the Bible epitomized the values embodied in the entire Christian tradition, and thus Western culture and civilization in general. Since these values had become obsolete and ultimately destructive, a rejection of the book of Revelation was a fundamental prerequisite for a new vision of life to emerge. In addition, and to complicate matters, *Apocalypse* also contains a reinterpretation of the very book he rejected. Finding in Revelation traces of the old pagan vision he wanted to revive, Lawrence reinterpreted its *cosmic* dimension – the apocalypse and the millennium – into a purely *individual* experience of death and resurrection. This is explicitly stated in the discussion of the seven seals. Strongly influenced by James Pryse's *The Apocalypse Unsealed*, Lawrence writes: 'The sixth seal, the divesting of the spirit from the last living quick of the "I", this has been turned by the apocalyptist into a muddled cosmic calamity. . . . This cosmic calamity no doubt corresponds to the original final death of the initiate, when his very spirit is stripped off him and he knows death indeed, yet still keeps the final flame-point of life, down in Hades' (104–5). As a result, Lawrence does away with the whole notion of the millennium of the beyond and secures the essential this-worldliness of his vision.

Thus *Apocalypse* is intended as a radical rejection of Revelation as it is generally perceived, but there remain several problems. Lawrence himself acknowledges the power of Revelation. In a famous passage from the introduction to Frederick Carter's *The Dragon of the Apocalypse*, he describes how, during his whole childhood, he was surrounded by apocalyptic language and apocalyptic images: 'I did not even listen attentively. But language has a power of echoing and re-echoing in my unconscious mind. . . . The very sound itself registers. And so the sound of Revelation had registered in me very early . . .' (*Ap*, 54–5). In *Apocalypse*, he says that these portions of the Bible 'became soaked in, they became an influence which affected all the processes of emotion and thought' (59).

This is the main reason why Lawrence's *Apocalypse* emerges, not as a consistent repudiation of Revelation, but rather as an alternative vision which retains all the basic elements of traditional apocalypticism. The apocalyptic framework was simply so powerful and so deeply ingrained in his consciousness that he was incapable of launching a new vision which was not itself based upon it.

There are several examples in *Apocalypse* of this slip into the very framework he rejected. For instance, having just described the sun and the moon as the two great points of contact between man and the cosmos, he writes: 'If we get out of contact and harmony with the sun and moon, then both turn into great dragons of destruction against us' (77). Lawrence thus envisages exactly the kind of 'cosmic calamity' which was earlier dismissed as an escapist invention of St. John. Just a couple of pages later, he relates how, particularly after the Reformation, the mechanistic principle has conquered the world: 'It is the long, slow death of society which parallels the quick death of Jesus and the other dying gods. It is death none the less, and will end in the annihilation of the human race – as John of Patmos so fervently hoped – unless there is a change, a resurrection and a return to the cosmos' (79). Lawrence then – like the prophets before him – raises a finger in warning, and calls for repentance. Clearly, the threat of annihilation of the human race is no less drastic than that of eternal fire. Also, John of Patmos was not alone in actively welcoming the Day of Wrath. Connie, in *John Thomas and Lady Jane*, was similarly longing for a world in ruins. Moreover, in the section on the meaning of the dragons, Lawrence presents a world view which is a direct reflection of the clear-cut division in Revelation between the forces of good and evil. The only difference is that evil, in Lawrence's Nietzschean transvaluation, has become good, and good evil. 'The green dragon [= good] becomes with time the red dragon [= evil]. What was our joy and our salvation becomes with time, at the end of the time era, our bane and our damnation. . . . And the Logos, the good dragon of the beginning of the cycle is now the evil dragon of today. . . . It is the red dragon, and it must once more be slain by the heroes, since we can expect no more from the angels' (125).

Essentially, Lawrence envisages only two ways of breaking away from the evil present into a new reality: either the religious *katharsis* of the apocalypse; or the more naive return, as in 'A Dream of Life', to a future modelled on a distant past. In *Apocalypse*, he claims that 'the consciousness of man always tends to revert to the original levels; though there are two modes of reversion: by degeneration and decadence; and by deliberate return in order to get back to the roots again, for a new start' (137).

The final and perhaps the clearest example of Lawrence's use of the vision he rejected, appears during his discussion of the individual and the state. Here he claims that Jesus – who was only concerned with the qualities of the individual – left it to John of

Patmos 'to formulate the Christian vision of the Christian State', and this vision 'entails the destruction of all earthly power, and the rule of an oligarchy of martyrs (the Millennium)' (146). As was mentioned earlier, Lawrence clearly rejected this 'cosmic calamity' as a product of St. John's envious imagination. Suddenly, however, he turns round and assumes the voice of a chapel preacher: 'This destruction of all earthly power we are now moving towards. The oligarchy of martyrs began with Lenin, and apparently Mussolini is also a martyr. . . . When every country has its martyr-ruler, . . . what a strange, unthinkable world it will be! But it is coming: the *Apocalypse* is still a book to conjure with' (ibid.). No doubt, this comes close to acknowledging the *Apocalypse* as a guide to the more far-reaching implications of contemporary politics.

In a condensed form *Apocalypse* also contains a number of the main themes of Lawrence's career, among them the glorification of aristocracy and power, and of pagan primitivism. Underneath them all, there is the perpetual crux of the relationship between the sexes.

Revelation symbolizes for Lawrence the root as well as the essence of the Christian message as it has ruled the world for two millennia. It is a religion of the weak, and of the will-to-power among the weak. It is a religion of the masses of democratic mediocrity, and of their hatred for the natural superiority of the aristocrat. These masses of the 'pseudo-humble' are the driving force behind the longing for the end of the world. Thus Lawrence sees the modern mass society, in all its fuming sordidness, as the logical consequence of the vision of St. John: 'This is the spirit of society today, religious and political' (65). He does not seem to realize, however, that his protest is largely moving in a circle; that he was himself born and raised in this society; that he was infused with the dream of another, more perfect world; and that the power of his natural aristocrat is therefore embarrassingly similar to the vulgar will-to-power of the masses. This becomes particularly evident in a section on Russia, in which, once more, his alternative vision of aristocratic splendour emerges as surprisingly similar to the one he repudiates. First, he claims that Lenin continued the tradition of St. John by accomplishing 'the triumph over worldly power' and that he, consequently, 'had every quality of a saint' (70–1). He then goes on to praise the time of the Tsar, when 'every peasant was consummated in the old dash and gorgeousness of the nobles, and in the supreme splendour of the Tsar' (71). Similarly, in the essay 'The Grand Inquisitor', written at the same time, Lawrence claims that ordinary beings can only be brought in touch with the sun by letting 'the many accept the decision [of the few], with gratitude, and bow down to the few, in the hierarchy' (*Ph*, 290). But what is actually the difference between the pseudo-humble vulgarity of John of Patmos and the sunlit grandeur of Lawrence's aristocrat? The answer is: not very much. According to Lawrence, in Revelation the pseudo-humble masses look to their god and take comfort from the promise of a splendid life in the beyond. According to Lawrence's own vision, the masses are not pseudo-humble, but properly humble, and they look to their *vicarius dei*, their lord and aristocrat, taking comfort from the promise that he will put the sun into their hearts. In both versions, the masses are the compliant instruments of the lord's will, and both are rewarded with a share in the glory which they can only attain through their lord. As with all aristocratic thinkers who praise the virtues of humble service, the uncomfortable fact remains that the aristocrat himself is the last person willing to accept the part of the servant. The defender of aristocracy invariably regards himself as an aristocrat, who would naturally assume the position of lord and master. This is precisely the case with Lawrence – 'life is more vivid in me, than in the Mexican who drives the wagon for me' (*RDP*, 357) – which leaves him open to the accusation that he is himself possessed by the same vulgar will-to-power and the same inferiority complex as the pseudo-humble followers of St. John.

This crucial flaw in Lawrence's argument is most evident in the relationship between the sexes. In *Apocalypse*, as in the leadership novels and *Lady Chatterley's Lover*, woman is granted only a subordinate role. According to old myth, 'it is woman who falls most absolutely into the power of the dragon, and has no power of escape till man frees her' (125). She is in the same position in relation to the man as the coarse majority in relation to the aristocrat. She receives her being from the man, like the moon which reflects the light of the sun. Furthermore, she is again connected to the dying wave of the feminine Christian culture, since no one is 'coiled more bitterly in the folds of the old Logos than woman' (126).

Once again, Lawrence's answer is a return to a pagan world dominated by the male power of the phallus. It remains unclear whether all men, or just a chosen few, are aristocrats of phallic splendour. However, the all-important role of the male seems to be beyond dispute. 'Suddenly we feel again the nostalgia for the old pagan world, long before John's day, we feel an immense yearning to be freed from this petty personal entanglement of weak life . . .'

(75–6). This period, which was 'perhaps the last phase of the great cosmic worship of power' (171), certainly contained for Lawrence all the glory and all the power that the pseudo-humble masses could ever manage to conjure up in their vision of the New Jerusalem. Only they were content with a heaven above, whereas Lawrence hoped for a heaven on earth.

Notes

Introduction

1 'Apocalypticism', *Encyclopædia Britannica*, 1985 ed.

Chapter 1

1 Frank Kermode (1971) p. 159.
2 Norman Cohn (1957), pp. 310–11.
3 Hans Blumenberg (1983), p. 42.
4 Frank Kermode (1967), p. 29.
5 Stephen Spender (1935), p. 224.
6 Admittedly, the terms 'this-worldly' and 'this-worldliness' are a rather unsatisfactory translation of the German 'diesseitig' and 'Diesseitigkeit' (contr. 'jenseitig' and 'Jenseitigkeit'). However, as the best English alternative seems to be 'secular', which contains only a part of the important contrast implied in the German terms, I have decided to prefer clarity of meaning before style. (Ref. p. 24.)
7 Marjorie Reeves (1985).
8 Karl Löwith (1949), p. 148.
9 Frank E. Manuel and Fritzie P. Manuel (1979), p. 57.
10 Ibid.
11 An interesting indication of this is Rolf Gardiner's claim that when he read *Twilight in Italy* as a young man, he immediately associated Lawrence's ideas of the Holy Ghost with Joachim, of whom Gardiner was aware. Edward Nehls ed. (1959), vol. III, p. 73.
12 In their book *Joachim of Fiore and the Myth of the Eternal Evangel in the Nineteenth Century*, which contains a whole chapter on Lawrence and Joachim, Marjorie Reeves and Warwick Gould (1987) offer a number of rather vague suggestions as to exactly how Lawrence came across Joachim. And in his review of this book in the *TLS*, Frank Kermode continues these speculations (No. 4,408, Sept. 25–Oct. 1, 1987, pp. 1054–5). This work by Salimbene, however, which seems to be the only certain reference, has so far been ignored.
13 It should also be mentioned that Joachim occurs in the Paradise of Dante's *Divine Comedy*, with which Lawrence was well acquainted.
14 An apropos to Lawrence and Poe: In October 1921 – well before the final rewriting of *Studies in Classic American Literature* – Lawrence read Emil Lucka's (1916) book *Grenzen der Seele* (see pp. 108–9), which contains a long section on Poe (pp. 111–26). At times Lucka and Lawrence argue along very similar lines – especially when discussing the role of murder in Poe's writings.

15 Marjorie Reeves and Warwick Gould (1987), p. 288.
16 Manuel and Manuel (1979), p. 57.
17 Arnold J. Toynbee (1948), p. 15.
18 Daniel Schneider (1984), p. 106.
19 Ibid.
20 Keith Sagar, ed. (1982), p. 82.
21 Frederick Copleston (1965), VII, Part 2, pp. 190–1.
22 Helena Blavatsky (1910), I, pp. 293–4.
23 Baruch Hochman (1970), p. 237.
24 Blavatsky (1910), vol. I, pp. 151–2. An almost identical passage is found in Carlyle (1887), pp. 18–19.
25 Zelia Nuttall (1901), pp. 252–3.
26 John Gross (1971), p. 84.
27 Graham Hough (1961; first published 1949), p. 246.
28 The language is certainly strange in this passage. Whereas the *Phoenix II* edition has the more likely 'That is one time when Jesus', etc., the new Cambridge edition has 'That is one thing where Jesus', etc.
29 Oswald Spengler (1923), I, p. 69.
30 H. Stuart Hughes (1952), p. 10.
31 The following section, dealing with heroic-totalitarian ideas in relation to universal history, will also serve as a general introduction to the more detailed discussion of the background to Lawrence's political ideas in chapter 4.
32 Walter E. Houghton (1959), pp. 314–15.
33 Arnold Hauser (1977), III, p. 201.
34 Houghton (1959), p. 337.
35 Friedrich Nietzsche (1987), p. 42.
36 Nietzsche (1979), p. 58.
37 Löwith (1949), p. 42.
38 Manuel and Manuel (1979), p. 760.
39 John A. Lester Jr. (1968), p. 41.
40 Lillian Feder (1971), p. 276.

Chapter 2

1 Though for the most part written in 1915, 'The Crown' was not published in full until 1925. In the new Cambridge edition, however, the 1915 variants have been provided, so that the original text can be reconstructed. Because the present chapter deals primarily with the war years, all quotes from 'The Crown' are taken from the 1915 version.
2 It is interesting to note here the connection between Loerke and the Norse god Loki (ref. note 4): significantly, Loki was the god who announced the end of the world.
3 Hochman (1970), p. 116.
4 It is not my intention, of course, to claim that Gerald, all through the novel, is solely modelled on Hades. Donald R. Eastman (1976) has very convincingly shown that Gerald also carries features of Geri, the wolf of the Norse god Odin, of another Norse god Loki, and of Hermes, Cain and Dionysus. The links with Hades, however, are a further demonstration of Gerald's close relationship with the forces of destruction.
5 Robert Chamberlain (1963, p. 410) gives a very different version of the name Minette, connecting it with Mino, the cat in the novel which puts his female in place. Lawrence changed the name from Pussum to Minette because of a threat of a libel suit from Philip Heseltine.

6 *New Larousse Encyclopedia of Mythology* (1987), p. 152.
7 Ibid.
8 For an alternative discussion of this chapter, see Colin Clarke (1969), pp. 76–9.
9 *New Larousse Encyclopedia of Mythology* (1987), p. 131.
10 Charles Ross (1977), p. 6.
11 Hochman (1970), p. 113.
12 Michael D. Biddiss (1977), p. 185.
13 As Lawrence would know from his reading of both Frazer and Tylor, the oak was a sacred tree, particularly to the Germans.
14 Luke, ii.19.
15 Having quoted Lawrence's verbal massacre of *Ghosts*, one is tempted to point out the obvious parallels, though probably accidental, between Ibsen's drama and *Women in Love*. Both the Criches and the Albings are haunted by a curse which cannot be put right. The life of Osvald, like that of Gerald, is a 'living death' (Ibsen, 1986, p. 73), and both of them regard their chosen woman as their 'only salvation' (ibid., p. 78). Altogether, it is difficult to see where Ibsen's criticism of contemporary society is radically different from that of Lawrence.
16 Miller (1985), p. 49.
17 Lester (1968), p. 4.
18 Esmé Wingfield-Stratford (1933), p. 27.
19 Samuel Hynes (1968), pp. 17–32.
20 J. B. Priestly (1972), p. 229.
21 Ibid., p. 253.
22 Wingfield-Stratford (1933), pp. 57–70.
23 Hynes (1968), p. 53.
24 Ibid., pp. 43–4.
25 Lascelles Abercrombie (1922), p. 148.
26 Ibid., p. 162.
27 *New Larousse Encyclopedia of Mythology* (1987), p. 276.
28 Vladimir Soloviev (1915), pp. 174–5.
29 Ibid., p. 180.
30 Josephine Preston Peabody (1917), p. 77.
31 Ibid., p. 37.
32 Holbrook Jackson (1976), p. 18.
33 *The New Age*, March 7, 1908.
34 William J. Brazill (1981), p. 533.
35 For a good summary of Nietzschean elements in Lawrence, see John B. Humma (1974), pp. 110–20 and Eleanor H. Green (1974), pp. 141–61. For a more recent and comprehensive study, see Colin Milton (1987).
36 Robert Lucas (1973), p. 131.
37 Wingfield-Stratford (1933), p. 121.
38 Houghton (1959), p. 58.
39 Alan D. Gilbert (1976), pp. 185–6.
40 Ibid., pp. 202–3.
41 Jessie Chambers (1980), p. 84.
42 Gilbert (1976), p. 174.
43 Lester (1968), pp. 30–1.
44 William Y. Tindall (1956), pp. 150–1.
45 Joseph Conrad, quoted by Edward Said (1966), p. 34.
46 Hough (1961), p. 106.
47 John Fowles, Introd., *After London*, by Richard Jefferies (1980), p. viii.
48 Blavatsky (1910), I, p. 5.
49 Ibid., p. 38.
50 Hynes (1968), p. 150.
51 Edward Carpenter (1902), p. 25.
52 Edward Carpenter (1912), p. 31.

53 Ernst Haeckel (1950), p. 6.
54 Ibid., pp. 10–11.
55 Ibid., p. 304.
56 Ibid., pp. 199–200.

Chapter 3

1 Lester (1968), p. 5.
2 For the sake of simplicity, the term *utopianism* will be used in the following to denote not only the above mentioned crossbreed of religious and secular ideas concerning society at large, but also ideas regarding the fate of the individual, or, to use a religious term, ideas of personal salvation.
3 Harry T. Moore (1980), p. 484.
4 W. H. G. Armytage (1961), pp. 394–5. The mentioning of Pantisocracy, of course, refers to the plans of Coleridge and Robert Southey to establish a utopian commune in New England. This may well have been a source of inspiration for the Rananim.
5 Anthony Burgess (1986), p. 64.
6 Keith Brown (1990), pp. 23–37.
7 Hochman (1970), p. 166.
8 Copleston (1965), p. 172.
9 Tindall (1956), p. 223.
10 A. L. LeQuesne (1982), p. 26.
11 In their book *Anti-Oedipus*, Deleuze and Guattari (1977) give a more positive evaluation of Lawrence's criticism of Freud: 'D. H. Lawrence – who does not struggle against Freud in the name of the rights of the Ideal, but who speaks by virtue of the flows of sexuality and the intensities of the unconscious, and who is incensed and bewildered by what Freud is doing when he closets sexuality in the Oedipal nursery – has a foreboding of this operation of displacement, and protests with all his might. No, Oedipus is not a state of desire and the drives, it is an idea, nothing but an idea that repression inspires in us concerning desire; not even a compromise, but an idea in the service of repression, its propaganda, or its propagation' (p. 115).
12 Hynes (1968), p. 147.
13 Lester (1968), pp. 83–4.
14 Carpenter (1912), pp. 113–14.
15 Ibid., p. 257.
16 As will be shown later, however, the sun is also closely connected with male power.
17 Edward B. Tylor (1873), II, p. 8.
18 Blavatsky (1910), II, p. 490.
19 The following section can be read as an introduction to the more comprehensive discussion of *Lady Chatterley's Lover* in chapter 6.
20 Hynes (1968), p. 171.
21 Horace Gregory (1934), p. 6.
22 Ibid.
23 Lester (1968), pp. 70–1.
24 I will return to Green's book in chapters 4 and 5.
25 Martin Green (1974), p. 54.
26 Revelations, xxi.5.
27 Ref. Genesis, vi.4.
28 James Hall (1979), pp. 291–2.

29 Father William Tiverton (1951), p. 96.
30 Percy B. Shelley (1927), II, p. 400.

Chapter 4

1 Cohn (1957), p. 307.
2 Ibid., p. 308.
3 Raymond Williams (1958), p. 202.
4 Paul Johnson (1984), p. 4.
5 Ibid., p. 11.
6 Ibid., p. 20.
7 F. L. Carsten (1973), p. 127.
8 Johnson (1984), p. 15.
9 Hynes (1968), p. 14.
10 Richard Thurlow (1987), p. 22.
11 Ibid., pp. 16–17.
12 Johnson (1984), p. 5.
13 Lucas (1973), p. 34.
14 Ibid., p. 20.
15 Ernst Nolte (1965), p. 10.
16 Robert Musil (1979), I, p. 70.
17 Fritz Stern (1974), p. xvi.
18 George L. Mosse (1964), p. 123.
19 Ibid., p. 108.
20 Ibid.
21 Ibid., pp. 111–12.
22 Ibid., p. 115.
23 Ibid., p. 116.
24 Ibid., p. 176.
25 Ibid., p. 212.
26 Ibid., p. 213.
27 Ibid.
28 Ibid., p. 214.
29 Ibid., pp. 214–15.
30 See especially Blüher (1921), vol. 2, part 1: 'Die Frau und die Familie', pp. 7–87. There is no doubt that the Wandervogel movement had a considerable following in Germany around the First World War. Blüher claims that: 'Heute zählt der Wandervogel nach vielen Zehntausenden', p. 113. As to the homo-erotic aspects of the movement – highly relevant for an understanding of short stories like 'The Prussian Officer' – see the chapter 'Die militärischen Kameraderien' in Blüher, pp. 154–77, which gives detailed descriptions, including diary notes by young soldiers, of life in the military *Kadettenhaus* and of the erotic relationships between the *Obertertianer* and the *Untertertianer*. As one soldier puts it: 'Es kam zu stürmischen Umarmungen, heissen Küssen, schliesslich zum geschlechtlichen Verkehr. Für uns war es alles so natürlich, keiner dachte an Pathologie oder Kriminalität; es war für uns ganz selbstverständlich' (p. 158). For a full bibliography of literature related to the German youth movement in general, see Karl Krausze (1939), pp. 151–7.
31 Stern (1974), p. xiv.
32 Ibid., p. xxviii.
33 Mosse (1964), p. 207.
34 Ibid., p. 210.
35 Ibid.

36 Eric R. Bentley (1947), p. 198.
37 Ibid., p. 204.
38 Mosse (1964), p. 284.
39 Nolte (1965), p. 150.
40 David D. Roberts (1979), p. 195.
41 Manuel and Manuel (1979), p. 750.
42 Ibid.
43 Ibid., p. 752.
44 Ibid. Another famous thinker, whose ideas resulted in a similar kind of heroic élitism, was the Italian Vilfredo Pareto, who claimed that the 'great revolutions had been no more than the struggle of one élite to displace an old one – with the "people" serving as its humble soldiers'. H. Stuart Hughes (1974), p. 81.
45 Nolte (1965), p. 149.
46 Roberts (1979), p. 179.
47 Nolte (1965), p. 187.
48 Johnson (1984), p. 96.
49 Manuel and Manuel (1979), p. 433.
50 Richard Gerber (1955), p. 11.
51 Winwood Reade (1910), p. 538.
52 Hauser (1977), III, p. 73.
53 Manuel and Manuel (1979), p. 444.
54 Stern (1974), p. xvii.
55 Jack J. Roth (1980), p. 160.
56 Ibid., p. 159.
57 F. M. Borras (1967), p. 48.
58 Ibid., p. 55.
59 Ibid., pp. 55–6.
60 Ibid., p. 56.
61 LeQuesne (1982), p. 64.
62 Ibid., p. 66.
63 Thomas Carlyle (1887), p. 14.
64 LeQuesne (1982), p. 55.
65 Hauser (1977), IV, p. 103.
66 Bentley (1947), p. 173.
67 Wilfred B. Trotter (1916), pp. 117–18.
68 Ibid., p. 163.
69 Ibid., p. 162.
70 Ibid., pp. 162–3.
71 Ibid., p. 163.
72 Biddiss (1977), p. 133.
73 A more humorous reference to Keyserling is found in a letter from 9 January 1930: 'Count Keyserling asked my sister-in-law to give him a copy of *Plumed Serpent* because he wants to write an article on it. Mean swine won't buy a copy!' (*Moore Letters*, vol. 2, p. 1232).
74 Franz Schoenberner (1965), p. 320.
75 Emile Delavenay (1972), p. 303.
76 Ibid., p. 255.
77 Emil Lucka (1916), p. 19.
78 Ibid., p. 20.
79 Armin Arnold (1963), p. 34.
80 Jethro Bithell (1909), p. xx.
81 *Zwei Menschen* offers interesting associations both to *Women in Love* and to a number of Lawrence's short stories and poems from Germany. Major parts of the novel are set in the mountains, with snow and moon as important images. The following passage, furthermore, gives an impression of the erotic frankness of Dehmel's verse (1908; vol. 5, pp. 119–20):

In uns, Seele, da träumt die Nacht;
aber hier, ein Hauch meines Mundes macht
diese dürre Insel – ja, schau sie an –
zum Paradies und Kanaan,
wo Adam sündlos bei Eva ruht,
wo der Tag glüht wie unser Fleish und Blut,
wo Alles Frucht ist am reinen Leib der Liebe,
selbst der Halm dort im Sandgetriebe!
selbst der Salzgeruch, der von der Küste
herquillt an deine braunen Brüste
und Milch aus deinem Mutterblut braut!
selbst deine honigwabengoldne Haut,
und deines Schoosses glückstrotzender Schwung,
und meiner Mannheit Verkörperung!

82 R. Ensor (1909), p. 448.
83 Ibid., p. 450.
84 Martin Green (1974), pp. 30–1.
85 Biddiss (1977), p. 161.
86 Anthony Rhodes (1959), p. 48.
87 A. L. French (1979), p. 66.
88 R. W. Flint, Introd., in Marinetti (1972), p. 7.
89 Ibid., p. 5.
90 Ibid., p. 33.
91 Filippo Tommaso Marinetti (1972), pp. 41–2. For a more comprehensive discussion of Lawrence and Futurism, see Kim A. Herzinger (1982), pp. 127–40.

Chapter 5

1 Some of course would argue that this is precisely Lawrence's point: *not* to arrive at a final conclusion, but rather to regard the movement, the vibrations and the flows as the objects of desire. Ref. Deleuze and Guattari (1977), who strongly emphasize this aspect of Lawrence's ideological exploration.
2 Mosse (1964), p. 215. The dialectic between sun and moon is an interesting one in Lawrence. In *Women in Love*, for instance, there is a passage which may indicate that Lawrence was aware of Lomer's ideas. In the chapter 'Snowed Up', in which Gerald dies, the moon is powerfully connected with Gudrun. While Gerald is climbing up the mountain, the moon, previously not mentioned, suddenly appears: 'To add to his difficulty, a small bright moon shone brilliantly just ahead, on the right, a painful brilliant thing that was always there, unremitting, from which there was no escape' (p. 473). Clearly, this is the ghost of Gudrun driving Gerald to his death, and it could be seen as a counterpart to Birkin's dramatic stoning of the image of the moon in the pond earlier in the novel, only Birkin does not succumb, the way Gerald does, to the power of the female.
3 One certain indication that Lawrence must have been aware of Weininger, is from October 1921. Then he read Emil Lucka's *Grenzen der Seele* (1916), which was discussed in the previous chapter. In this book Lucka has a number of references to Weininger's work *Sex and Character*. It should also be added that Lucka was a close friend of Weininger, and that he wrote a book about him as early as 1905: *Otto Weininger: Sein Werk und seine Persönlichkeit*. Lawrence also mentions Weininger in his review from February 1929 of V. V. Rozanov's *Fallen Leaves, Phoenix*, p. 392.
4 Delavenay (1972), p. 342.

5 In Lawrence the word occurs both as *Blutbruderschaft* and *Blutbrüderschaft*. Both forms are valid in German.
6 Jeffrey Meyers (1990) claims that this and other 'overt homosexual scenes' in Lawrence are 'modeled on the biblical friendship of David and Jonathan' (p. 207). Though this point should not be ignored, it does not take into consideration Lawrence's explicit use of the German term, which clearly points in another direction.
7 Marinetti (1972), p. 42.
8 Leviticus, viii.12.
9 R. P. Draper (1959), p. 211.
10 Graham Hough (1975), p. 112.
11 Manuel and Manuel (1979), p. 351.
12 Apropos of Whitman, Lawrence started rewriting *Studies of Classic American Literature* a month after finishing *Kangaroo*.
13 Robert Darroch (1981), p. 84.
14 Ibid., p. 88.
15 Chambers (1980), p. 202.
16 Mosse (1964), p. 313.
17 John, xx.15.
18 Luke, xxiv.30.

Chapter 6

1 In *John Thomas and Lady Jane* the verb is 'fallen' instead of 'happened', suggesting more strongly the religious character of the event.
2 It may not be a coincidence that the name Wragby is actually connected with a word meaning a 'burial-mound'. Ref. Eilert Ekwall (1985), p. 537.
3 Stephen Gill (1971), p. 359.
4 *New Larousse Encyclopedia of Mythology* (1987), p. 161.
5 Ibid., p. 123.
6 Ibid., p. 161.
7 Moore (1980), p. 532.
8 Knut Merrild (1964), p. 88.
9 Despite the limited interest in Hamsun in Britain, Lawrence was clearly aware of his towering position on the Continent, particularly in Germany, where *Pan* had gone through eighteen editions by the time it was first translated into English. Thus, Lawrence may have read *Pan* in German before 1920. It is also interesting that Lawrence mentions another of Hamsun's works as early as May 1920. In a letter he says that he has seen the manuscript of a translation of '*Love's Tragedy* – by Knut Hamsun, 4 act – a famous thing, unknown in England'. (*The Letters*, vol. III, p. 532). And the translator was Maurice Magnus, Lawrence's acquaintance who committed suicide at Malta a few months later.
10 Knut Hamsun (1920), p. 60. The quotes are taken from the 1920 edition, which Lawrence most probably read – unless he read it in German.
11 Ibid., p. 29.
12 Ibid., pp. 3–4.
13 Ibid., p. 81.
14 As mentioned in chapter 2, 'The Crown', which is one part of *Reflections*, was mainly written in 1915, and is therefore largely irrelevant to the present discussion.
15 Kenneth Muir (1961), p. 21.
16 Gill (1971), p. 356.

17 Ref. the apocalyptic game played by Loerke and Gudrun in *Women in Love*, in which they envisage a world split in two.
18 Nehls (1957–59), III, p. 72.
19 Ibid., p. 82.
20 Ibid., p. 83.
21 W. J. Keith (1974), pp. 127–38.
22 Karl Scheffler (1869–1951) was a prominent German art historian who also wrote essays of cultural criticism.
23 Mosse (1964), p. 313.

Bibliography

This bibliography includes all the works quoted from or referred to in the book, but only the more important of the additional works consulted.

LAWRENCE'S WORK

Aaron's Rod. Ed. Mara Kalnins. 1922; Cambridge: Cambridge University Press, 1988 (*AR*).

Apocalypse and the Writings on Revelation. Ed. Mara Kalnins. Cambridge: Cambridge University Press, 1980 (*Ap*).

A Propos of Lady Chatterley's Lover and Other Essays. Harmondsworth: Penguin Books, 1967 (*APLCL*).

Collected Letters of D. H. Lawrence, The. Ed. Harry T. Moore. 2 vols. London: Heinemann, 1965 (*CL*).

England, My England and Other Stories. Ed. Bruce Steele. 1922; Cambridge: Cambridge University Press, 1990 (*EME*).

Escaped Cock, The. Paris: The Black Sun Press, 1929 (*TEC*).

Etruscan Places. In *D. H. Lawrence and Italy*. 1932; Harmondsworth: Penguin Books, 1985 (*EP*).

Fantasia of the Unconscious and Psychoanalysis and the Unconscious. 1922, 1921; Harmondsworth: Penguin Books, 1986 (*FU*).

First Lady Chatterley, The. 1944; Harmondsworth: Penguin Books, 1986 (*TFLC*).

John Thomas and Lady Jane. 1972; Harmondsworth: Penguin Books, 1986 (*JTLJ*).

Kangaroo. 1923; Harmondsworth: Penguin Books, 1985 (*Ka*).

Lady Chatterley's Lover. 1928; Harmondsworth: Penguin Books, 1987 (*LCL*).

Letters of D. H. Lawrence: September 1901–May 1913, The. Ed. James T. Boulton. Vol. I. Cambridge: Cambridge University Press, 1979 (*Le I*).

Letters of D. H. Lawrence: June 1913–October 1916, The. Eds. George J. Zytaruk and James T. Boulton. Vol. II. Cambridge: Cambridge University Press, 1981 (*Le II*).

Letters of D. H. Lawrence: October 1916–June 1921, The. Eds. James T. Boulton and Andrew Robertson. Vol. III. Cambridge: Cambridge University Press, 1984 (*Le III*).

Letters of D. H. Lawrence: June 1921–March 1924, The. Eds. Warren Roberts, James T. Boulton and Elizabeth Mansfield. Vol. IV. Cambridge: Cambridge University Press, 1987 (*Le IV*).

Letters of D. H. Lawrence: March 1924–March 1927, The. Eds. James T. Boulton and Lindeth Vasey. Vol. V. Cambridge: Cambridge University Press, 1989 (*Le V*).

Lost Girl, The. Ed. John Worthen. 1920; Cambridge: Cambridge University Press, 1981 (*TLG*).

Mornings in Mexico. In *Mornings in Mexico and Etruscan Places*. 1927; Harmondsworth: Penguin Books, 1967 (*MM*).
Mortal Coil and Other Stories, The. Harmondsworth: Penguin Books, 1980 (*TMC*).
Movements in European History. 1921; Oxford: Oxford University Press, 1981 (*MEH*).
Phoenix: The Posthumous Papers of D. H. Lawrence. Ed. Edward D. McDonald. 1936; London: Heinemann, 1967 (*Ph*).
Phoenix II: Uncollected, Unpublished and Other Prose Works by D. H. Lawrence. Eds. Warren Roberts and Harry T. Moore. London: Heinemann, 1968 (*Ph II*).
Plumed Serpent, The. Ed. L. D. Clarke. 1926; Cambridge: Cambridge University Press, 1987 (*TPS*).
Princess and Other Stories, The. Harmondsworth: Penguin Books, 1981 (*TP*).
Rainbow, The. Ed. Mark Kinkead-Weekes. 1915; Cambridge: Cambridge University Press, 1989 (*TR*).
Reflections on the Death of a Porcupine and Other Essays. Ed. Michael Herbert. Cambridge: Cambridge University Press, 1988 (*RDP*).
Sea and Sardinia. In *D. H. Lawrence and Italy*. 1921; Harmondsworth: Penguin Books, 1985 (*SS*).
Selected Poems. Ed. Keith Sagar. 1972; Harmondsworth: Penguin Books, 1984 (*SP*).
Studies in Classic American Literature. N.Y., 1923; Harmondsworth: Penguin Books, 1986 (*SCAL*).
Study of Thomas Hardy and Other Essays. Ed. Bruce Steele. Cambridge: Cambridge University Press, 1985 (*SThH*).
Twilight in Italy. In *D. H. Lawrence and Italy*. 1916; Harmondsworth: Penguin Books, 1985 (*TI*).
Virgin and the Gipsy, The. 1930; Harmondsworth: Penguin Books, 1974 (*TVG*).
Women in Love. Eds. David Farmer, Lindeth Vasey and John Worthen. 1920; Cambridge: Cambridge University Press, 1987 (*WL*).

OTHER SOURCES

Abercrombie, Lascelles. 1922. *Four Short Plays*. London: Martin Secker.
Armytage, W. H. G. 1961. *Heavens Below: Utopian Experiments in England 1560–1960*. London: Routledge & Kegan Paul.
Arnold, Armin, ed. 1962. *The Symbolic Meaning: The Uncollected Versions of 'Studies in Classic American Literature'*. Fontwell: Centaur Press.
Arnold, Armin. 1963. *D. H. Lawrence and German Literature: With Two Hitherto Unknown Essays by D.H.Lawrence*. Montreal: Heinemann.
Belt, Thomas. 1911. *The Naturalist in Nicaragua*. 1874; London: J. M. Dent & Sons.
Bentley, Eric R. 1947. *The Cult of the Superman: A Study of the Idea of Heroism in Carlyle and Nietzsche, with Notes on Other Hero-Worshippers of Modern Times*. London: Robert Hale Ltd.
Biddiss, Michael D. 1977. *The Age of the Masses: Ideas and Society in Europe Since 1870*. New York: Harper & Row.
Bithell, Jethro, ed. 1909. *Contemporary German Poetry*. London: The Walter Scott Publishing Co.
Blavatsky, Helena P. 1910. *Isis Unveiled: A Master-Key to the Mysteries of Ancient and Modern Science and Theology*. 2 vols. 1877; London: The Theosophical Publishing Society.

Blüher, Hans. 1921. *Die Rolle der Erotik in der männlichen Gesellschaft: Eine Theorie der menschlichen Staatsbildung nach Wesen und Wert*. 2 vols. 1917; Jena: Eugen Diederichs.

Blüher, Hans. 1922. *Die deutsche Wandervogelbewegung als erotisches Phänomen: Ein Beitrag zur Erkenntnis der sexuellen Inversion*. 1912; Prien: Kampmann & Schnabel.

Blüher, Hans. 1922. *Wandervogel: Geschichte einer Jugendbewegung*. 1912; Prien: Kampmann & Schnabel.

Blumenberg, Hans. 1983. *The Legitimacy of the Modern Age*. Trans. R. M. Wallace (Frankfurt am Main, 1966) London: MIT Press.

Borras, F.M. 1967. *Maxim Gorky the Writer: An Interpretation*. Oxford: Clarendon Press.

Bradbury, Malcolm and James McFarlane, eds. 1986. *Modernism. 1890–1930*. Harmondsworth: Penguin Books.

Brazill, William J. 1981. 'Art and "The Panic Terror"'. In *The Turn of the Century: German Literature and Art 1890–1915*. Eds. Gerald Chapple and Hans H. Schulte. Bonn: Bouvier Verlag.

Brown, Keith. 1990. 'Welsh Red Indians: D. H. Lawrence and *St. Mawr*'. In *Rethinking Lawrence*. Ed. Keith Brown. Milton Keynes: Open University Press.

Burgess, Anthony. 1986. *Flame into Being: The Life and Work of D. H. Lawrence*. 1985; London: Heinemann.

Carlyle, Thomas. 1887. *On Heroes, Hero-Worship and the Heroic in History*. 1841; London: Chapman & Hall.

Carpenter, Edward. 1902. *Civilization Its Cause and Cure and Other Essays*. 1889; London: Swan Sonnenschein & Co.

Carpenter, Edward. 1912. *The Drama of Love and Death: A Study of Human Evolution and Transfiguration*. London: George Allen & Co.

Carsten, F. L. 1973. 'The Historical Roots of National Socialism'. In *Upheaval and Continuity: A Century of German History*. Ed. E. J. Feuchtwanger. London: Oswald Wolff.

Chamberlain, Robert L. 1963. 'Pussum, Minette, and the Africo-Nordic Symbol in Lawrence's *Women in Love*'. *PMLA*, 78, pp. 407–16.

Chambers, Jessie. 1980. *D. H. Lawrence: A Personal Record*. Cambridge: Cambridge University Press.

Clark, L. D. 1970. 'The Apocalypse of Lorenzo'. *D. H. Lawrence Review*, vol. 3, no. 2 (Summer), pp. 141–60.

Clarke, Colin. 1969. *River of Dissolution: D. H. Lawrence & English Romanticism*. London: Routledge & Kegan Paul.

Cohn, Norman. 1957. *The Pursuit of the Millennium: Revolutionary Messianism in Medieval and Reformation Europe and Its Bearing on Modern Totalitarian Movements*. London: Secker & Warburg.

Copleston, Frederick. 1965. *Modern Philosophy: Schopenhauer to Nietzsche*. Vol. VII, Part II of *A History of Philosophy*. 1963; New York: Image Books.

Coulton, G. G. 1907. *From St. Francis to Dante: Translations from the Chronicle of the Franciscan Salimbene*. London: David Nutt.

Daleski, H. M. 1965. *The Forked Flame: A Study of D. H. Lawrence*. London: Faber & Faber.

Darroch, Robert. 1981. *D. H. Lawrence in Australia*. South Melbourne: Macmillan.

Dehmel, Richard. 1908. *Aber die Liebe: Zwei Folgen Gedichte*. Vol. 2; *Zwei Menschen: Roman in Romanzen*. Vol. 5. *Gesammelte werke von Richard Dehmel*. 10 vols. Berlin: S. Fischer Verlag.

Delany, Paul. 1979. *D. H. Lawrence's Nightmare: The Writer and His Circle in the Years of the Great War*. Stanford Terrace, Sussex: The Harvester Press.

Delavenay, Emile. 1972. *D. H. Lawrence: The Man and His Work, The Formative Years: 1885–1919*. Trans. K. M. Delavenay. Paris, 1969; London: Heinemann.

Delavenay, Emile. 1987. 'Lawrence, Otto Weininger and "Rather Raw Philosophy"'. In *D. H. Lawrence New Studies*. Ed. Christopher Heywood. London: Macmillan Press, pp. 137–57.

Deleuze, Gilles and Felix Guattari. 1977. *Anti-Oedipus: Capitalism and Schizophrenia*. Trans. Robert Hurley. New York: Viking Press.

Draper, R. P. 1959. 'Authority and the Individual: A Study of D. H. Lawrence's "Kangaroo"'. *Critical Quarterly*, vol. 1 (Autumn), pp. 208–15.

Eastman, Donald R. 1976. 'Myth and Fate in the Characters of *Women in Love*'. *D. H. Lawrence Review*, vol. 9, no. 2 (Summer), pp. 177–93.

Ekwall, Eilert. 1985. *The Concise Oxford Dictionary of Place-names*. Oxford: Clarendon Press.

Ensor, R. C. K. 1909. 'Detlev von Liliencron'. *The Contemporary Review*, no. 526 (October), pp. 448–57.

Feder, Lillian. 1971. *Ancient Myth in Modern Poetry*. Princeton: Princeton University Press.

Frazer, Sir James George. 1983. *The Golden Bough: A Study in Magic and Religion*. 1890–1915; Abbr. ed. London: Macmillan Press.

French, A. L. 1979. '"The Whole Pulse of Social England": *Women in Love*'. *The Critical Review*, vol. 21, pp. 57–71.

George, Stefan. 1928. *Das neue Reich*. Berlin: Georg Bondi.

Gerber, Richard. 1955. *Utopian Fantasy: A Study of English Utopian Fiction since the End of the Nineteenth Century*. London: Routledge & Kegan Paul.

Gilbert, Alan D. 1976. *Religion and Society in Industrial England: Church, Chapel and Social Change 1740–1914*. London: Longman.

Gill, Stephen. 1971. 'The Composite World: Two Versions of *Lady Chatterley's Lover*'. *Essays in Criticism*, vol. 21, no. 4 (October), pp. 347–64.

Goodheart, Eugene. 1971. *The Utopian Vision of D. H. Lawrence*. 1963; Chicago: The University of Chicago Press.

Green, Eleanor H. 1974. 'Blueprints for Utopia: The Political Ideas of Nietzsche and D. H. Lawrence'. *Renaissance and Modern Studies*, vol. 18, pp. 141–61.

Green, Martin. 1974. *The von Richthofen Sisters: The Triumphant and the Tragic Modes of Love. Else and Frieda von Richthofen, Otto Gross, Max Weber, and D.H.Lawrence, in the Years 1870–1970*. London: Weidenfeld & Nicolson.

Gregory, Horace. 1934. *Pilgrim of the Apocalypse: A Critical Study of D. H. Lawrence*. London: Martin Secker.

Gross, John. 1971. *Joyce*. London: Fontana.

Gutierrez de Lara, L. and Edgeumb Pinchon. 1914. *The Mexican People: Their Struggle for Freedom*. Trans. E. Pinchon. New York: Doubleday, Page & Co.

Haeckel, Ernst. 1950. *The Riddle of the Universe*. Trans. Joseph McCabe. 1899; London: Watts & Co.

Hall, James. 1979. *Dictionary of Subjects and Symbols in Art*. New York: Harper & Row.

Hamsun, Knut. 1920. *Pan*. Trans. W. Worster. London: Gyldendal.

Hauser, Arnold. 1977. *The Social History of Art*. 4 vols. Trans. Stanley Godman and Arnold Hauser. 1951; London: Routledge & Kegan Paul.

Herzinger, Kim A. 1982. *D. H. Lawrence in His Time: 1908–1915*. Lewisburg: Bucknell University Press.

Hochman, Baruch. 1970. *Another Ego: The Changing View of Self and Society in the Work of D. H. Lawrence*. Columbia, S.C.: University of South Carolina Press.

Holy Bible, The: Authorized King James Version.

Hough, Graham. 1961. *The Last Romantics*. 1949; London: Methuen.

Hough, Graham. 1975. *The Dark Sun: A Study of D. H. Lawrence*. 1956; London: Duckworth.

Houghton, Walter E. 1959. *The Victorian Frame of Mind: 1830–1870*. 1957; New Haven: Yale University Press.

Hughes, H. Stuart. 1952. *Oswald Spengler: A Critical Estimate*. London: Charles Scribner's Sons.
Hughes, H. Stuart. 1974. *Consciousness and Society: The Reorientation of European Social Thought 1890–1930*. 1958; Frogmore, St.Albans: Granada.
Humma, John B. 1974. 'D. H. Lawrence as Friedrich Nietzsche'. *Philological Quarterly*, vol. 53 (Jan.), pp. 110–20.
Hynes, Samuel L. 1968. *The Edwardian Turn of Mind*. Princeton: Princeton University Press.
Ibsen, Henrik. 1986. *Ghosts*. In *Ghosts, A Public Enemy, When We Dead Wake*. Trans. Peter Watts. Oslo, 1881; Harmondsworth: Penguin Books.
Jackson, Holbrook. 1976. *The Eighteen Nineties: A Review of Art and Ideas at the Close of the Nineteenth Century*. 1913; Hassocks, Nr. Brighton: The Harvester Press.
Jefferies, Richard. 1980. *After London: or Wild England*. Intro. John Fowles. 1885; Oxford: Oxford University Press.
Johnson, Paul. 1984. *A History of the Modern World From 1917 to the 1980s*. London: Weidenfeld & Nicolson.
Jones, Alun R. 1960. *The Life and Opinions of T. E. Hulme*. London: Victor Gollancz.
Keith, W. J. 1974. 'Spirit of Place and *Genius Loci*: D. H. Lawrence and Rolf Gardiner'. *D. H. Lawrence Review*, vol. 7, no. 2 (Summer), pp. 127–38.
Kermode, Frank. 1967. *The Sense of an Ending: Studies in the Theory of Fiction*. New York (Oxford: Oxford University Press, 1968).
Kermode, Frank. 1971. *Modern Essays*. London: Fontana.
Kermode, Frank. 1976. *Lawrence*. 1973; London: Fontana.
Krausze, Karl. 1979. *Die Jugendbewegung im Spiegel Deutscher Dichtung*. Würzburg-Aumühle: Konrad Trieltsch Verlag.
Lawrence, Frieda. 1983. *'Not I, But the Wind'*. 1935; London: Granada.
LeQuesne, A. L. 1982. *Carlyle*. Oxford: Oxford University Press.
Lester Jr., John A. 1968. *Journey Through Despair 1880–1914: Transformations in British Literary Culture*. Princeton: Princeton University Press.
Löwith, Karl. 1949. *Meaning in History*. Chicago: Chicago University Press.
Lucas, Robert. 1973. *Frieda Lawrence: The Story of Frieda von Richthofen and D. H. Lawrence*. Trans. Geoffrey Skelton. Munich, 1972; London: Secker & Warburg.
Lucka, Emil. 1905. *Otto Weininger: Sein Werk und seine Persönlichkeit*. Wien: Wilhelm Braumüller.
Lucka, Emil. 1916. *Grenzen der Seele*. 1914; Berlin: Schuster & Loeffler.
MacDonald, James Ramsay. 1912. *Syndicalism: A Critical Examination*. London: Constable & Co.
Manuel, Frank E. and Fritzie P. Manuel. 1979. *Utopian Thought in the Western World*. Oxford: Basil Blackwell.
Marinetti, Filippo Tommaso. 1972. *Marinetti: Selected Writings*. Ed. and intro. R. W. Flint. London: Secker & Warburg.
Merrild, Knut. 1964. *With D. H. Lawrence in New Mexico: A Memoir of D. H. Lawrence*. 1938; London: Routledge & Kegan Paul.
Meyers, Jeffrey. 1990. *D. H. Lawrence: A Biography*. London: Macmillan.
Michaels-Tonks, Jennifer. 1976. *D. H. Lawrence, The Polarity of North and South: Germany and Italy in His Prose Works*. Bonn: Bouvier Verlag.
Miller, Henry. 1985. *The World of Lawrence: A Passionate Appreciation*. London: John Calder.
Milton, Colin. 1987. *Lawrence and Nietzsche: A Study in Influence*. Aberdeen: Aberdeen University Press.
Moore, Harry T. 1980. *The Priest of Love: A Life of D. H. Lawrence*. 1974; Harmondsworth: Penguin Books.
Mosse, George L. 1964. *The Crisis of German Ideology: Intellectual Origins of the Third Reich*. New York: Grosset & Dunlap.

Muir, Kenneth. 1961. 'The Three Lady Chatterleys'. *The Literary Half-Yearly*, vol. 2, no. 1 (Jan.), pp. 18–25.

Musil, Robert. 1979. *The Man Without Qualities*. Vol. I. Trans. Eithne Wilkins and Ernst Kaiser. 1930; London: Pan Books.

Nash, Christopher. 1980. 'Myth and Modern Literature'. In *The Context of English Literature 1900–1930*. Ed. Michael Bell. London: Methuen.

Nehls, Edward, ed. 1957–59. *D. H. Lawrence: A Composite Biography*. 3 vols. Madison: The University of Wisconsin Press.

New Larousse Encyclopedia of Mythology. 1987. Trans. Richard Aldington and Delano Ames. 1959; London: Hamlyn.

Nietzsche, Friedrich. 1979. *Ecce Homo: How One Becomes What One Is*. Trans. R. J. Hollingdale. 1908; Harmondsworth: Penguin Books.

Nietzsche, Friedrich. 1987. *Thus Spoke Zarathustra: A Book for Everyone and No One*. Trans. R. J. Hollingdale. 1883–5; Harmondsworth: Penguin Books.

Nolte, Ernst. 1965. *Three Phases of Fascism: Action Francaise, Italian Fascism, National Socialism*. Trans. Leila Vennewitz. Munich, 1963; London: Weidenfeld & Nicolson.

Nordau, Max. 1913. *Degeneration*. No trans. 1895; London: William Heinemann.

Nuttall, Zelia. 1901. *The Fundamental Principles of Old and New World Civilizations*. Cambridge, Mass.: Harvard University Press.

Peabody, Josephine Preston. 1917. *Harvest Moon*. London: Longmans, Green & Co.

Priestley, J. B. 1972. *The Edwardians*. 1970; London: Sphere Books.

Pryse, James M. 1910. *The Apocalypse Unsealed: Being an Esoteric Interpretation of the Initiation of Iônnês*. London: John M. Watkins.

Reade, Winwood. 1910. *The Martyrdom of Man*. 1872; London: Kegan Paul.

Reeves, Marjorie. 1985. 'Joachim of Fiore'. *Encyclopedia Britannica*.

Reeves, Marjorie and Warwick Gould. 1987. *Joachim of Fiore and the Myth of the Eternal Evangel in the Nineteenth Century*. Oxford: Clarendon Press.

Rhodes, Anthony. 1959. *The Poet as Superman: A Life of Gabriele D'Annunzio*. London: Weidenfeld & Nicolson.

Roberts, David D. 1979. *The Syndicalist Tradition and Italian Fascism*. Manchester: Manchester University Press.

Ross, Charles L. 1977. 'D. H. Lawrence's Use of Greek Tragedy: Euripides and Ritual'. *D. H. Lawrence Review*, vol. 10, no. 1 (Spring), pp. 1–19.

Roth, Jack J. 1980. *The Cult of Violence: Sorel and the Sorelians*. Berkeley, L.A.: University of California Press.

Sagar, Keith. 1979. *D. H. Lawrence: A Calendar of His Works*. Manchester: Manchester University Press.

Sagar, Keith. 1982. *A D. H. Lawrence Handbook*. Manchester: Manchester University Press.

Sagar, Keith. 1985. *D.H.Lawrence: Life into Art*. Harmondsworth: Penguin Books.

Said, Edward W. 1966. *Joseph Conrad and the Fiction of Autobiography*. Cambridge, Massachusetts: Harvard University Press.

Scheffler, Karl. 1926. *Zeit und Stunde: Neue Essays*. Leipzig: Insel-Verlag.

Schneider, Daniel J. 1983. '"Strange Wisdom": Leo Frobenius and D. H. Lawrence'. *D. H. Lawrence Review*, vol. 16, no. 2 (Summer), pp. 183–93.

Schneider, Daniel J. 1984. 'D. H. Lawrence and the Early Greek Philosophers'. *D. H. Lawrence Review*, vol. 17, no. 2 (Summer), pp. 97–109.

Schoenberner, Franz. 1965. *Confessions of a European Intellectual*. 1946; New York: Collier Books.

Shelley, Percy B. 1927. *The Complete Works of Percy Bysshe Shelley*. Eds. Roger Ingpen and Walter E. Peck. 10 vols. London: Ernest Benn Ltd.

Soloviev, Vladimir. 1915. *War, Progress, and the End of History: Including a Short Story of the Anti-Christ*. Trans. Alexander Bakshy. London: University of London Press.

Spender, Stephen. 1935. *The Destructive Element: A Study of Modern Writers and Beliefs*. London: Jonathan Cape.

Spengler, Oswald. 1923. *Der Untergang des Abendlandes: Umrisse einer Morphologie der Weltgeschichte*. 2 vols. 1918–1922; München: C. H. Becksche Verlagsbuchhandlung.

Squires, Michael. 1983. *The Creation of Lady Chatterley's Lover*. Baltimore: Johns Hopkins Press.

Stern, Fritz. 1974. *The Politics of Cultural Despair: A Study in the Rise of the Germanic Ideology*. 1961; Berkeley, L.A.: University of California Press.

Strong, James. 1985. *The New Strong's Concordance of the Bible*. Nashville: Thomas Nelson Publishers.

Thomson, David. 1978. *England in the Nineteenth Century: 1815–1914*. Vol. 8 in *The Pelican History of England*. 1950: Harmondsworth: Penguin Books.

Thurlow, Richard. 1987. *Fascism in Britain: A History 1918–1985*. Oxford: Basil Blackwell.

Tindall, William York. 1956. *Forces in Modern British Literature 1885–1956*. New York: Vintage Books.

Tiverton, Father William. 1951. *D. H. Lawrence and Human Existence*. London: Rockliff.

Toynbee, Arnold J. 1948. *Civilization on Trial*. Oxford: Oxford University Press.

Trotter, Wilfred B. 1916. *Instincts of the Herd in Peace and War*. London: T. Fisher Unwin.

Tuveson, Ernest Lee. 1964. *Millennium and Utopia: A Study in the Background of the Idea of Progress*. 1949; New York: Harper & Row.

Tylor, Edward B. 1873. *Primitive Culture: Researches into the Development of Mythology, Philosophy, Religion, Art and Custom*. 2 vols. 1871; London: John Murray.

Urang, Sarah. 1983. *Kindled in the Flame: The Apocalyptic Scene in D. H. Lawrence*. Ann Arbor, Michigan: UMI Research Press.

Williams, Raymond. 1958. *Culture and Society 1780–1950*. New York: Columbia University Press.

Williams, Raymond. 1975. *The Country and the City*. Frogmore: Paladin.

Williams, Raymond. 1984. *The English Novel from Dickens to Lawrence*. London: The Hogarth Press.

Wingfield-Stratford, Esmé. 1933. *The Victorian Aftermath 1901–1914*. London: George Routledge & Sons.

Index

Besides names, this index includes all of Lawrence's works mentioned in the book. Boldface indicates where more in-depth discussion can be found.

Aaron's Rod ix, 11, 77, 99, 108, 120, **121–3**, 131–3 *pass.*, 145, 146
Abercrombie, Lascelles 47–8, 49, 50
Aldington, Richard 101
Ambris, Alceste de 102
Andrews, Esther 64
D'Annunzio, Gabriele 99, 101–2, **110**, 119
Apocalypse viii, ix, 7, 8, 10, 17, 18, 33, 48, 70, 72, 78, 94, 145, 146, 148, 159, 160, **170–5**
Apollinaire, Guillaume 111
'A Propos of *Lady Chatterley's Lover*' 80, 81
'Aristocracy' 159
Armytage, W. H. 65
Arnold, Armin 109
Asquith, Lady Cynthia 28, 30

Bacon, Francis 103
Baden-Powell, Sir Robert 46
Baudelaire, Charles 50
Belt, Thomas 69
Bentley, Eric 98, 125
Bergson, Henri 24, 73, 100
Bertram, Ernst 97–8
Biddiss, Michael 40
Bismarck, Otto von 112
Bithell, Jethro 109
Blatchford, Robert 52
Blavatsky, Helena P. (Madame) viii, 17, 18, 55, 69, 75, 78
'Blessed Are the Powerful' 159
Blüher, Hans 96–8, 115, 181 n.
Blumenberg, Hans 6, 8
Brazill, William J. 50
Brett, Dorothy 65, 66
Brown, Keith 70
Bruck, Moeller van den 97
Bulwer-Lytton, Edward 103
Burgess, Anthony 67
Burnet, John 16, 52, 103
Burrows, Louie 105
Burwell, Rose Marie 102
Butler, Samuel 103
Buzzi, Paolo 111
Byron, George Gordon, Lord 21, 22

Campbell, Gordon 63
Cannan, Mary 65
Carlyle, Thomas 21, 73, 104, 105–6
Carpenter, Edward 55, 56, 75, 79, 103
Carsten, F. L. 91
Carswell, Catherine 63–5 *pass.*
Carter, Frederick 171
Chamberlain, Houston S. 108, 115, 116
Chamberlain, Robert 178 n.
Chambers, Jessie 52
Charles I, King 116
Clark, L. D. 1
Clarke, Colin 179 n.
Cohn, Norman vii, ix, 5, 88–9
Coleridge, Samuel T. 180 n.
Comte, Auguste viii
Conrad, Joseph 54
Copleston, Frederick 16
Corradini, Enrico 99
Coulton, G. G. 11
Cromwell, Oliver 116
'Crown, The' viii, 6, 7, 15, 19, 23, 24, 27, 28, 31, 32–4, 36, 43, 54, 57, 70, 71, 72, 76, 88, 116, 117, 184 n.
Cusa, Nicholas of 71

Dante Alighieri 103, 177 n.
Darroch, Robert 125, 127

Darwin, Charles 23, 52, 90, 93
Defoe, Daniel 103
Dehmel, Richard **109**, 110, 182–3 n.
Delany, Paul 43
Delavenay, Emile 43, 56, 108, 115, 116
Deleuze, Gilles 180 n., 183 n.
Derby, Edward George Villiers, Lord 30
Dostoevsky, Fyodor 48, 50
Draper, R. P. 116
'Dream of Life, A' **168–70**, 172

Eastman, Donald R. 178 n.
'Education of the People' 119, **120–1**, 122
Edward VII, King 46
Einstein, Albert 90
Eisner, Kurt 95
Eliot, George viii
Ellis, Havelock 79
Eliot, T. S. 85
Empedocles 16
Ensor, R. 110
Escaped Cock, The (*The Man Who Died*) 3, 77
Etruscan Places 70, 78–9

Fantasia of the Unconscious 2, 18, 60, 68–9, 70, 73, 74, 77, 80, 84, 86, 106, 122
Fichte, Johann Gottlieb 105
Fiedler, H. G. 109
First Lady Chatterley, The 20, 150, 154–5, 157, **160–1**
Flint, R. W. 111
Forster, E. M. 62
Frank, Waldo 64
Frazer, Sir James George 8, 18, 69, 179 n.
Freud, Sigmund 67, 73, 82, 90, 95, 96, 97, 180 n.

Garden, Jock 127
Gardiner, Rolf 116, **165–7**, 170, 177 n.
George, Lloyd 30
George, Stefan 98, 110
Gerber, Richard 103
'German Books: Thomas Mann' 51
'Germans and English' 166–7
'Germans and Latins' 166–7
Gertler, Mark 30, 65
Gibbon, Edward 46
Gilbert, Alan D. 52
Gill, Stephen 150, 160
Godwin, William 103
Goethe, Johann Wolfgang von 22
Gorky, Maxim 104–5
Gould, Warwick 11, 177 n.
Gramsci, Antonio 111
'Grand Inquisitor, The, by F. M. Dostoievsky' 173
Green, Eleanor H. 179 n.
Green, Martin 82, 110, 112–13
Gregory, Horace 79
Gross, John 19
Gross, Otto 82, 95, 115
Guattari, Felix 180 n., 183 n.

Haeckel, Ernst 55, **56–7**, 96
Hamsun, Knut x, 154–6, 184 n.
Hardy, Thomas 115
Harrison, Jane 69
Hauser, Arnold 106
Hawthorne, Nathaniel 11, 103
Hegel, Georg W. F. 14, 21
Hentschel, Willibald 96
Heraclitus 16
Herder, Johann G. von 14
Herzinger, Kim A. 183 n.
Heseltine, Philip 178 n.
Hesiod 103
Hitler, Adolf 97, 106
Hochman, Baruch 18, 39
Hofmannsthal, Hugo von 50
Homer 103
Hopkin, William 62, 101
Hough, Graham 55
Houghton, Walter E. 20
Hulme, T. E. 101
Humma, John B. 179 n.
Hynes, Samuel 56, 74, 79

Ibsen, Henrik viii, 44, 179 n.
'Introduction to *The Dragon of the Apocalypse* by Frederick Carter' 171

Jaffe, Edgar 95
Jaffe, Else (b. von Richthofen) 95, 109, 110
Jefferies, Richard 55, 103
Jesus 71, 77, 135, 136, 150, 172
Joachim of Fiore vii, viii, **9–13**, 103
John of Patmos (St John) vii, ix, 171–4 *pass.*
John Thomas and Lady Jane 20, 147–57 *pass.*, **161–4**, 172, 184 n.
Johnson, Paul 93
Joyce, James 19
Jung, Carl Gustav 67

Kangaroo ix, 25, 36, 88, 89, 92, 99, 112, **123–9**, 130, 131, 134, 137, 138, 184 n.
Keats, John 86
Keith, W. J. 166
Kermode, Frank 1, 5, 6, 177 n.
Keyserling, Hermann Graf 108, 182 n.
Klee, Paul 50
Kokoschka, Oskar 50
Koteliansky, Samuel S. 30, 62–5 *pass.*, 104, 160
Krausze, Karl 181 n.

Lady Chatterley's Lover ix, x, 20, 54, 79–85 *pass.*, 145, **146–58**, 159–66, 168, 170, 174, 180 n.
Lagarde, Paul de 97
Lambert, Cecily 65
Langbehn, Julius 97
Lawrence, Frieda von Richthofen 51, 66, 82, 92, 94–5, 109, 112–13, 115, 133
Lederhandler, D. V. 150
Lenin, Vladimir I. 94, 105, 138, 173
Lester Jr., John A. 23, 65, 75
'Letter from Germany, A' 139
Liliencron, Detlev von 110
Lomer, Georg 115, 135, 183 n.
Lost Girl, The 103
Löwith, Karl 7–10 *pass.*, 14, 25
Lucas, Robert 51, 95
Lucka, Emil 108–9, 177 n., 183 n.

MacDonald, Ramsay 101
Magnus, Maurice 184 n.
Mahler, Gustav 53
Man Who Died, The, see *Escaped Cock, The*
Mann, Thomas 51
Mansfield, Katherine 63, 101, 120
Manuel, Frank and Manuel, Fritzie 10, 100, 103, 126
Marinetti, Filippo Tommaso **111**, 120
Marsh, Sir Edward 31, 47, 101
Marx, Karl vii, 22, 90, 100
'Matriarchy' 170
Mazzini, Guiseppe 100
Merrild, Knud 154
Meyers, Jeffrey 184 n.
Miller, Henry 44
Milton, Colin 179 n.
Milton, John 29, 103
Monroe, Harriet 49
Moore, Harry T. 3, 65
Mornings in Mexico 19, 71, 76, 78
Morrell, Lady Ottoline 11, 29, 36–7, 62, 63, 120
Morris, William 55, 103, 132
Mosse, George L. 95, 167
Mountsier, Robert 64
Movements in European History 11, 16, 100, 104
Muir, Kenneth 160
Munch, Edvard 50, 53
Murry, John Middleton 65, 101, 120
Musil, Robert 95
Mussolini, Benito 99, 100, 102, 106, 173

Napoleon I 21
Nietzsche, Friedrich 16, 21–2, 24, 51, 73, 97, 98, 100, **107–8**, 109, 110, 120, 135
'Nobody Loves Me' 113
Nolte, Ernst 95, 99, 101
Nordau, Max 50
'Novel, The' 146
Nuttall, Zelia 18–19

'On Being Religious' 13, 50
Orage, A. R. 101, 107

'Pan in America' 153
Pareto, Vilfredo 182 n.
'Paris Letter' 139
Peabody, Josephine Preston 49–50
Plato 102
Plumed Serpent, The ix, 11–12, 18, 25, 69, 70, 73, 74, 77, 78, 86, 89, 112, 114, 117, **129–44**, 145, 146, 150, 153, 157–60 *pass.*, 170, 182 n.
Poe, Edgar Allan 11, 177 n.
'Prologue to *Women in Love*' 36, **117–18**, 122
'Prussian Officer, The' 181 n.
Pryse, James 74, 171
'Psychoanalysis and the Unconscious' 73

Rainbow, The x, 32, 51, 61, 76, 81, 82, 83, 109, 112, 114, 116, 117, 122, 123, 143
Reade, Winwood 103
'Red Trousers' 113
Reeves, Marjorie 11, 177 n.
Reid, Robert 52
Renan, Ernest viii, 52
'Resurrection' 7, 13, 53
'Return to Bestwood' 159

'Review of *The Oxford Book of German Verse* edited by H. G. Fiedler, A' 109
Rhodes, Anthony 110
Rilke, Rainer Maria 50
Roberts, David D. 100
Robertson, J. M. 52
Rosenberg, Alfred 108
Ross, Charles 38
Roth, Jack J. 104
Rousseau, Jean Jacques 103–4
Rozanov, V. V. 183 n.
Russell, Bertrand 52, 62, 63, 117, 120

Sagar, Keith 102, 108
Saint-Simon, Henri de vii
St Mawr ix, 70
Salimbene de Adam (Salimbene Parmensis) 11, 177 n.
Scheffler, Karl 167, 185 n.
Schelling, Friedrich W. J. 14
Schneider, Daniel 16
Schoenberner, Franz 108
Schopenhauer, Arthur 24, 73, 107
Scott, Robert Falcon 46
Sea and Sardinia 70, 102
Secker, Martin 159
Shakespeare, William 35
Shaw, George Bernard 50, 75, 106
Shelley, Percy B. 86
'Snake' 78
Socrates 100
Soloviev, Vladimir 48–9, 50
Sons and Lovers 133
Sorel, Georges **100–1**, 111, 127, 138, 140, 141
Southey, Robert 180 n.
Spencer, Herbert 16, 52
Spender, Stephen 7
Spengler, Oswald 20, 24, 45, 108, 149
Stern, Fritz 95, 104
Strindberg, August 44
Studies in Classic American Literature 72, 184 n.
Study of Thomas Hardy, A viii, 12, 60, 68, 82, 108, **115–16**
'Sun' 76–7

Thoreau, Henry David 103
Thurlow, Richard 92, 93
Tindall, William 54, 73
Tiverton, Father William 85
Tolstoi, Leo 115
Toynbee, Arnold 13
Trotter, Wilfred B. 106–7
Twilight in Italy 11, 28, 36, **42–5**, 116, 177 n.
Tylor, Edward B. 8, 18, 69, 77, 179 n.

Urang, Sarah 1

Vico, Giambattista 100
Virgil 103
Vivian, Philip (Harry V. M. Phillips) 52

Wagner, Richard 50, 108
Weber, Alfred 95
Weber, Max 95
Weekley, Ernest 95
Weininger, Otto 115–16, 183 n.
Wells, H. G. 47, 79, 103, 168
Whitman, Walt 127, 184 n.
Williams, Raymond 90
Wingfield-Stratford, Esmé 46
Winstanley, Gerrard 126
Women in Love ix, 6, 16, 28, **31–42**, 43, 46, 54, 66, 70, 72, 75, 82, 84, 85–6, 111, 113, 117, 122, 123, 124, 130–2 *pass.*, 179 n., 182 n., 183 n., 184 n.

Yeats, William Butler viii, 19